Aggression in Personality Disorders and Perversions

AGGRESSION IN PERSONALITY DISORDERS AND PERVERSIONS

OTTO F. KERNBERG, M.D.

YALE UNIVERSITY PRESS   NEW HAVEN AND LONDON

Designed by Sonia L. Scanlon
Set in Trump type by The Composing Room of Michigan, Inc.
Printed in the United States of America by Vail-Ballou Press, Binghamton, N.Y.

Library of Congress Cataloging-in-Publication Data
Kernberg, Otto F., 1928–
    Aggression in personality disorders and perversions
  / Otto F. Kernberg.
        p.   cm.
    Includes bibliographical references and index.
    ISBN 0-300-05003-8 (cloth)
            0-300-06508-6 (pbk.)
      1. Personality disorders.   2. Personality disorders—
  Treatment.   3. Aggressiveness (Psychology)
  4. Sexual deviation.   I. Title.
      [DNLM: 1. Aggression—psychology.
  2. Personality Disorders—psychology.
  3. Psychoanalytic Theory.   4. Psychosexual
  Disorders—psychology.   WM 600   K39a]
  RC554.K45   1992
  616.85'8—dc20
  DNLM/DLC
  for Library of Congress   92-18118
                                CIP

A catalogue record for this book is available from the British Library.

The paper in this book meets the guidelines for permanence and durability of the Committee on Production Guidelines for Book Longevity of the Council on Library Resources.

10   9   8   7   6   5   4   3   2

CONTENTS

PREFACE

In this book I present the most recent of my continuing explorations of the etiology, nature, and treatment of personality disorders. Essential to such explorations is an understanding of the dynamics of severely pathological human behavior. My book therefore opens with an examination of the psychoanalytic theory of motivation, with a particular focus on aggression.

Taking into consideration the contemporary developments in the studies of affects, I am proposing modification but not abandonment of Freud's drive theory. The modification I am suggesting recognizes the fundamental role of affects in the organization of drives and in bringing together the neuropsychological determinants of affects with the earliest interpersonal experiences of infancy and childhood as determinants of personality formation.

I follow these broad considerations of affects with a specific emphasis on aggression, undertaking the task of clarifying the relationship between aggression and rage and between rage and hatred.

Underlying all my work is the conviction that the psychopathology of personality is determined by the psychic structures erected under the impact of affective experiences with significant early objects. This conviction is expressed in my emphasis on the need to integrate a diagnostic system based upon description of behavior with a psychodynamic approach centered on psychic structure formation. I describe several prevalent personality disorders in the light of this approach.

In the central sections of this book, I have updated and spelled out my ego psychology—object relations theory as it applies to the clinical situation. In this context, my focus is on the specific distortions in the transference and countertransference induced by structured aggression in the form of chronic hatred and secondary defenses against this hatred. The interplay among identity diffusion, reality testing, and treatment stalemates is explored through the entire spectrum of personality disorders from neurotic through borderline and psychotic organizations. I apply my theoretical conclusions regarding aggression and hatred to new technical approaches for severe personality disorders ranging from psychoanalysis proper through psychoanalytic psychotherapy to hospital milieu treatment.

Further exploring the implications regarding the primacy of the nature of psychic structure and aggression in determining psychopathology, the final section of this book deals with perversions. The psychodynamics of perversions and personality disorders are outlined—both their commonalities and the differences. Emphasized in this discussion is the unique position occupied by the homosexualities in current psychoanalytic thinking.

For their contributions to my ideas on object relations theory and affect theory, I am indebted to Doctors Selma Kramer, Rainer Krause, Joseph and Anna-Marie Sandler, Ernst and Gertrude Ticho, and the late John Sutherland. Regarding the psychoanalytic theories of perversion, I have been stimulated and helped by Doctors Janine Chasseguet-Smirgel, Andre Green, Joyce McDougall, and most especially the late Robert Stoller. My thinking on the subject of structural change has benefited significantly from my discussions with Doctors Mardi Horowitz, Lester Luborsky, and Robert Wallerstein.

In my work with patients as well as in my efforts to contribute to psychoanalytic and psychotherapeutic techniques, I have been privileged by my ongoing professional dialogue with a group of close friends and colleagues in New York, including Doctors Martin and Maria Bergman, Harold Blum, Arnold Cooper, William Frosch, William Grossman, Donald Kaplan, Robert Michels, and Ethel Person, all of whom have patiently read and criticized many of the chapters included in this volume. Dr. Paulina Kernberg, in her multiple roles as psychoanalyst, professional co-worker, and wife, not only influenced the content of my writings but must also be credited for creating the space that has permitted me to dedicate myself to this work.

Formal research on intensive psychotherapy with borderline patients has formed the background to the theoretical explanations contained in this book. I owe much to the enthusiasm, dedication, and unwaveringly critical review of our joint research enterprise on the part of the members of the Psychotherapy Research Project on Borderline Patients at the Department of Psychiatry of Cornell University Medical College and the Westchester Division of New York Hospital throughout the entire body of work reported in this volume. I am deeply indebted to Doctors John Clarkin and Harold Koenigsberg, the codirectors of this project, and to Doctors Ann Appelbaum, Steven Bauer, Arthur Carr, Lisa Gornick, Lawrence Rockland, Michael Selzer, and Frank Yoemans, colleagues in this endeavor, whose critical evaluation of our group's evolving clinical experiences has shaped my approach to particularly challenging technical problems. Although I thank all these colleagues for the stimulation, suggestions, and criticisms, I assume personal responsibility for all the formulations of this book.

I am deeply appreciative to Miss Louise Taitt and Miss Becky Whipple for their endless patience in typing, revising, proofreading, and organizing the seemingly endless versions of the manuscript. Miss Whipple's indefatigable attention to every small detail of this manuscript saved the day on many occasions. Ms. Rosalind Kennedy, my administrative assistant, provided the overall organizational frame that permitted me to carry out this work in the context of my clinical, academic, and administrative functions; she protected the working ambience that made it all possible.

This is the second book I have produced with the assistance of both my editor over many years, Mrs. Natalie Altman, and the senior editor at Yale University Press, Mrs. Gladys Topkis. Both of them tactfully respected my investment in what I wanted to say while helping me to express it as clearly as possible. I am immensely grateful to them both.

Part I THE ROLE OF AFFECTS IN PSYCHOANALYTIC THEORY

Chapter 1 NEW PERSPECTIVES ON DRIVE THEORY

Marjorie Brierley (1937) was the first to point to a strange paradox regarding the role of affects in psychoanalytic theory and practice. Affects, she said, play a central role in the clinical situation but a peripheral and ambiguous one in psychoanalytic theory. Brierley thought that if the part played by affects could be clarified, this might help to clarify still unresolved issues in drive theory. The paradox Brierley described a half century ago seems to have persisted until recently. Only in the past ten years has this situation begun to change. After reexamining the relation between affects and drives in psychoanalytic theory, including Freud's changing theories of drives and affects and recent psychoanalytic contributions—including my own—to these issues, I am offering a revised psychoanalytic theory of affects and drives. I then examine the nature of affects as they emerge in the psychoanalytic situation and their distortions under the impact of defensive processes. Finally, I offer a developmental model based upon my conceptual frame.

DRIVES AND INSTINCTS

Although Freud believed that the drives, which he saw as the ultimate psychic motivational systems, had biological sources, he repeatedly stressed the lack of available information regarding the process that would transform these biological sources into psychic motivation. He conceived of libido, or the sexual drive, as a hierarchically supraordinate organization of partial sexual drives from an earlier developmental phase. This idea is in accordance with his concept of drives as psychic in nature. According to Freud (1905), the partial drives (oral, anal, voyeuristic, sadistic, and so on) are psychologically integrated in the course of development and are not physiologically linked to each other. The dual drive theory of sexuality and aggression (1920) represents his final classification of drives as the ultimate source of unconscious psychic conflict and psychic structure formation.

While Freud described biological sources of the sexual drives according to the excitability of the erotogenic zones, he did not describe such specific and concrete biological sources for aggression. In contrast to the fixed sources of libido, he characterized the aims and objects of both libidinal and aggressive drives as changing throughout psychic development; he described continuity of sexual and aggressive motivations in a broad variety of complex psychic developments.

As Holder (1970) has pointed out, Freud clearly differentiated drives from instincts. He saw the drives as supraordinate; they were constant rather than intermittent sources of motivation. Instincts, on the other hand, were biological, inherited, and intermittent in that they were activated by physiological and/or environmental stimulation. Libido is a drive; hunger is an instinct. Freud conceived of drives as on the boundary between the physical and the mental, as psychic processes rooted in biology; he proposed (1915b, 1915c) that the only way we can know about drives is through their psychic representatives—ideas and affects.

Both Holder and Laplanche and Pontalis (1973, pp. 214–217) have stressed the purely psychic nature of Freud's dual drive theory and have charged that the distinction between psychological drives and biological instincts is lost in the *Standard Edition*'s translation of both *Instinkt* and *Trieb* as "instinct." I would add that the Strachey translation has had the unfortunate effect of linking Freud's drive concept too closely with biology, inhibiting psychoanalytic research into the nature of the mediating processes that bridge biological instincts with drives, defined as purely psychic motivation. The very term *instinct* stresses the biological realm of this concept and thus discourages psychoanalytic exploration of motivation. In my opinion, the concept of drives as hierarchically supraordinate psychic motivational systems is valid, and Freud's dual drive theory is satisfactory to explain such motivation.

As Laplanche and Pontalis (1973) appropriately note, Freud always referred to instincts as discontinuous inherited behavior patterns that vary little from one member of the species to another. It is impressive how closely Freud's concept of instinct parallels modern instinct theory in biology, as represented, for example, by Lorenz (1963), Tinbergen (1951), and Wilson (1975). These investigators consider instincts to be hierarchical organizations of biologically determined perceptive, behavioral, and communicative patterns released by environmental factors that activate inborn releasing mechanisms. This biological-environmental system is considered epigenetic. Lorenz and Tinbergen showed in their animal research that the maturational and developmental linkage of discrete inborn behavior patterns, their overall organization within a particular individual, is very much determined by the nature of environmental stimulation: hierarchically organized instincts represent the integration of inborn dispositions with environmentally determined learning. Instincts, in this view, are hierarchically organized biological motivational systems. They are usually classified along the lines of feeding behavior, fight-flight behavior, mating, and other such dimensions.

Rapaport (1953) describes how Freud changed his concept of affects over the years. He originally (1894) considered them pretty much equivalent to drives; by 1915 (1915b, 1915c) he considered them (particularly their pleasurable or painful, psychomotor, and neurovegetative features) to be discharge processes of drives; eventually (1926), he considered them to be inborn dispositions (thresholds and channels) of the ego.

In my view, affects are instinctive structures—that is, biologically given, developmentally activated psychophysiological patterns. It is the psychic aspect of the patterns that becomes organized to constitute the aggressive and libidinal drives Freud described. The partial sexual drives, in this view, are more limited, restricted integrations of corresponding affect states, and libido as a drive is the hierarchically supraordinate integration of them—that is, the integration of all erotically centered affect states. In contrast to the still quite prevalent view within psychoanalysis of affects as merely discharge processes, I consider them to be the bridging structures between biological instincts and psychic drives. Supporting arguments for this conclusion will follow further elaboration of my definitions of affects and emotions.

AFFECTS AND EMOTIONS

Following Brierley (1937) and Jacobson (1953) from the clinical psychoanalytic field, and Arnold (1970a, 1970b), Izard (1978), Knapp (1978), and Emde (1987; Emde et al. 1978) from the field of empirical research on affective behavior in neuropsychology, I define affects as psychophysiological behavior patterns that include a specific cognitive appraisal, a specific facial pattern, a subjective experience of a pleasurable and rewarding or painful and aversive nature, and a muscular and neurovegetative discharge pattern. The expressive facial pattern is part of the general communicative pattern that differentiates each particular affect.

There is fairly general agreement today that affects from their very origin have a cognitive aspect, that they contain at least an appraisal of the "goodness" or "badness" of the immediate perceptive constellation, and that this appraisal, in Arnold's (1970a, 1970b) formulation, determines a felt motivation for action either toward or away from a certain stimulus or situation. In contrast to the older James-Lange theory (James 1884; Lange 1885), which held that the subjective and cognitive aspects of affects follow or are derived from the perception of the muscular and neurovegetative discharge phenomena, and in contrast to the derived position of Tomkins (1970) that the cognitive and felt aspects of affects follow or are derived from the perception of their facial expression, I think that the subjective quality of felt appraisal is the core characteristic of each affect.

I see affects as either primitive or derived. Primitive affects make their appearance within the first two or three years of life and have an intense, global quality and a diffuse, not well-differentiated cognitive element. Derived affects are more complex, consisting of combinations of the primitive affects, cognitively elaborated. Unlike primitive affects, they may not display all their original components with equal strength, and their psychic aspects gradually come to dominate the psychophysiological and facial communicative ones. For these more complex phenomena I would reserve the term *emotions* or *feelings*. This distinction corresponds to the clinical observations regarding primitive affect states and complex emotional developments in the psychoanalytic situation.

AFFECTS AND DRIVES

In Freud's first theory of affect the concepts of affect and drive were practically interchangeable. In his second affect theory, Freud proposed that drives are manifest by means of psychic representations or ideas— that is, cognitive expressions of the drive—and affects. Affects, he postulated, are discharge processes that may reach consciousness but do not undergo repression; only the mental representation of the drive is repressed, together with a memory of or a disposition to activate the corresponding affect (1915b, 1915c).

In clinical psychoanalysis, the idea that affects cannot be dynamically unconscious has been a conceptual problem, and it is possible that Freud's exclusive stress on the discharge aspects of affects in his second theory was to some extent a consequence of the then-dominant James-Lange theory. In any case, we now have important neuropsychological evidence that affects may be stored in the limbic brain structures as affective memory (Arnold 1984, chaps. 11, 12).

If affects and emotions include subjective experiences of pain or pleasure and cognitive and expressive-communicative elements as well as neurovegetative discharge patterns, and if they are present—as infant research has demonstrated (Emde et al. 1978; Izard 1978; Stern 1985; Emde 1987)—from the earliest weeks and months of life, are they the primary motivational forces of psychic development? If they include both cognitive and affective features, what does the broader concept of drive contain that is not contained in the concept of affect? Freud implied that the drives are present from birth on, but he also implied that they mature and develop. It may be argued that the maturation and development of affects are expressions of the underlying drives, but if all the functions and manifestations of drives can be included in the functions and manifestations of developing affects, it would be difficult to sustain a concept of independent drives underlying the organization of affects. In fact, the transformation of affects throughout development, their integration with internalized object relations, their overall developing dichotomy into pleasurable affects building up the libidinal series and painful affects building up the aggressive series, all point to the enormous richness and complexity of their cognitive as well as affective elements.

I believe the traditional psychoanalytic concept of affects as discharge processes only and the assumption that decrease of psychic tension leads to pleasure and increase to unpleasure have unnecessarily complicated the understanding of affects in the clinical situation. Jacobson (1953) called attention to the fact that tension states (such as sexual excitement) may be pleasurable and discharge states (such as anxiety) may be unpleasurable; she concluded, in agreement with Brierley (1937), that affects are not solely discharge processes but complex and sustained intrapsychic tension phenomena.

Jacobson also described how the cognitive aspects of affects refer to their investment of self and object representations in both ego and superego. She concluded that affective investments of these representations constitute the clinical manifestations of drives. In other words, whenever a drive derivative is diagnosed in the clinical situation—for example, a sexual or aggressive impulse—the patient is invariably experiencing at that point an image or representation of the self relating to an image or representation of another person ("object") under the impact of the corresponding sexual or aggressive affect. And whenever a patient's affect state is explored, a cognitive aspect is found, usually a relation of the self to an object under the impact of the affect state. The cognitive elements of drives, Jacobson said, are represented by the cognitive relations between self and object representations, and between self and actual objects. Sandler (Sandler and Rosenblatt 1962; Sandler and Sandler 1978) reached similar conclusions regarding the intimate connection between effects and internalized object relations.

In clarifying the relationship between affects and moods, Jacobson (1957b) defined moods as a temporary fixation and generalization of affects throughout the entire world of internalized object relations—that is, a generalization of an affect state throughout all the individual's self and object representations for a limited time span: moods are thus extended yet relatively subdued affect states that color, for a time, the entire world of internalized object relations.

AFFECT AND OBJECT

I propose that early affect development is based on a direct fixation of early, affectively imbued object relations in the form of affective memory. Indeed, the works of Emde, Izard, and Stern all point to the central function of object relations in activating affects.

Different affect states toward the same object are activated under the dominance of various developmental tasks and biologically activated instinctive behavior patterns. The variety of affect states directed to the same object may provide an economic explanation for how affects are linked and transformed into a supraordinate motivational series, which becomes the sexual or aggressive drive. For example, the pleasurable oral stimulations during nursing and the pleasurable anal stimulation during toilet training may bring about a condensed memory of pleasurable interactions with mother, linking oral and anal libidinal developments. In contrast, enraged reaction to frustrations during the oral period and power struggles during the anal period may link consonant aggressive affect states, thus integrating the aggressive drive. Further, the infant's intense positive affective investment of mother during the practicing stage of separation-individuation may later link up with a sexually imbued longing for her derived from the activation of genital feelings in the oedipal stage of development. In general, the affects of sexual excitement and rage may be considered, respectively, as the central organizing affects of libido and aggression.

If we consider affects the primary psychobiological building blocks of drives and the earliest motivational systems, we still have to explain how affects become organized into supraordinate hierarchical drive systems. Why not say that the primary affects themselves are the motivational systems? In my view, a multitude of complex secondary combinations and transformations of affects exists, so that a theory of motivation based on affects rather than on two basic drives would be complex and clinically unsatisfactory. I also believe that the unconscious organization and integration of affectively determined early experience assumes a higher level of motivational organization than that represented by affect states per se. We need to assume a motivational organization that does justice to the complex integration of all affective developments in relation to the parental objects.

An effort to replace both drive and affect theory with an attachment theory or an object relations theory that rejects the concepts of drives leads to a simplification of intrapsychic life by stressing only the positive or libidinal elements of attachment and neglecting the unconscious organization of aggression. Although in theory this should not necessarily be so, in practice those object relations theoreticians who have rejected drive theory have, in my view, also seriously neglected the motivational aspects of aggression.

AFFECT AND INTRAPSYCHIC FORCES

For all these reasons, I think we should not replace a drive theory by an affect theory or an object relations theory of motivation. It seems eminently reasonable to me to consider affects the link between biologically determined instinctive components, on the one hand, and intrapsychic organization of the overall drives, on the other. The correspondence of the series of rewarding and aversive affect states with the dual lines of libido and aggression makes sense from both clinical and theoretical perspectives.

The concept of affects as the building blocks of drives I believe, resolves some persistent problems in the psychoanalytic theory of drives. It broadens the concept of erotogenic zones as the source of libido into a general consideration of all physiologically activated functions and bodily zones that become involved in affectively invested interactions of the infant and child with mother. These functions include the shift from concerns with bodily functions to concerns with social functions and role enactments. My proposed concept also provides the missing links within psychoanalytic theory among the "sources" of aggressively invested infant-mother interactions, the "zonal" function of aggressive rejection of oral ingestion, anal control, direct physical power struggles linked with temper tantrums, and the like. I am suggesting that it is affectively invested object relations that energizes physiological "zones."

The id, according to this concept of the relation between drives and affects, consists of repressed, intensely aggressive or sexualized internalized object relations. The condensation and displacement characteristic of the contents of the id reflect the linkage of affectively imbued self and object representations with a similar positive or negative valence, thus constituting the corresponding aggressive, libidinal, and, later on, combined series.

My proposal permits us to do justice to the biologically determined input of new affective experiences throughout life. These experiences include the activation of intense sexual excitement during adolescence, when erotically tinged affect states become integrated with the genital excitement and with erotically charged emotions and fantasies derived from the oedipal stage of development. In other words, the intensification of drives (both libidinal and aggressive) at various stages of life is determined by the incorporation of new psychophysiologically activated affect states into preexistent, hierarchically organized affect systems.

More generally, once the organization of drives has been consolidated as the supraordinate hierarchical motivational system, any particular activation of drives in the context of intrapsychic conflict is represented by the activation of a corresponding affect state. This affect state includes an internalized object relation, basically a particular self representation relating to a particular object representation under the impact of a particular affect. The reciprocal role relation of self and object that is framed by the affect is usually expressed as a concrete fantasy or wish. Affects, in short, become the signals or representatives of drives as well as their building blocks.

This view of affects, while in contrast to Freud's second theory of affects, is in consonance with his first and third theories: with the first theory, in linking affects and drives; with the third theory, in stressing the inborn disposition to affects that characterizes the original ego-id matrix.

AFFECTS IN THE PSYCHOANALYTIC SITUATION

Having described a theory of drive development, I return to the clinical manifestations of affects to support Brierley's and Jacobson's suggestions that clinically we always work with affects or emotions and that affects are complex intrapsychic structures rather than simply discharge processes.

The psychoanalytic situation provides a unique way of exploring all kinds of affects—from primitive (such as rage or sexual excitement) to cognitively differentiated, compounded ones. As Brierley (1937) and Jacobson (1953) pointed out, affects include a basic subjectively pleasurable or painful experience. The subjective experiences of pleasure and pain are usually but not always differentiated from each other.

Affects differ quantitatively as well as qualitatively: the intensity of subjective experiences varies, as is usually observable in physiological discharge patterns and/or psychomotor behavior. The patient's behavior also serves to communicate his subjective experience to the analyst. Indeed, the communicative functions of affects are central to the transference and permit the analyst to empathize with and (internally) respond emotionally to the patient's experience. The ideational content of affects is important in relation to the psychoanalytic exploration of all affects, particularly primitive ones, which may give the initial impression of being almost devoid of cognitive content. Psychoanalytic exploration of intense affect storms in regressed patients, in my experience, consistently demonstrates that there is no such thing as a "pure" affect without cognitive content.

The affects we observe in the psychoanalytic situation not only always have cognitive content but—and this is, I think, a crucial finding—always have an object relations aspect as well; that is, they express a relation between an aspect of the patient's self and an aspect of one or another of his object representations. Furthermore, affect in the psychoanalytic situation either reflects or complements a reactivated internal object relation. In the transference, an affect state recapitulates the patient's significant past object relation. Indeed, all actualizations of an object relation in the transference contain a certain affect state as well.

DEFENSIVE DISTORTIONS

The manifestations of impulse/defense configurations in the psychoanalytic situation may be conceptualized as the activation of certain object relations in conflict. One side of the configuration is defensive; the other reflects the impulse or drive-derivative side. The masochistic suffering of a hysterical patient who experiences the analyst as frustrating and punitive may serve as a defense against the patient's underlying sexual excitement, fantasies, and positive oedipal strivings: the mixture of sorrow, rage, and self-pity may reflect an affect state with defensive functions directed against repressed sexual excitement. In fact, whenever, clinically speaking, we point to the defensive use of one drive against another, we are actually referring to the defensive function of one affect against another.

The defensive process itself, however, frequently disrupts the affect state. For example, the patient may repress the cognitive aspects of the affect, its subjective experience, or everything except its psychomotor aspects. When the affect state is disrupted, the predominant object relation in the transference is interfered with, and the patient's full awareness of his own subjective experience is obscured. The analyst's capacity for empathic understanding is also thereby thwarted. Consider, for example, listening to an obsessive patient's sexual thoughts without their affective, sexually excited qualities, which remain in repression; or to a hysterical patient's intense and dramatic affect storm, which obscures the cognitive content of the experience; or to a narcissistic patient's speaking in what sounds like highly emotional tones while his total behavior conveys the absence or unavailability of any emotional communication. This dissociation of various components of affects in the service of defense may give the impression that the subjective experience of affects is separate from their cognitive, behavioral, communicative aspects, particularly in the initial stages of treatment or when resistance is strong.

This defensive dissociation seems to illustrate the traditional psychological view that affect, perception, cognition, and action are separate ego functions. But when these defensive operations are worked through, and as the deeper layers of the patient's intrapsychic experience gradually emerge, the psychoanalyst encounters the integration of the various components of the affects. When the nature of the unconscious conflict that develops in the transference is on the primitive side, then the affects appear full-blown and centered upon a subjective experience, but with a full complement of cognitive, physiological, behavioral, and communicative aspects, and expressing a specific relation between the patient's self and the corresponding object representation in the transference.

These observations confirm recent neuropsychological research on affects, which contradicts the traditional idea that affects, cognition, communicative behavior, and object relations develop separately (Emde et al. 1978; Hoffman 1978; Izard 1978; Plutchik 1980; Plutchik and Kellerman 1983; Stern 1985; Emde 1987). Affects thus can be seen as complex psychic structures indissolubly linked to the individual's cognitive appraisals of his immediate situation and containing a positive or negative valence with regard to the relation of the subject to the object of the particular experience. Affects, therefore, because of this cognitive appraisal component, have a motivational aspect.

Arnold's (1970a, 1970b) definition of emotions—that they are a felt action tendency based on appraisal—is relevant here. "Emotion" in this context corresponds to what I refer to as "affect." (As I said earlier in this chapter, I prefer to reserve the term *emotion* for affects with highly differentiated cognitive contents and relatively mild or moderate psychomotor and/or neurovegetative components.) Arnold described two constituents of emotion: one static, the appraisal; and one dynamic, the impulse toward what is appraised as good or away from what is appraised as bad. If Arnold's work reflects a general trend of contemporary neuropsychological research on affects, as I believe it does, this trend is remarkably concordant with the clinical findings on affects in the psychoanalytic situation as spelled out by Brierley (1937) and Jacobson (1953).

THE ORIGINS OF FANTASY AND PEAK-AFFECT STATES

When intense affect states are activated in the transference, a corresponding gratifying or frustrating past object relation is recalled, together with the effort to reactivate that object relation if it was gratifying or escape from it if it was painful. This process of juxtaposition, in fact, illustrates the origin of fantasy—namely, the juxtaposition of an evoked remembered state with a future desired state in the context of a current perception that activates the desire for change. The formation of fantasy thus reflects the simultaneity of past, present, and future that is characteristic of the id, predating the awareness and acceptance of objective space-time constraints that characterize the differentiated ego (Jaques 1982).

From a primordial integration of primitive affective memory linking "all-good" or "all-bad" peak-affect states stems the development of specific wishful fantasies linking self and object that characterize unconscious fantasy. Peak-affect states occur in connection with highly desirable (pleasurable) or undesirable (painful) experiences that motivate intense desires to respectively reinstate or avoid similar affective experiences. These desires, expressed as concrete unconscious wishes, constitute the motivational repertoire of the id. "Desire" expresses a more general motivational urge than "wish": we might say that unconscious desire is expressed in concrete wishes. Unconscious fantasy centers around wishes that concretely express desire and ultimately the drives.

Peak-affect experiences may facilitate the internalization of primitive object relations organized along the axis of rewarding, or all-good, or aversive, or all-bad, ones. In other words, the experience of self and object when the infant is in a peak-affect state acquires an intensity that facilitates the laying down of affective memory structures. Originally, in these internalizations, self and object representations are not yet differentiated from each other. Fused, undifferentiated, or condensed all-good self and object representations are built up separately from equally fused, undifferentiated, or condensed all-bad self and object representations. These earliest intrapsychic structures of the symbiotic stage of development (Mahler and Furer 1968) would correspond both to the beginning of structure formation of internalized object relations and to the beginning of overall organization of libidinal and aggressive drives. At the same time, the internalization of object relations represents the origin of the tripartite structure as well: internalized object relations and their corresponding affective investment constitute the substructure of the ego, the id, and the superego. I see the structural characteristics associated with the id as based on a combination of several factors: the primitive, diffuse, and overwhelming nature of early affective memory derived from peak affects and the corresponding internalized object relations; the undifferentiated quality of early subjectivity and early consciousness; and the rudimentary nature of symbolic functions in the process of condensation of past, present, and evoked "future" in early fantasy formation.

Affect states may have very different developmental consequences. Modulated affect states may contribute directly to ego development. Parallel mother-infant interaction and learning under conditions of mild or modulated affect states might set up memory structures reflecting more discriminatory and instrumental relations to the immediate psychosocial environment.

AFFECTS AND EARLY SUBJECTIVE EXPERIENCE

What evidence do we have affirming the fact that infants display of affects means that they have a subjective awareness of pain or pleasure? This question implicitly argues against early subjectivity, early intrapsychic experience before the development of linguistic capacities, and early activation of intrapsychic motivational systems. The study of tension states in infants following the presentation of stimuli that activate affects (as, for example, in the study of heart rate) indicates modification in tension—either increase or decrease, according to the cognitive implications of the stimuli. In other words, we are beginning to find evidence of an increase or decrease in intrapsychic tension prior to the time when the expressive and discharge patterns of affect become apparent (Sroufe 1979; Sroufe et al. 1974).

There is also evidence that the diencephalic centers that mediate the experience of aversive or rewarding qualities of perception are fully mature at birth, which supports the assumption of an early capacity for experiencing pleasure and pain. In addition is the surprisingly early infant capacity for cognitive differentiation, suggesting the potential for affective differentiations as well. It seems reasonable to assume that a three-month-old is able to experience emotions as well as show behavioral evidence of pleasure, rage, or disappointment (Izard 1978), a point developed at great length by Plutchik and Kellerman (1983).

Recent advances in the observations of infant-mother interactions (Stern 1977, 1985) point to the activation, within the first few weeks of life, of a capacity for discrimination of properties belonging to mother, indicating that the infant is "prewired" to begin to form distinct schemas of self and of others. The cognitive potential of infants, in other words, is much more sophisticated than has traditionally been assumed, and the same is true of the infant's affective behavior.

Affective behavior strongly influences the infant's relation with mother from birth on (Izard 1978; Izard and Buechler 1979). A central biological function of inborn affective patterns—with their behavioral, communicative, and psychophysiological manifestations—is to signal the infant's needs to the environment (the mothering person) and thus to initiate the communication between the infant and mother that marks the beginning of intrapsychic life (Emde et al. 1978). Recent research has surprised us by describing a high degree of differentiation in infant-mother communications from very early on (Hoffman 1978). Neuropsychological theorizing now assumes that affective memory is stored in the limbic cortex; as direct brain-stimulation experiments indicate, this permits the reactivation of not only the cognitive aspects of past experience but also the affective aspects, particularly the subjective, affective coloring of that experience (Arnold 1970a). I have proposed earlier that affects, operating as the earliest motivational system, are intimately linked with the fixation by memory of an internalized world of object relations (Kernberg 1976).

Insofar as current neuropsychological theorizing about the nature of affects implies that their subjective quality—basically, pleasure and pain—is a central feature that integrates their psychophysiological, behavioral, and communicative aspects, and as highly differentiated behavioral, communicative, and psychophysiological aspects of affects are observable from the first weeks of life, it seems reasonable to assume that the capacity for subjective experience of pleasure and pain exists very early on. In fact, granting that affective schemas as well as perceptual and motor schemas are operant from birth on, the subjective experience of pleasure and pain (subjectivity) can be assumed to constitute the first stage of consciousness and, by that token, the first stage of development of the self as well.

Piaget's statements that "affective states that have no cognitive elements are never seen, nor are behaviors found that are wholly cognitive" and that "affectivity would play the role of an energy source on which the functioning but not the structures of intelligence would depend" (1954, p. 5) probably reflect generally accepted principles of psychological functioning. I have suggested earlier in this chapter that affective subjectivity, the primordial experience of self, helps to integrate—in the form of affective memory—perceptual, behavioral, and interactional experiences, as well as the affective schemata themselves, particularly when the infant is in an extremely pleasurable or unpleasurable affective state (peak-affect state), which maximizes his alertness and attention.

It would also seem reasonable to assume that such an assembly of memory structures during peak-affect states may spur the earliest symbolic activities, in that one element of such peak-affective constellations stands for the entire constellation. A light turned on in a room, for example, represents the presence of the feeding mother even before she herself is perceived. One could argue about the point at which simple association and conditioned reflexes are transformed into symbolic thinking—in the sense that one element stands for an entire constellation of evoked experience outside the rigid linkage of conditioned associations—but, in any case, it seems reasonable to assume that the earliest symbolic function, an active representation of an entire sequence by one of its elements, placed outside the rigid associative chain, would occur under precisely such conditions.

Peak-affect states, then, would constitute the conditions under which purely affective subjectivity would be transformed into mental activity with symbolic functions, clinically represented by affectively imbued memory structures of pleasurable relations of infant and mother, in which self and object representations, in spite of their highly differentiated, cognitive inborn schemata, are as yet undifferentiated. Affective memory structures derived from the unpleasurable or painful peak-affect states in which self and object representations are also undifferentiated would be built up separately.

Memory structures acquired during peak-affect states will be very different from those acquired during quiescent or low-level affect states. When the infant is in the latter state, the memory structures established will be largely of a cognitive, discriminatory nature and will contribute directly to ego development. Ordinary learning thus occurs under conditions in which alertness is focused on the immediate situation and tasks, with little distortion derived from affective arousal and no particular defense mechanism interfering with it. These memory structures constitute the early precursors, we might say, of more specialized and adaptive ego functioning—the "primary autonomy" structures of early consciousness, which are gradually integrated into the affective memory structures and also contribute to the later stages of integration of total consciousness.

In contrast, peak-affect experiences facilitate the internalization of primitive object relations organized along the axes of rewarding, or all-good, and aversive, or all-bad, objects. The experiences of self and object under the impact of extreme affect activation acquire an intensity that facilitates the laying down of affectively impregnated memory structures. These affective memory structures, constituted in essence of self and object representations in the context of a specific peak-affect experience, represent the earliest intrapsychic structures of the symbiotic stage of development (Mahler and Furer 1968). They mark the beginning of internalized object relations as well as of the organization of libidinal and aggressive drives.

I am thus proposing a first stage of consciousness characterized by peak-affect states and the beginning of symbolization. This early stage has essentially subjective features and cannot be considered equivalent to the data indicating the early capacity for cross-model differentiation, which presumably corresponds to prewired potentials optimally observable under experimental conditions characterized by mild or modulated affect dispositions. Subjectivity implies experiencing, and experiencing should logically be maximal under conditions of peak affects. Subjectivity also implies thinking and therefore requires, as a minimum, the manipulation of symbols. That minimum, I propose, implies a breaking out from the rigid chain of conditioned associations.

Perhaps of particular importance here is the gradual development of two parallel series of all-good and all-bad fantasied characteristics of this symbiotic world: the pleasure connected with the presence of the "good" feeding mother is in sharp contrast to the pain related to the "bad" mother when the infant is frustrated, discomfited, or enraged. By the same token, the transformation of painful experiences into the symbolic image of an undifferentiated "bad self–bad mother" obviously contains an element of fantasy that transcends the realistic character of the "good" self-object representations. The original fantasy material of what later becomes the repressed unconscious may reflect a predominance of aggressive imagery and affects.

Subjective experience in peak-affect states may initiate the construction of an internal world that gradually separates out into a deep layer of fantastic imagery linked to internalized object relations acquired during the peak states and a more superficial layer that "infiltrates" the cognitively more realistic perceptions of external reality built up under ordinary states of low-level affect when the infant is in alert exploration of the surround. Eventually, symbol formation and affective organization of reality would develop in this surface layer of perception as well, transforming wired-in organization of perception into symbolically manipulated information: that is, "conscious thinking," the origin of secondary-process thinking, evolves on the surface of the deep layer.

The dynamic unconscious originally includes unacceptable states of self-awareness under the influence of aggressively invested relations with object representations similarly perceived by means of primitive defensive operations, particularly projective identification. The early peak-affect states resulting from frustration activate primitive fantasies of frustrating "objects" represented by sensoriperceptive experiences that also come to symbolize efforts to "expel" such intolerable objects and rageful wishes to destroy them, together with transformation of the experience of frustration into the fantasy of being attacked and endangered. The repression of peak-affect experiences of a pleasurable nature—particularly of sexually excited states related to unacceptable fantasies involving parental objects—follows the earlier aggressive wishes and fantasies of the dynamic unconscious. The unconscious defenses connected with primitive fantasies and the later defenses that secondarily reinforce repression eventually "encapsulate" the deepest, unconscious layer of aggressively and libidinally invested object relations—the id.

Insofar as the earliest pleasurable peak-affect experiences of an undifferentiated self and object representation under the condition of an all-good object relation may be considered a core self experience, the awareness of self and of others is intimately linked in the area of self experience that will be incorporated into ego functions and structure as well. Although affectively modulated experiences may foster the mapping out of areas of differentiation between self and objects from early on, a core of fused or undifferentiated primitive experiences is rooted in the early ego as well as in the id.

Peak-affect experiences thus give birth to a core structure of intersubjectivity, both in the earliest identification with an object of love (an "introjective identification") and in the earliest identification with an object of hatred at the "periphery" of self experience (a "projective identification"), which is later dissociated, projected more effectively, and eventually repressed.

Intersubjectivity, whether incorporated in the self experience or rejected by projective mechanisms, is therefore an inseparable aspect of the development of normal identity. The psychoanalyst, too, by means of "concordant identification"—that is, empathy with the patient's central subjective experience—and "complementary identification"—that is, empathy with what the patient cannot tolerate within himself and activates by means of projective identification—may diagnose the patient's world of internalized object relations, which is part of his ego identity.

The subjective experience of the self, with its component aspects of self-awareness or self-reflection, its sense of subjective continuity cross-sectionally and longitudinally, and its sense of responsibility for its actions, is more than a subjective fantasy. It constitutes an intrapsychic structure, a dynamically determined, internally consistent, stable frame for organizing psychic experience and behavioral control. It is a channel for various psychic functions that actualizes itself in these functions, a substructure of the ego that gradually acquires supraordinate functions within the ego. It represents an intrapsychic structure of the highest order, whose nature is confirmed by its behavioral consequences, its expression in character formations, and its human depth and moral commitment in relations with others.

Defenses push the dynamic unconscious deeper and deeper into the psychic apparatus, a development that culminates with the establishment of repressive barriers that simultaneously signify the mutual rejection and the consolidation of the id and the ego. The dynamic unconscious of the neurotic patient and of the normal person is the end-product of a long evolution of psychic functioning, within which the qualities of consciousness and the dynamic unconscious are more closely interwoven than one might think on the basis of observation. But the eruption of the dynamic unconscious into consciousness is not reserved to patients with severe character pathology or psychoses. Interpersonal behavior in small unstructured groups, and to an even greater extent in large unstructured groups that temporarily eliminate or blur ordinary social role functions, may activate, sometimes in frightening ways, primitive contents of the repressed in the form of fantasies and behaviors shared by the entire group. This leads to the question of the ultimate nature of the motivational forces of the dynamic unconscious and to the psychoanalytic theory of drives.

ORIGIN AND STRUCTURE OF DRIVES AS MOTIVATIONAL FORCES

In my view, affects are the primary motivational system in that they are at the center of each of the infinite number of gratifying and frustrating concrete experiences the infant has with his environment. Affects link the series of undifferentiated self/object representations so that gradually a complex world of internalized object relations, some pleasurably tinged, others unpleasurably tinged, is constructed. But even while affects are linking internalized object relations in two parallel series of gratifying and frustrating experiences, "good" and "bad" internalized object relations are themselves being transformed. The predominant affect of love or hate of the two series of internalized object relations is enriched and modulated and becomes increasingly complex.

Eventually, the internal relation of the infant to the mother under the sign of "love" is more than the sum of a finite number of concrete loving affect states. The same holds true for hate. Love and hate thus become stable intrapsychic structures in the sense of two dynamically determined, internally consistent, stable frames for organizing psychic experience and behavioral control in genetic continuity through various developmental stages. By that very continuity, they consolidate into libido and aggression. Libido and aggression, in turn, become hierarchically supraordinate motivational systems, expressed in a multitude of differentiated affect dispositions under different circumstances. Affects are the building blocks, or constituents, of drives; they eventually acquire a signal function for the activation of drives.

Again, it needs to be stressed that drives are manifest not simply by affects but by the activation of a specific object relation, which includes an affect and in which the drive is represented by a specific desire or wish. Unconscious fantasy, the most important being oedipal in nature, includes a specific wish directed toward an object. The wish derives from the drive and is more precise than the affect state—an additional reason for rejecting a concept that would make affects rather than drives the hierarchically supraordinate motivational system.

Chapter 2 THE PSYCHOPATHOLOGY OF HATRED

Having offered a general theory of affects as the component substructures of drives, I turn now to a specific affect that occupies a central position in human behavior. I am referring to hatred, the core affect of severe psychopathological conditions, particularly severe personality disorders, perversions, and functional psychoses. Hatred derives from rage, the primary affect around which the drive of aggression clusters; in severe psychopathology, hatred may evolve into an overwhelming dominance directed against the self as well as against others. It is a complex affect that may become the major component of the aggressive drive, overshadowing other universally present aggressive affects such as envy or disgust.

In what follows, I focus for the most part on the developmental vicissitudes of rage, which lead to the dominance of hatred in certain patients with severe character pathology, resulting in the emergence of hatred as an overriding affect in the transference. This development permits the psychoanalytic exploration of hatred, but it also presents formidable challenges to the analyst, who must resolve the corresponding psychopathology in the transference. The formulations that follow are based, on the one hand, on the relation between the pathology of mother-infant relationships in infants at high risk and the development of inordinate aggression in such infants (Massie 1977; Gaensbauer and Sands 1979; Call 1980; Roiphe and Galenson 1981; Fraiberg 1983; Galenson 1986; Osofsky 1988) and, on the other hand, on the psychopathology of excessive aggression in the transference in patients with borderline personality organization and narcissistic and antisocial personality disorders (Winnicott 1949; Bion

1957a, 1959, 1970; A. Green 1977; Moser 1978; Ogden 1979; Krause 1988; Krause and Lutolf 1988; Grossman 1991). Observations of extreme regression in patients who show a predominance of hatred in the transference constitute the principal source for the formulations that follow.

RAGE

Clinically, the basic affect state characterizing the activation of aggression in the transference is that of rage. Irritation is a mild aggressive affect that signals the potential for rage reactions and, in chronic form, presents as irritability. Anger is a more intense affect than irritation, usually more differentiated in its cognitive content and in the nature of the object relationship that is activated. A full-fledged rage reaction—its overwhelming nature, its diffuseness, its "blurring" of specific cognitive contents and corresponding object relations—may convey the erroneous idea that rage is a "pure" primitive affect. Clinically, however, the analysis of rage reactions—as of other intense affect states—always reveals an underlying conscious or unconscious fantasy that includes a specific relation between an aspect of the self and an aspect of a significant other.

Infant research documents the early appearance of rage as an affect and its primordial function: to eliminate a source of pain or irritation. A later developmental function of rage is to eliminate an obstacle to gratification; the original biological function of rage—signaling to the caregiver to facilitate elimination of an irritant—now becomes a more focused appeal to the caregiver to restore a desired state of gratification. In the unconscious fantasies that develop around rage reactions, rage comes to signify both activation of an all-bad object relation and the wish to eliminate it and restore an all-good one. At a still later developmental stage, rage reactions may function as last-ditch efforts to restore a sense of autonomy in the face of highly frustrating situations unconsciously perceived as the threatening activation of all-bad, persecutory object relationships. A violent assertion of will functions to restore a state of narcissistic equilibrium; this act of self-assertion represents an unconscious identification with an idealized—all-good—object.

Clinically, the intensity of the aggressive affects—whether irritation, anger, or rage—correlates roughly with their psychological function: to assert autonomy, to eliminate an obstacle or barrier to a desired degree of satisfaction, or to eliminate or destroy a source of profound pain or frustration. But the psychopathology of aggression is not limited to the intensity and frequency of rage attacks. The most severe and dominant of the affects that together constitute aggression as a drive is the complex or elaborated affect of hatred. As we move from the transference develop-ments of patients with neurotic personality organization to those of patients with borderline personality organization, particularly those with severe narcissistic pathology and antisocial features, we are increas-ingly faced not only with rage attacks in the transference but with hatred, which emerges along with certain typical secondary characterological expressions of and defenses against awareness of this affect.

HATRED

Hatred is a complex aggressive affect. In contrast to the acuteness of rage reactions and the easily varying cognitive aspects of anger and rage, the cognitive aspect of hatred is chronic and stable. Hatred also presents with characterological anchoring that includes powerful rationalizations and corresponding distortions of ego and superego functioning. The primary aim of one consumed by hatred is to destroy its object, a specific object of unconscious fantasy, and this object's conscious derivatives; the object is at bottom both needed and desired, and its destruction is equally needed and desired. Understanding this paradox is at the center of the psychoana-lytic investigation of this affect. Hatred is not always pathological: as a response to an objective, real danger of physical or psychological destruc-tion, a threat to the survival of oneself and those one loves, hatred is a normal elaboration of rage aimed to eliminate that danger. But uncon-scious motivations usually enter and intensify hatred, as in the search for revenge. When it is a chronic characterological predisposition, hatred always reflects the psychopathology of aggression.

An extreme form of hatred demands the physical elimination of the object and may be expressed in murder or in a radical devaluation of the object that may generalize in the form of a symbolic destruction of all objects—that is, all potential relationships with significant others— as is clinically observable in antisocial personality structures. This form of hatred is sometimes expressed in suicide, where the self is identified with the hated object and self-elimination is the only way to destroy the object as well.

Clinically, some patients with the syndrome of malignant narcissism (narcissistic personality, ego-syntonic aggression, paranoid and anti-social tendencies) and "psychopathic" transferences (deceptiveness as a dominant transference feature) may consistently attempt to exploit, destroy, symbolically castrate, or dehumanize significant others— including the therapist—to an extent that defies the therapist's efforts to protect or recapture some island of an idealized primitive, all-good object relationship. At the same time, the transference may appear to be remarkably free from overt aggression; chronic deceptiveness and the search for a primitive all-good self state that eliminates all objects—by means of alcohol or drugs, for example, and by unconscious and conscious efforts to coopt the therapist in the exploitation or destruction of others—dominate the scene. The therapist's efforts to stand up against this diffuse, generalized destruction or corruption of everything valuable may be experienced by the patient (by projective mechanisms) as a brutal attack, which leads to the emergence of direct rage and hatred in the transference; we witness the transformation of a "psychopathic" into a "paranoid" transference (see chap. 14). Paradoxically, this transformation offers a glimmer of hope for these patients.

A less severe degree of hatred is expressed in sadistic tendencies and wishes; the patient has an unconscious or conscious desire to make the object suffer, with a sense of profound conscious or unconscious enjoyment of that suffering. Sadism may take the form of a sexual perversion with actual physical damaging of the object, or it may be part of the syndrome of malignant narcissism, sadomasochistic personality structure, or, sometimes, a rationalized, intellectualized form of cruelty that includes wishes to humiliate the object. In contrast to the earlier, more encompassing form of hatred, sadism is characterized by the wish not to eliminate but to maintain the relationship with the hated object in an enactment of an object relationship between a sadistic agent and a paralyzed victim. The desire to inflict pain and pleasure in doing so are central here, representing an implicit condensation of aggression and libidinal excitement in inducing such suffering.

A still milder form of hatred centers around the desire to dominate the object, a search for power over it that may include sadistic components but in which attacks on the object tend to be self-limited by the object's submission and its implied reconfirmation of the subject's freedom and autonomy. Anal-sadistic components predominate over the more primitive oral-aggressive ones found in the more severe forms of hatred; the assertion of hierarchical superiority and "territoriality" in social interactions and the aggressive aspects of regressive small- and large-group processes are the most frequent manifestations of this milder level of hatred.

Finally, in those with relatively normal superego integration and a neurotic personality organization with a well-differentiated tripartite structure, hatred may take the form of a rationalized identification with a strict and punitive superego, the aggressive assertion of idiosyncratic but well-rationalized systems of morality, justified indignation, and primitive levels of commitment to vindictive ideologies. Hatred at this level, of course, bridges over to the sublimatory function of courageous aggressive assertion in the service of commitment to ideals and ethical systems.

At this level of integration there is usually also a tendency toward self-directed hatred in the form of cruelty of the superego; clinically we see a potential for a transformation of transferences from the primitive "paranoid" into the more advanced "depressive" type. Masochistic and sadomasochistic personality structures and mixed neurotic constellations including paranoid, masochistic, and sadistic traits may experience relatively sudden shifts between depressive and paranoid transference regression. In contrast, at more severe levels of psychopathology, the transference is overwhelmingly paranoid, except when psychopathic transferences defend the patient against the paranoid ones.

The entire spectrum of affective and characterological components of hatred may be observed in the transference of patients of the second level of pathology, patients who have at least a wish to preserve the hated object. The chronicity, stability, and characterological anchoring of hatred is matched by the desire to inflict pain upon the object, characterological—and sometimes sexual—sadism, and cruelty.

Primitive hatred also takes the form of an effort to destroy the potential for a gratifying human relationship and for learning something of value in that human interaction (see chap. 13). Underlying this need to destroy reality and communication in intimate relationships is, I believe, unconscious and conscious envy of the object, particularly of an object not dominated from within by similar hatred.

It was Melanie Klein (1957) who first pointed to envy of the good object as a significant characteristic of patients with severe narcissistic psychopathology. Such envy is complicated by the patient's need to destroy his own awareness of it, lest his terror over the savagery of his hatred of what, *au fond*, he values in the object be exposed. Behind the envy of the object and the need to destroy and spoil anything good that might come from contacts with it lies unconscious identification with the originally hated—and needed—object. Envy may be considered both a source of a primitive form of hatred, intimately linked with oral aggression, greed, and voracity, and a complication of the hatred that derives from the fixation to trauma.

At the surface, hatred of the unconsciously—and consciously—envied object is usually rationalized as fear of the object's destructive potential, deriving both from actual aggression inflicted by essentially needed objects in the patient's past (in patients who have been severely traumatized) and from projection of his own rage and hatred.

Tendencies toward chronic and potentially severe self-mutilation and nondepressive suicidal behaviors frequently accompany the syndrome of malignant narcissism. Self-mutilation typically reflects unconscious identification with a hateful and hated object. Hatred and the inability to tolerate communication with the object may protect the patient from what might otherwise emerge as a combination of cruel attacks on the object, paranoid fears of that object, and self-directed aggression in identification with the object.

Clinically, the transference characterized by arrogance, curiosity, and pseudostupidity (incapacity to reflect on what the therapist says), described by Bion (1957a), illustrates the patient's acting out of envy of the therapist, destruction of meaning, and sadism.

One of the most consistent features in transferences dominated by acting out deep hatred is the patient's extraordinary dependence on the therapist, manifested simultaneously with aggression toward the therapist—an impressive demonstration of "fixation to the trauma." At the same time, the patient's fantasies and fears reflect his assumption that unless he consistently fights off the therapist, he will be subjected to a similar onslaught of hatred and sadistic exploitation and persecution from the therapist. Obviously, by means of projective identification, the patient is attributing his own hatred and sadism to the therapist; the situation illustrates the intimate link between persecutor and persecuted, master and slave, sadist and masochist, all referring in the last resort to the sadistic, frustrating, teasing mother and the helpless, paralyzed infant.

Basically, the patient is enacting an object relation between persecutor and victim, alternating these roles in his identifications while projecting the reciprocal role onto the therapist. In the most pathological cases, it is as if the only alternative to being victimized is to become a tyrant, and the repeated assertions of hatred and sadism would appear to be the only form of survival and meaning, aside from murder, suicide, or psychopathy. In milder cases, an additional dynamic factor, envy, emerges—intolerance of the good object who escapes from that savagery and who is hated for willfully withholding (as the patient fantasizes) what could transform the object from a persecuting one into an ideal one. Here the search for an ideal object (an ideal mother) lies behind the unending onslaught of hatred in the transference.

In still milder cases, with more sophisticated and elaborated types of sadomasochistic behavior within a neurotic personality organization, we discover the unconscious potential for pleasure in pain, the temptation to experience pain as a precondition for experiencing pleasure, in the context of castration anxiety, unconscious guilt over oedipal strivings, and as the ultimate transformation of passively experienced pain into an active compromise solution of the corresponding unconscious conflicts.

All these dynamics may emerge intimately condensed and combined, with differences in degree and proportion. What they have in common is the intense motivation to maintain a link with the hated object, a link that gratifies these various primitive transferences and is, in my view, responsible for the powerful fixation to this traumatic relationship.

FIXATION TO THE TRAUMA

I believe that peak-affect states organize internalized object relationships not only under conditions of love—the elation that corresponds to a primitive idealized fusion between an all-good self and an all-good object—but also under conditions of rage, in the internalization of originally undifferentiated all-bad self and object representations, which are gradually sorted out into the typical object relation under the domination of hatred. A powerful link to the traumatizing object under the dominance of hatred has been observed in studies of battered children and of infants at high risk, and also in studies of persons in extremely traumatic circumstances, such as hijacked airplane passengers who end up defending their captors (the "Stockholm Syndrome"). Research by Fraiberg (1983) and Galenson (1986) is particularly instructive regarding infants' internalization of the aggressive behavior of the mother toward them and their replication of the mother's behavior in relationship with her and with other objects.

Intense attachment to the frustrating mother is the ultimate origin of the transformation of rage into hatred. The cause of this transformation is the fixation to a traumatic relationship with a fundamentally needed object that is experienced as all-bad and as having destroyed or swallowed up the ideal, all-good object. The revengeful destruction of this bad object is intended to magically restore the all-good one, but in the process it leads to the destruction of the very capacity of the self to relate to the object. This transformation takes the form of identifying not simply with the object (mother) but with the *relationship* to her, so that the hatred of mother as victimizer, with its painful, impotent, paralyzing implications, also is transformed into identification with her as the cruel, omnipotent, destructive object. At the same time a search develops for other objects onto whom the attacked, depreciated, and mistreated self can be projected. In identifying with both suffering self and sadistic object, the subject is himself swallowed up by the all-encompassing aggression in the relationship.

Hatred as a reversal of suffering is a basic type of revengeful triumph over the object, a triumph also over the terrifying self representation achieved by projective identification, and symbolic revenge for past suffering condensed in the fixation to sadistic behavior patterns. Patients so motivated mistreat others sadistically because they experience themselves as being mistreated, again, by sadistic objects; unconsciously, they become their own persecutory objects while sadistically attacking their victims. They cannot escape being victim and perpetrator at the same time. As victimizer, they cannot live without their victim—the projected, disowned persecuted self; as victim, they remain attached to their persecutors internally and sometimes, in behavior shocking to an observer, externally as well.

Extremely contradictory, unreliable behaviors on the part of mother probably reinforce the psychopathic end of the spectrum of hatred by permitting the interpretation of her behavior as a betrayal by the potentially good object, which thus becomes unpredictably and overwhelmingly bad. Identification with a betraying object initiates the path to a revengeful destruction of all object relations. The ultimate source of the paranoid urge to betray (Jacobson 1971a, pp. 302–318) probably lies here. The most severely psychopathological attachment behavior has been described in infants whose mothers' behavior combined abandonment, violence, chaos, and a teasing overstimulation together with chronic frustration (Fraiberg 1983; Galenson 1986).

Elsewhere (Kernberg 1991b) I have described the inclusion of an aggressive component of sexual excitement—the aggressive implication of penetrating and being penetrated—as a means of incorporating aggression in the service of love, utilizing the erotogenic potential of the experience of pain as a crucial contributor to the gratifying fusion with the other in sexual excitement and orgasm. This normal capability for transforming pain into erotic excitement miscarries when severe aggression has characterized the mother-infant relationship and is probably a crucial bridge to the erotic excitement of inducing suffering in others, which consolidates the pleasurable characteristics of sadistic hatred. If, at the same time, as Braunschweig and Fain (1971, 1975) have suggested, the alternatingly erotically stimulating and withdrawing attitudes of mother toward her infant form the basis of his unconscious identification with a teasing mother as well as with being teased and in the process activate his own sexual excitement as a basic affect, then a mother whose behavior includes exaggerated teasing of the infant may orient his hatred particularly toward the sadomasochistic perversions.

More generally, to cause deep pain in the infant and small child leads first to rage and then, by the identificatory and transformational mechanisms mentioned, to the development of hatred. Thus, as Grossman (1991) has proposed, pain may lead, by a series of intrapsychic transformations, to the intensification and psychopathology of aggression.

Excessive activation of aggression as a drive (to which characterologically fixated hatred contributes fundamentally) interferes with the normal integration of the mutually dissociated, all-good and all-bad internalized object relations at the conclusion of the developmental phase of separation-individuation and therefore with the initiation of object constancy and the advanced stage of oedipal development. In disrupting these processes, excessive aggression leads to fixation at a point when all-good and all-bad internalized object relations were not integrated, while self and object representations within each of these all-good and all-bad object relationships were differentiated from each other. These constitute the psychostructural conditions of borderline personality organization, characteristic of severe personality disorders in which preoedipal and oedipal aggression is dominant.

Under more favorable circumstances, integration of all-good and all-bad internalized object relations may proceed and object constancy may develop, leading to integration of the ego and superego structures and to the establishment of repressive boundaries separating ego from id: the tripartite structure consolidates.Under such conditions the pathological hatred is absorbed by the superego. The integration of early sadistic superego precursors with the preoedipal ego ideal, on the one hand, and of oedipal prohibitions and demands with those earlier superego structures, on the other, leads to sadistic superego demands, depressive-masochistic psychopathology, and secondarily rationalized characterological sadism correlated with the integration of cruel and sadistic ethical systems. Or perhaps various sexual pathologies, including perversions at a neurotic level of personality organization, may contain hatred as a relatively harmless, eroticized symptom.

The wish to humiliate is another manifestation of hatred potentially integrated into superego-mediated character features. An obsessive-compulsive patient needs to control and dominate others to feel protected against threatening outbreaks of aggressive rebelliousness and chaos in others—thus enacting his identification with a hated object and his projection of unacceptable, repressed, and projected aspects of his self at a relatively high level of psychic functioning. Fixation to specific hated objects can be seen along the entire spectrum of psychopathology and illustrates, sometimes almost in caricature, attachment to the enemy or persecutor. It says something about the common origins of the basic affects of rage and sexual excitement in the symbiotic phase that the highest tendency for sustained mutual gaze exists under conditions of intense hatred and intense love.

SOME COMMENTS ABOUT TREATMENT

What follows are some general considerations regarding the treatment of patients with severe psychopathology of aggression, particularly intense hatred in the transference. Elsewhere (chap. 3), I point to the importance of interpreting consistently and in depth the nature of the unconscious fantasies implied in the activation of rage in the transference, particularly to the importance of interpreting secondary defenses against acknowledging the pleasurable aspects of rage. In considering the spectrum of the psychopathology of hatred, I would first stress the countertransference consequences of this affect.

I have pointed out in earlier work (1975, 1984) that the patient, particularly the narcissistic patient with antisocial features, hates most what he most needs to receive from the therapist: unwavering dedication to him. The patient also hates, because he envies it, the creativity contained in the therapist's efforts to gain understanding and to communicate this understanding to the patient. The analyst's sense of being exhausted, that his efforts are going to waste, his sense of the enormity of the patient's lack of gratitude, may result in a countertransference that tends to perpetuate or even obscure the patient's acting out of hatred and envy.

The therapist may attempt to escape from his discouragement by emotionally disconnecting from the patient. The restoration of the therapist's tranquillity may be at the cost of an internal surrender that, not surprisingly, the patient often perceives but easily tolerates because he rightly experiences it as the therapist's defeat. An uneasy equilibrium may ensue in which a surface friendliness obscures the "parasitic" (Bion 1970) nature of the therapeutic relationship.

Or the therapist may enter into collusion with the splitting process in the patient, facilitating the displacement of aggression elsewhere and fostering the creation of a pseudotherapeutic alliance that ensures a friendly surface relationship in the transference.

Another solution frequently adopted by the therapist is to absorb the patient's aggression, in full awareness of what is going on but without finding a way to transform this acting out into viable interpretations. This development, which amounts to a masochistic submission to the "impossible" patient, is sometimes engaged in quite consciously by a therapist who believes that with sufficient love most things can be cured.

The counterpart to such a masochistic submission to the patient is often the eventual acting out of aggression in the countertransference, either by dismissing the patient or by unconsciously provoking him to leave.

It is most likely, however, that the therapist, even the experienced therapist, will oscillate in his internal stance from day to day, from session to session, between efforts to resolve the activation of hatred in the transference analytically and giving up or withdrawing. These natural oscillations may actually reflect a reasonable compromise formation that permits the therapist to step back and evaluate the effects of his various interventions and gives him some breathing space before he returns to an active interpretive stance.

In all cases, I think it is extremely important to diagnose secondary defenses against hatred at the most pathological end of the spectrum of aggression in the transference—that is, the development of antisocial or psychopathic transferences. The patient's conscious or unconscious corruption of all relationships, particularly the therapeutic one, must be examined consistently, with the therapist fully aware that such an examination will probably shift the apparently "quiet" psychopathic transference relationship into a severely paranoid one and activate intense hatred in the transference. The therapist's normal superego functions, his being moral but not moralistic (E. Ticho, personal communication), will be experienced by patients with antisocial tendencies as devastating attacks and criticisms.

It is important to interpret the patient's paranoid reaction as part of the interpretation of the antisocial transferences. Such an interpretation might run as follows: "I am under the impression that, if I point out to you that I believe (such and such behavior) is an expression of your profound need to destroy (a certain relationship), you might interpret my comment as if I were attacking you rather than trying to help you understand what I consider a very important aspect of your difficulties at this time."

Once the transferences have shifted from a dominantly antisocial into a paranoid mode, the general technical approach to severe paranoid regression is indicated, the characteristics and management of which I discuss elsewhere (chap. 4). I want only to stress the need to acknowledge openly to the patient who is convinced of a paranoid distortion of reality that the therapist sees that reality in a completely different way but respects the temporary incompatibility of his and the patient's perceptions of it: in other words, a "psychotic nucleus" is identified, circumscribed, and tolerated in the transference before any attempt is made to resolve it interpretively. It is usually only at advanced stages of the treatment of patients with severe psychopathology that integration of idealized and persecutory internalized object relations can take place, with a corresponding shift of paranoid into depressive transferences—that is, the emergence in the patient of guilt feelings, concern over the dangerous effects of aggression, and wishes to repair the psychotherapeutic relationship.

Where the sadistic elements are particularly marked, it is important that the patient become aware of his pleasure in hatred, a subject I deal with extensively in chapter 3. This requires that the therapist be able to empathize with the pleasure implied in the patient's aggression. When power relations are the dominant issue in the transference and hatred is expressed as an inordinate need to assert power and autonomy, analysis of this aspect of the transference is usually facilitated by the fact that ordinary anal-sadistic components are involved and the therapist is dealing with the "healthier" end of the spectrum of psychopathology of aggression.

Again, the most difficult patients are those in whom intense aggression goes hand in hand with deep psychopathology of superego functioning, so that internal constraints against dangerous enactment of aggression are missing, and the therapist may be realistically afraid of unleashing destructive forces beyond the capacity of the treatment to contain them. This applies to some patients who present the syndrome of malignant narcissism and is probably a major reason that the antisocial personality proper is unapproachable by means of psychoanalytic modalities of treatment. It is important that the therapist have a reasonable sense of security that the analysis of powerful aggressive forces will not create new risks for the patient or others, including himself. A realistic assessment of this possibility and a realistic structuring of the treatment situation to protect patient, therapist, and others from inordinate and dangerous, potentially irreversible effects of the acting out of aggression are preconditions for successful work in this area.

Part II DEVELOPMENTAL ASPECTS OF BROAD-SPECTRUM PERSONALITY DISORDERS

Chapter 3 CLINICAL DIMENSIONS OF MASOCHISM

Masochism cannot be understood without taking into consideration the vicissitudes of both libidinal and aggressive strivings, superego development and pathology, levels of ego organization and pathology of internalized object relations, and the extent to which normal or pathological narcissistic functions predominate. Because of the universality of masochistic behaviors and conflicts, it is not always easy to know when masochism is psychopathological. Recent tendencies to overextend the concept of masochism make it essential to circumscribe this field more precisely (Grossman 1986).

In what follows, I propose a general classification of masochistic psychopathology based on the level of personality organization; I also describe the relationship between this clinical domain and other types of psychopathology that might be confused with it. My objective is to provide a description of masochistic pathology relevant for diagnostic, prognostic, and treatment considerations.

Laplanche and Pontalis (1973) provide the briefest and, in my view, most satisfactory definition of masochism in the psychoanalytic literature: "Sexual perversion in which satisfaction is tied to the suffering or humiliation undergone by the subject." They add: "Freud extends the notion of masochism beyond the perversion as described by sexologists. In the first place, he identifies masochistic elements in numerous types of sexual behaviour and sees rudiments of masochism in infantile sexuality. Secondly, he describes derivative forms, notably 'moral masochism,' where the subject, as a result of an unconscious sense of guilt, seeks out the position of victim without any sexual pleasure being directly involved" (p. 244). This definition has the virtue of including the basic elements common to a broad spectrum of masochistic behaviors.

"NORMAL" MASOCHISM

The price paid for the integration of normal superego functions is the disposition to develop unconscious guilt feelings when repressed infantile drive derivatives are activated. Therefore a proneness to minor self-defeating behaviors—for example, in response to what is unconsciously perceived as oedipal triumph—is virtually universal. Obsessive behaviors that unconsciously express magical reassurance against the threatened activation of infantile prohibitions and their clinical correlates, such as characterological inhibitions and self-imposed restrictions of a full enjoyment of life, are also ubiquitous. The tendency for realistic self-criticism to expand into a general depressive mood is another manifestation of such self-defeating superego pressures (Jacobson 1964). In short, minor manifestations of "moral masochism" are an almost unavoidable correlate of normal integration of superego functions. The sublimatory capacity to endure pain (in the form of hard work) as the price of future success or achievement also has roots in this generally normal masochistic predisposition.

In the sexual realm, the ability to tolerate the preservation of polymorphous perverse infantile sexuality should permit the capacity for sexual arousal with masochistic and sadomasochistic fantasies and experiences. As I note in chapter 16, the sadomasochistic aspect of infantile sexuality is of particular importance in maintaining an equilibrium between libidinal and aggressive strivings because it represents a primitive form of synthesis between love and hatred. In sadomasochistic pleasure, sexual excitement and pain become one; therefore, to give or receive aggression in the form of pain may also signify to give or receive love in the form of erotic stimulation. It is this condensation of physical pleasure and pain that leads, by means of transformational processes still unexplored, to the predisposition to experience a condensation of psychological pleasure and pain as well, when superego-determined accusations and attacks are directed against the self.

MASOCHISTIC CHARACTER PATHOLOGY
The Depressive-Masochistic Personality Disorder

This constellation of pathological character traits constitutes one of the three most common personality disorders of high-level or neurotic character pathology ("neurotic personality organization"; Kernberg 1984). The others are obsessive-compulsive personality disorder and the hysterical personality disorder. All these personality disorders present a well-integrated ego identity, nonspecific manifestations of ego strength (good anxiety tolerance, impulse control, and sublimatory functioning), and a strict but well-integrated superego. These patients are also able to establish well-differentiated object relations in depth.

The depressive-masochistic personality disorder is characterized by three particular types of character traits: (1) those reflecting an intransigent superego, (2) traits reflecting overdependency on support, love, and acceptance from others, and (3) traits reflecting difficulties in the expression of aggression.

The "superego" features of the depressive-masochistic personality are reflected in a tendency to be excessively serious, conscientious, and concerned about work performance and responsibilities. These patients are highly reliable and dependable, tend to judge themselves harshly and to set extremely high standards for themselves. They are somber and may lack a sense of humor. But in contrast to their usually considerate, tactful, and concerned behavior, they may occasionally show harshness in their judgment of others, a harshness that may be tinged with justified indignation. When these patients do not live up to their own high standards and expectations, they may become depressed. They may even, when their inordinate demands on themselves are matched by their unconscious tendency to put themselves into circumstances that will induce suffering or exploitation, unconsciously create or perpetuate an external reality that will justify their sense of being mistreated, demeaned, or humiliated.

The traits that reflect overdependency on support, love, and acceptance from others also reveal, on psychoanalytic exploration, a tendency to feel inordinately guilty toward others because of unconscious ambivalence toward loved and needed objects and to overreact to frustration when these patients' expectations are not met. They show an abnormal vulnerability to being disappointed by others, often going far out of their way to obtain sympathy and love. In contrast to the narcissistic personality, who is overdependent on external admiration but does not respond with love and gratitude, the depressive-masochistic personality typically is able to respond deeply with love and to be grateful. The sense of being rejected and mistreated in reaction to relatively minor slights may lead these patients to unconscious behaviors geared to making the objects of their love feel guilty. A chain reaction is set up of heightened demandingness, feelings of rejection, and an unconscious tendency to try to make others feel guilty; consequent actual rejection from others may spiral into severe problems in intimate relations and may also trigger depression connected to loss of love.

The patients in this category have trouble expressing aggression and tend to become depressed under conditions that would normally produce anger or rage. In addition, unconscious guilt over expressing anger to others may further complicate their interpersonal relations, adding to the chain reaction already described: a tendency toward "justified" attacks on those they need and feel rejected by, followed by depression and abject, submissive, and/or compliant behavior, and then by a second wave of anger over the way they are treated and their own submissiveness.

What I have described corresponds to the description of "moral masochism" in the psychoanalytic literature (Freud 1916, 1919, 1924; Fenichel 1945, pp. 501–502; Berliner 1958; Brenner 1959; Laughlin 1967; Gross 1981; Asch 1985). Typically, the corresponding unconscious dynamics center on excessive superego pressures derived from infantile, particularly oedipal, conflicts and may express themselves in an unconscious defensive regression to preoedipal dynamics and general masochistic behaviors that are at a considerable distance from infantile sexual conflicts. In some cases, however, unconscious sexual conflicts are closely related to the masochistic behaviors, so that it is particularly in the sexual realm that these patients manifest self-punitive behaviors as a reflection of unconscious prohibitions against oedipal impulses. These patients may tolerate a satisfactory sexual experience only under conditions of objective or symbolic suffering, and the depressive-masochistic personality structure may be accompanied by an actual masochistic perversion at a neurotic level. In any event, it is patients with this personality structure who most frequently present masochistic masturbation fantasies and masochistic sexual behaviors without a masochistic perversion per se. The masochistic behaviors that directly express unconscious guilt over oedipal impulses link the depressive-masochistic and the hysterical personality disorders (see chap. 4).

Sadomasochistic Personality Disorder

These patients typically show alternating masochistic and sadistic behavior toward the same object. I am not referring here to the individual who submits to his superiors and tyrannizes his inferiors—social behavior compatible with various pathological character constellations. The patients I refer to alternate self-demeaning, self-debasing, self-humiliating behaviors with sadistic attacks on the same objects they feel they need and are deeply involved with.

Sadomasochistic personalities usually present borderline personality organization with identity diffusion, nonspecific manifestations of ego weakness (lack of anxiety tolerance, impulse control, and sublimatory channeling), predominance of part-object relations, and prevalence of primitive defensive mechanisms (splitting, projective identification, denial, primitive idealization, omnipotent control, and devaluation). Within the chaos of their object relations, the intensification of chaotic interactions with their closest intimates stands out. These patients usually experience themselves as the victims of others' aggression, bitterly complain about being mistreated, and adamantly justify their own aggressions toward those upon whom they are dependent. The "help-rejecting complainer" (Frank et al. 1952) is typical; these patients' interpersonal and social difficulties may lead to chronic failure at work and socially as well as in intimate relations.

In contrast to the impulsive, chaotic, arrogant, and devaluating behaviors of the narcissistic personality functioning on an overt borderline level, the sadomasochistic personality has much more capacity for investment in depth in relations with others; he is dependent and clinging, unlike the aloof narcissistic personality.

The dynamic features of these patients include severe conflicts, both oedipal and preoedipal, particularly an internal dependency on primitive maternal images experienced as sadistic, dishonest, and controlling; such images exacerbate oedipal fears and condense unconscious oedipal and preoedipal issues in these patients' behaviors much more than occurs with preoedipal regression of patients with depressive-masochistic personality and essentially oedipal dynamics.

One male patient experienced intense feelings of insecurity and inferiority toward his analyst while berating him continually. In his relationships with girlfriends, he was both extremely afraid that they would drop him for more attractive men and extremely demanding of their time and attention; his breakups with girlfriends were followed by pathological mourning with intense paranoid reactions, alternating with a depressive sense of having been abandoned.

The lack of integration of superego functions, the projection of primitive superego precursors in the form of paranoid traits, and the tolerance of contradictory behaviors—in fact, the rationalization of aggressive behaviors—all illustrate the failure of superego functions to integrate in these patients, in marked contrast to the rigid superego integration of the depressive-masochistic personality disorder.

Primitive Self-Destructiveness and Self-Mutilation

In earlier writing (1975) I described a group of patients who tend to discharge aggression indiscriminately toward the outside or onto their own bodies. These patients, clearly self-destructive, lack superego integration and show a remarkable absence of the capacity for experiencing guilt; they present the general characteristics of borderline personality organization. The most typical examples are patients who obtain nonspecific relief of anxiety by some form of self-mutilation or by impulsive suicidal gestures carried out with great rage and almost no depression.

These self-destructive patients fall into three groups (Kernberg 1984). In patients with predominantly histrionic or infantile personality disorder, those who correspond closely to the descriptive disorder of borderline personality disorder in DSM-III-R (1987), the self-destructiveness emerges at times of intense rage or rage mixed with temporary flare-ups of depression. This behavior frequently represents an unconscious effort to reestablish control over the environment by evoking guilt feelings in others—for example, when a relationship with a sexual partner breaks up or when the patient's wishes are opposed.

A more severe type of self-mutilating behavior and/or suicidal tendencies can be seen in patients with malignant narcissism (see chap. 5). In contrast to the first group, these patients do not show intense dependency or clinging behavior and are rather aloof from and uninvolved with others. Their self-destructive behavior occurs when their pathological grandiosity is challenged, resulting in their experiencing a traumatic sense of humiliation or defeat. It is often accompanied by overtly sadistic behavior. Grandiosity is fulfilled by a feeling of triumph over the fear of pain and death and by a sense of superiority over those who are shocked or chagrined by their behavior.

A third type of chronic self-destructive behavior is found in certain atypical psychotic conditions that mimic borderline pathology. These patients' history of bizarre suicide attempts marked by an unusual degree of cruelty or other highly idiosyncratic features may actually alert the clinician to the possibility of an underlying psychotic process.

All of these self-destructive patients experience conscious or unconscious pleasure in connection with the pain they inflict upon themselves, aggression directed against themselves that is neither centered in their superego pathology (an unconscious sense of guilt) nor linked directly or primarily with erotic strivings. These patients illustrate clinically a self-destructiveness that is dependent on the intensity of primitive aggression, primitivization of all intrapsychic structures, lack of superego development, and a recruitment of libidinal and erotic strivings in the service of aggression. They derive a sense of power from their diffuse destructiveness, a triumphant sense of autonomy and the absence of need for others; clinically they show blatant efforts to destroy love and relatedness, gratitude and compassion, in themselves and in others. It is questionable whether this group of patients may still be considered part of masochistic psychopathology in a strict sense: unconscious guilt, as well as erotization of pain, is usually absent.

In more general terms, as we move toward the more severe pole of this spectrum of masochistic character pathology, we find a gradual decrease of integration of the superego and of participation of the superego in the consolidation of masochistic pathology, and an increase of primitive and severe aggression together with primitivization of object relationships and defensive operations. Eroticism also fades out at this pole of the masochistic spectrum.

THE SYNDROMES OF PATHOLOGICAL INFATUATION

Freud asserted that in the act of falling in love the ego is depleted of libidinal cathexes, which are invested in the love object as a replacement of the ego ideal (1921, pp. 111–116). I am convinced by Chasseguet-Smirgel (1985), who disagrees with Freud, pointing to the enrichment of libidinal investment of the self of the person in love. Particularly under normal circumstances, a love object who does not reciprocate the subject's love is abandoned in a process of mourning. When love is reciprocated, the self-esteem of the lovers is enhanced. The difference between normal and masochistic falling in love is precisely that masochistic personalities may be irresistibly attracted to unresponsive objects. In fact, the unconscious selection of an object who is clearly unable or unwilling to respond to love characterizes masochistic infatuations.

It is important to differentiate such impossible love affairs from a masochistic sexual perversion, in which a love object provides sexual gratification together with physical pain, debasement, and/or humiliation. Although these patterns may coincide, such is rarely the case. The description of sexual masochism by Sacher-Masoch in *Venus in Furs* (from which the word *masochism* derives; 1881) corresponds to the writer's relation to his first wife (and later to his second wife as well) and illustrates typically perverse practices in the context of a stable relationship with a loved object.

To sacrifice oneself and all one's interests for someone who does not reciprocate (dramatically illustrated in the 1932 novel by Heinrich Mann and the film *The Blue Angel*) may suggest the presence of a depressive-masochistic personality disorder. But the dramatic self-sacrifice and the ease with which the subject seems to brush aside an entire life pattern in pursuit of the idealized, unavailable love object may impress the clinician as presenting quasi-narcissistic qualities: the neglect of all others except the love object, the total self-involvement of the afflicted individual. In fact, the patient presenting such pathological infatuation manifests a sense of narcissistic gratification and fulfillment in his enslavement to an unavailable object. He takes unmistakable pride in the image of himself as the greatest sufferer on earth, dynamically related to the narcissistic gratification of being "the *greatest* sinner" or "the *worst* victim."

In this type of pathological infatuation, love for the unavailable object represents submission to the ego-ideal aspects of the superego that were projected onto the object, and this painful and unsatisfactory love fills the individual with pride and emotional intensity. Masochistic involvement with unavailable love objects may also be present in patients with a hysterical personality structure, such as the woman who can fall in love only with men who mistreat her. In other cases, it is not an unavailable love object but a clearly sadistic one the patient must choose.

The rejection of all those who would interpose themselves between the patient and his or her self-sacrificing love affair may impress the observer as narcissistic but in my view, it reflects normal infantile and not pathological narcissism. The masochistic patient's sense of superiority ("I am the greatest sufferer in the world") refers to the specific area of suffering but not to all other areas of the patient's life.

One woman, for example, conducted an unsatisfactory relationship with a sadistic, largely unavailable man while maintaining stable relationships in depth with other friends and social acquaintances, as well as cultural interests and commitments to her work and family. In the transference, her critical and belittling behavior toward any analytic effort to point to the self-demeaning aspects of her relationship with her sadistic lover corresponded to her effort to keep the psychoanalytic relationship unsatisfactory because of unconscious guilt feelings over oedipal longings for the analyst.

At the second, more severe level of pathological infatuation the opposite development has taken place—namely, the patient masochistically pursues an impossible love relationship while all his or her other object relations are narcissistic. For example, a young woman of considerable charm and beauty mercilessly denigrated and devalued men and was interested only in those who were physically attractive, socially prestigious, wealthy, or powerful—attributes she hoped to acquire for herself through association. Rejection by such a man triggered deep depression, attempts at suicide, and/or denial that she had been rejected. To deny the man's lack of interest she even went so far as to misinterpret, over a period of many months, any conventional friendliness from him as a sign that their relationship had a future.

Not surprisingly, when any of these men did reciprocate the patient's love, within weeks she was devaluing him as she had denigrated all the other men in her life. In fact, her growing awareness of this pattern led her to search for men who were even more unavailable and unconsciously to set up a situation that was certain to leave her rejected so that her investment in the "ideal man" could continue unchallenged. Her other object relations contained features typical of a narcissistic personality disorder.

Here we find the projection not of a normal ego ideal onto the unavailable love object but of a pathological grandiose self, with an effort to establish a relationship that unconsciously would confirm the stability of the patient's own grandiosity. On analytic exploration, these masochistic love affairs of narcissistic personalities may represent an unconscious effort to consolidate a symbolic integration within the grandiose self of the characteristics of both sexes by trying to establish a symbiotic unit with the idealized object.

In such cases the relation to the idealized love object typically reflects a condensation of oedipal and preoedipal issues, the idealized positive oedipal love object, and the superimposed sadistic yet needed preoedipal love object as well. Cooper (1985) has drawn our attention to the combination in clinical practice of narcissistic and masochistic character features. Although I disagree with his proposal that these two character constellations correspond to one basic type of character pathology, and I think he underestimates the differences between normal infantile and pathological narcissism in these patients, I do believe that the syndrome of pathological infatuation requires careful evaluation of both its masochistic and narcissistic characteristics.

MASOCHISTIC SEXUAL BEHAVIOR AND PERVERSION

Masochism as a sexual perversion is characterized by the restrictive, obligatory enactment of masochistic behavior to achieve sexual excitement and orgasm (Freud 1905; Laplanche and Pontalis 1973). Masochistic behavior may include the need to experience physical pain, emotional suffering, self-debasement, and/or humiliation. Levels of severity of sexual perversion can be seen in parallel to the levels of severity of masochistic character pathology already referred to.

Masochistic Perversion at a Neurotic Level

Sexual masochism at this level typically takes the form of a scenario enacted in the context of an object relation that is experienced as safe.

Typical unconscious dynamics, centering upon oedipal conflicts, include the need to deny castration anxiety and to assuage a harsh superego in order to obtain sexual gratification that has incestuous meanings. Unconscious scenarios also include enactment of conflictual identifications with the other sex and identification with a punishing, sadistic incestuous object. The "as if," play-acting quality of the sexual scenario, as I observe in chapter 16, is common to all perversions at this level. The sexual perversion may include symbolic enactment of the primal-scene experiences, such as the oedipal triangle in the form of a ménage à trois, in which the masochistic subject is forced to witness sexual relations between his love object and a rival as a condition for sexual intercourse and gratification.

Masochistic perversion usually but not necessarily involves a partner. There are masochistic forms of masturbation in which the individual ties himself up and watches himself in a mirror while experiencing pain as a precondition for orgasm, and masturbation fantasies may have an obligatory masochistic quality. The actual presence or absence of an object is, in my view, less important than the fact that an object relation underlies all sexual behavior; the manifest characteristics are less important than the conscious and unconscious fantasies that reflect the obligatory structure of the perversion. Usually the perverse scenario is spelled out in great detail by the individual, and the repetitive and punctilious enactment of that scenario is a source of reassurance against unconscious anxieties as well as a prerequisite for sexual pleasure and orgasm.

Sexual Masochism with Self-Destructive or Other Regressive Features

In contrast to the level of masochism just described are patients whose behavior seems devoid of safety features and has a quality of danger that may lead to mutilation, self-mutilation, and even accidental death. These behaviors are found in patients with borderline personality organization.

One patient, a narcissistic personality with overtly borderline features, demanded that he be tied up by men he met casually in bars frequented by sadomasochists. He provoked these men into serious fights in which he was sometimes physically hurt. On several occasions he had been threatened at gunpoint and robbed while engaging in such casual sexual encounters.

Another patient, a white, middle-class woman in her early twenties, was able to experience sexual excitement only when prostituting herself to much older men or to black men in dangerous neighborhoods. She was aware that the potential danger to her life was one source of excitement in such encounters. She also suffered from a narcissistic personality with infantile and masochistic features.

In these cases the sexual perversion breaks out of the "as if" or play-acting frame and reflects serious pathology of object relations. Sometimes there is no actual self-mutilating behavior but a bizarre quality of sexual activity in which undisguised anal, urethral, or oral contents color the masochistic pattern, giving it a primitive, pregenital quality. One patient had the following preferred mode of sexual relations with his wife: in order to achieve orgasm through masturbation, he had her sit on a specially constructed toilet that permitted her to defecate on his face while he was watching her. This patient had severely paranoid personality features in addition to a sadomasochistic personality structure.

Another patient's preferred mode of masturbatory gratification was to wade in a local brook so muddy that he sank knee deep in the mud while masturbating in the water, which he did at night to avoid being observed by neighbors. This patient also presented borderline personality organization, with paranoid, schizoid, and hypochondriacal personality features and social isolation.

These cases have in common (1) strong, primitive aggressive impulses, (2) severe pathology of object relations, (3) a predominance of preoedipal conflicts and aims in the sexually masochistic scenario, and (4) lack of integration of superego functions. These patients also revealed confusion of sexual identity, so that homosexual and heterosexual interactions were part of their sexual life, with the masochistic scenario representing its primary organizing feature.

Extreme Forms of Self-Mutilation and Self-Sacrifice

The most severe level of masochistic sexual perversion is illustrated by patients who are intent upon self-castration as part of a religious ritual or submission to an idealized, extremely sadistic primitive object. I have not personally seen any such cases, although I have seen patients whose self-mutilating wishes and behavior were part of a clearly psychotic pathology. I would also place at this level some borderline patients with self-mutilating behavior that has an erotic quality—for example, patients who bite and swallow their buccal mucosa or their fingernails, or who engage in self-mutilation of fingers and toes, or whose masturbation is linked to self-mutilating damage to their genitals. The patients I have seen with these characteristics presented the syndrome of malignant narcissism and pretty much overlap with the self-destructive, impulsively suicidal, and/or self-mutilating group described earlier. The major difference resides in the repetitive quality of the self-mutilating behavior; it seems more insidious and bizarre than the explosive self-destructive crises of the former group. The erotization of pain and self-mutilation seems to have acquired the meaning of a triumph over life and death, over pain and fear, and, unconsciously, over the entire world of object relations. These patients usually have a poor prognosis for psychotherapeutic treatment.

In summary, I propose the following grouping of masochistic syndromes:

A. At a neurotic level of personality organization
   1. Depressive-masochistic personality disorder
   2. Masochistic infatuation
   3. Masochistic perversion
B. At a borderline level of personality organization
   1. Sadomasochistic personality disorder
   2. Sexual masochism with self-destructive and/or other regressive features
   3. Extreme forms of self-mutilation and self-sacrifice

SOME IMPLICATIONS OF THE PROPOSED GROUPING

The preceding nosology points to the broad spectrum of pathology that can be classified as masochism and to the various structural and psychodynamic conditions that codetermine the clinical features and severity of each of these syndromes.

One major and obvious dimension is the universality of sexual masochistic features as part of sexual life at all levels of normality and pathology (chaps. 15, 16, 17). The intimate relation between erotic masochism and aggression in both sadomasochistic fantasies and behavior and the crucial function of aggression in determining the severity of masochism point to a basic dynamic of instinctual conflicts at all levels of psychopathology: the interplay and recruitment of libidinal and aggressive impulses.

At neurotic levels of masochism, aggression is recruited in the service of eroticism; at borderline levels of masochism, eroticism is recruited in the service of aggression; at the deepest level of masochism, eroticism fades out altogether and leaves the field to what seems to be an almost pure culture of aggression.

The quality and degree of superego integration appear to constitute an additional central organizing aspect of masochism not only in the gradual transformation of erotic into moral masochism but in the provision of a frame for both erotic and moral masochism that clearly differentiates higher-level masochistic pathology with good superego integration from lower-level syndromes with severe superego pathology. The general level of ego organization—whether borderline or neurotic—colors both the quality of object relations that constitute the matrix for masochistic fantasies and behavior and the extent to which sexual masochism may be contained within an integrated love relation. Finally, the consolidation of a pathological grandiose self as part of a narcissistic personality structure leads to completely different idealization processes from those of normal narcissistic functioning in the context of an integrated tripartite intrapsychic structure. Erotic idealization that reflects the projection of an ego ideal produces very different results from erotic idealization that reflects the projection of a pathological grandiose self.

In short, ego organization, object relations, superego development, narcissistic organization, and the extent of integration of polymorphous perverse infantile sexuality codetermine the level and clinical features of masochistic pathology. Oedipal psychodynamics, including castration anxiety and incestual conflicts, are central in moral masochism and masochistic perversion in neurotic personality organization; the condensation of these conflicts with pathologically dominant preoedipal conflicts centering around preoedipal aggression produces the regressive conditions characteristic of masochistic syndromes at the level of borderline personality organization.

The clinical syndromes I have described illustrate how, at the extremes of the spectrum, the concept of masochism dissolves into other diagnostic categories and psychodynamic considerations. For example, the normal tolerance of pain (in hard work, postponement of gratification, acknowledgment of one's own aggression) as part of sublimatory efforts is no longer masochism in a strict sense; the erotic excitement of milder forms of pain, playful debasement, and humiliation as part of normal sexual interactions serves so many functions and contains so many developmental features that the term *masochism* no longer says anything specific about such behavior. At the other extreme, the self-destructive and self-defeating effects of borderline and psychotic psychopathology may no longer warrant the term *masochism* either: in such cases there may be self-destructive aspects but hardly any erotization of pain and even less moral masochism. It is true that Freud (1920, 1924, 1937) linked masochism to the death instinct, so that, in his view, primary masochism represents the instinctual origin of self-destructiveness; but the equation of masochism and self-destructiveness at the severest levels of psychopathology dilutes the specific meaning of masochism as a psychopathological entity.

Another factor that affects our understanding of the concept of masochism is that of normal and pathological narcissism. Masochistic surrender provides narcissistic gratification; the depressive-masochistic personality obtains narcissistic gratification from the sense of being unjustly treated and thus implicitly morally superior to the object. The self-punitive price paid for normal sexual gratification or for success or creativity also produces approval from the superego and hence an increase in self-esteem. Insofar as the normal and the neurotic superego regulate self-esteem by self-directed approval or criticism, masochistic behavior patterns have important functions in neurotically maintaining self-esteem and, in metapsychological terms, in assuring the ego's narcissistic supplies. But then, all neurotic character formations have such a narcissistic function; there is no unique linkage here between masochism and narcissism. The self-idealization in fantasy linked to masochistic infatuations may be considered an example of the narcissistic consequence of an underlying masochistic structure.

In contrast, at the more severe level of pathological infatuation, the projection of the pathological grandiose self creates a narcissistic aspiration that has self-defeating qualities and impresses the observer as profoundly masochistic. Yet here the masochism restricted to one object relation is essentially a reflection of narcissistic psychopathology characteristic of the patient's other object relations and does not have the punitive function of moral masochism and pleasure in pain.

In earlier work I defined the negative therapeutic reaction as a worsening of the patient's condition, particularly when he is "consciously or unconsciously perceiving the therapist as a good object who is attempting to provide him with significant help" (1984, p. 241). I suggested three levels of negative therapeutic reaction, deriving from (1) "an unconscious sense of guilt," typical of depressive-masochistic personalities, (2) "the need to destroy what is received from the therapist because of unconscious envy of him," typical of narcissistic personalities, and (3) "the need to destroy the therapist as a good object because of the patient's unconscious identification with a primitive sadistic object who requires submission and suffering as a minimal condition for maintaining any significant object relation" (p. 241).

In light of the findings presented here, I would now restate that the first and mildest level of negative therapeutic reaction—that derived from an unconscious sense of guilt—is indeed typical of depressive-masochistic personality structures and may also emerge in the psychoanalysis of a masochistic perversion at a neurotic level. In contrast, the second and third levels of negative therapeutic reactions are related to other types of masochistic pathology.

The negative therapeutic reaction owing to unconscious envy of the therapist is typical of patients with narcissistic personality structure, but it may also develop in patients with sadomasochistic personalities whose unconscious sense of guilt at being helped is reinforced by their envy and resentment of the therapist for his freedom from the destructive and self-destructive potential from which these patients cannot escape. I would therefore suggest that a negative therapeutic reaction resulting from unconscious envy is not as specifically linked to narcissistic pathology as I suggested earlier.

Regarding the most severe type of negative therapeutic reaction— linked to the experience of a primary love object as destructive, so that love can be expressed only as destruction—this would seem to me an essential dynamic of the most severe case of masochistic pathology, in terms of both diffuse self-destructive behaviors that have characterological implications and primitive sexual masochistic perversions with dangerous—even life-threatening—primitivization of aggression. In earlier work based on Jacobson's (1964) description of superego development, I suggested what I thought was responsible for these patients' pathology of object relations and superego development:

(1) the experience of external objects as omnipotent and cruel; (2) a sense that any good, loving, mutually gratifying relationship with an object is frail, easily destroyed, and, even worse, contains the seeds for attack by the overpowering and cruel object; (3) a sense that total submission to that object is the only condition for survival and that, therefore, all ties to a good and weak object have to be severed; (4) once identification with the cruel and omnipotent object is achieved, an exhilarating sense of power and enjoyment, of freedom from fear, pain, and dread, and the feeling that the gratification of aggression is the only significant mode of relating to others; and (5) as an alternative, the discovery of an escape route by the adoption of a completely false, cynical, or hypocritical mode of communication, an erasing of all judgment that implies a comparison between good and bad objects, and negation of the importance of any object relation or successful maneuvering in the chaos of all human relations. (1984, p. 299)

I have also found helpful Fairbairn's (1954) idea of setting up a "moral defense against bad objects" in the form of an intrapsychic transformation of internalized relations with bad primary objects. In fact, Jacobson's (1964) description of early levels of superego development and Fairbairn's description of the vicissitudes of the internalization of bad objects have striking correspondences—once one gets beyond semantic barriers and their basic metapsychological incompatibilities. Let me quote Fairbairn at some length:

> In becoming bad he is really taking upon himself the burden of badness which appears to reside in his objects. By this means he seeks to purge them of their badness; and, in proportion as he succeeds in doing so, he is rewarded by that sense of security which an environment of good objects so characteristically confers. To say that the child takes upon himself the burden of badness which appears to reside in his objects is, of course, the same thing as to say that he internalizes bad objects. The sense of outer security resulting from this process of internalization is, however, liable to be seriously compromised by the resulting presence within him of internalized bad objects. Outer security is thus purchased at the price of inner insecurity; and his ego is henceforth left at the mercy of the band of internal fifth columnists or persecutors, against which defences have to be first hastily erected, and later laboriously consolidated. . . .
>
> In so far as the child leans towards his internalized bad objects, he becomes conditionally (i.e., morally) bad *vis-à-vis* his internalized good objects (i.e., his superego); and insofar as he resists the appeal of his internalized bad objects, he becomes conditionally (i.e., morally) good *vis-à-vis* his superego. It is obviously preferable to be conditionally good than conditionally bad; but, in default of conditional goodness, it is preferable to be conditionally bad than unconditionally bad. . . .
>
> It is better to be a sinner in a world ruled by God than to live in a world ruled by the Devil. . . . In a world ruled by the Devil the individual may escape the badness of being a sinner; but he is bad because the world around him is bad. Further, he can have no sense of security and no hope of redemption. The only prospect is one of death and destruction. (pp. 65–66)

Whichever model one finds congenial, the persistent influence of early sadistic superego precursors, an essential feature of the deepest levels of masochistic pathology, has devastating effects upon all subsequent internalization of object relations. In these patients' internal world, and therefore in their perceptions of their interpersonal reality, one is either extremely powerful and ruthless or threatened with being destroyed or exploited. If good object relations are in constant danger of destruction by such malignant forces, they may be devalued because of their implicit weakness. In this way primitive superego pathology and the pathology of all other internalized object relations reinforce each other. The activation of these sadistic superego precursors in the transferences of the more severe types of masochism within the total spectrum explored is reflected in sadomasochistic relations with the analyst that determine the severest types of negative therapeutic reactions. The patient requires the therapist to be bad as a primitive defense against otherwise diffuse and dangerous aggression; but this very badness of the therapist threatens the patient with the inability to receive anything good from him. The analyst's persevering interpretation of this regressive level of transference is of crucial importance in helping patients to overcome deeply regressive masochistic psychopathology.

Chapter 4 HYSTERICAL AND HISTRIONIC PERSONALITY DISORDERS

Two related personality disorders are described in this chapter. The first is the hysterical personality disorder, characterized by an essentially intact sense of identity, the capacity for stable, discriminating, emotionally rich, and empathic relations with others, including the capacity to tolerate ambivalence and complexity, and a predominance of defense mechanisms centering on repression. The hysterical personality disorder as here defined is not listed in DSM-III-R.

The second is the Histrionic Personality Disorder, which is included here as defined under that heading in DSM-III-R. This disorder corresponds to what others have called the "infantile," "hysteroid," "hysteroid dysphoric," "emotionally unstable," and "Zetzel type 3 and 4" hysterics (Zetzel 1968): patients whose manifest hysterical symptoms disguise deeper pathology. The Histrionic Personality Disorder falls into the category of borderline personality organization; that is, it is characterized by the syndrome of identity diffusion, severe pathology of object relations, and a predominance of primitive defensive operations centering around splitting.

CONTROVERSIAL ISSUES

Confusing and overlapping terminology and shifting clinical and theoretical frames of reference plague this area of the personality disorders, formerly brought together under the heading of "hysteria." A number of empirical studies carried out here and abroad (comprehensively summarized by Mersky [1979], the contributors to Roy's [1982] volume on Hysteria, and Cavenar and Walker [1983]) have provided some clarification of these questions while pointing to areas in which lack of agreement and information persists.

On the one hand, agreement seems to be emerging that the more severe the patient's personality disorder within the hysterical spectrum, the more likely it is that somatic symptoms corresponding to "conversion hysteria" will be present. By the same token, patients with severe "dissociative reactions" or even psychotic reactions who might once have been classified as "hysterical psychoses" also present severe personality disturbances within the broad spectrum previously called "hysterical." These disturbances, however, appear to overlap with the personality disturbances now classified in the "borderline" spectrum.

On the other hand, the more the personality disorder corresponds to the "hysterical personality" of the psychoanalytic literature (that is, personality disturbances close to the better functioning or "neurotic" end of the "hysterical" personality spectrum), the weaker are the connections among conversion symptoms, dissociative reactions, and the hysterical personality disorder proper. In short, the paradoxical impression conveyed by the literature on hysteria in the past is that the relations among personality disorder, conversion reaction, and dissociative symptoms are strongest when the personality disturbances are most severe and merge with other severe personality types and weakest when the most distinctive characteristics of the hysterical personality appear.

To make sharper distinctions among the conversion syndrome, the dissociative syndrome, and the personality disorder seems a reasonable first step in clarifying this area of psychopathology.

The chief problem that has been debated in the literature over the years (Marmor 1953; Chodoff and Lyons 1958; Easser and Lesser 1965, 1966; Lazare et al. 1966, 1970; Lazare 1971; Luisada et al. 1974; Chodoff 1974; Blacker and Tupin 1977; Krohn 1978; Millon 1981; Tupin 1981) is whether the hysterical personality should be considered in terms of severity of pathological character traits or whether a distinction should be made between the "hysterical personality disorder" that corresponds to the classical descriptions formulated by Reich (1933), Abraham (1979), Wittels (1931), and Fenichel (1945) and the personality disorder corresponding to the more regressive, "borderline" level of personality organization, referred to as the "hysteroid" (Easser and Lesser 1965), "Zetzel type 3 and 4" (Zetzel 1968), or "infantile" personality (Kernberg 1975).

The DSM-III-R definition places the Histrionic Personality Disorder clearly within this second, more disturbed type. It could be argued that

DSM-III-R has chosen to subsume the entire spectrum of the hysterical personality disorder under the heading "Histrionic Personality Disorder" rather than adopt the restrictive, two-type solution that seems indicated by clinical data. The clinical description of this disorder in DSM-III-R, however, negates this assumption: the description corresponds only to the regressive end of the spectrum and leaves out what might be called the "hysterical personality."

Regardless of where one stands in terms of the conceptual, clinical, and research issues that may influence one's view regarding this area of psychopathology, I suggest the following as a reasonable approach to clarifying at least the semantic issues: (1) the classical hysterical personality includes a broad spectrum of related pathological character traits ranging from the Hysterical Personality Disorder proper at the "higher" level to the "histrionic" (in the sense of DSM-III-R), or hysteroid, or infantile, or Zetzel types 3 and 4 personality disorder at the lower level; and (2) this "lower-level" personality disorder also corresponds to what DSM-III-R and the empirical researchers working in this area have designated the "borderline personality disorder." The psychostructural concept of Stone (1980; see also Kernberg 1984) considers the infantile personality (Borderline Personality Disorder in the DSM-III-R sense) as one type within the broader spectrum of "borderline personality organization."

For heuristic reasons, I shall use the term *hysterical personality disorder* to describe the higher level of this continuum and will treat it separately from the "histrionic personality disorder," which corresponds to the lower level of this spectrum. In actuality, however, the clinician will find patients who present intermediary levels of psychopathology, so that these "pure" types may be considered as either extremes of a continuum or discrete personality types with intermediary forms.

CLINICAL DESCRIPTIONS

Both the hysterical and the histrionic personality disorders present different characteristics in men and women. The features of the disorders that are common to the two genders will become apparent in the following descriptions.

The Hysterical Personality in Women

A dominant characteristic in these women is their emotional lability. They relate easily to others and are capable of warm and sustained emotional involvements—with the important exception of an inhibition in their sexual responsiveness. They are usually dramatic and even histrionic, but their display of affects is controlled and has socially adaptive qualities. The way they dramatize their emotional experiences can give the impression that their emotions are superficial, but exploration reveals otherwise: their emotional experiences are authentic; they may be emotionally labile, but they are not inconsistent or unpredictable in their emotional reactions. They lose emotional control only vis-à-vis those with whom they have intense conflicts, especially of a sexual and competitive nature.

With these people, hysterical women are prone to develop emotional crises, but they always have the capacity to recover themselves and evaluate such crises realistically afterward. They may cry easily and tend toward sentimentality and romanticism, but their cognitive capacities are intact, and their understanding of complex human reactions is in sharp contrast to the apparent immaturity of their emotional display. The difference between their generally appropriate social interactions and the specific object relations that have sexual implications represents a tendency to show infantile, regressive behavior only in circumstances that are either actually or symbolically sexual or that are concerned with persons they experience as having parental roles. Their impulsiveness is restricted to such specific interactions or to occasional temper tantrums.

Hysterical patients tend to be essentially outgoing and involved with others. This extroversion shows in easy social contacts and blends with a tendency to exhibitionism and excessive dependence on others. They want to be loved, to be the center of attention and attraction, particularly in circumstances with sexual implications. Their dependence on other people's evaluation of them is balanced by a clear sense of what socially realistic requirements they must meet to obtain such love and approval, and their childlike, clinging dependency is confined to sexual contexts. In fact, childlike attitudes in intimate relations and generally mature attitudes in ordinary social interactions are key characteristics of the hysterical personality. Some hysterical women seem shy or timid but nonetheless subtly convey a provocative sexual seductiveness that may even be accentuated by this timidity.

Women with hysterical personality typically show a pseudohypersexuality in combination with sexual inhibition; they are both sexually provocative and frigid. Their sexual involvements have triangular qualities in that they are with men who are unavailable or involved with other women. Their provocative behavior may induce sexual responses from men, which they may then experience as intrusive or shocking and to which they react with fear, indignation, and rejection.

The hysterical woman is competitive both with men and with other women for men. The competitiveness with men contains implicit fears and conflicts having to do with a consciously or unconsciously assumed inferiority to them. Subtypes of a submissive or competitive hysterical personality reflect characterological fixations of these submissive—often masochistic—and competitive patterns. Psychoanalytic exploration typically reveals that these women use regressive infantile behavior defensively against the guilt aroused by the adult aspects of sexual involvement. Some women tend to submit to men whom they experience as sadistic in expiation of guilt feelings and as a price to be paid for sexual gratification. What is of great interest is the difference between the nature of these patients' competitiveness with men and with women, in contrast to the more regressively undifferentiated patterns of pathological reactions toward men and women in patients with histrionic personality disorder.

Some additional aspects of the hysterical personality described in the early literature have recently been questioned. For instance, it had earlier been assumed that hysterical patients were highly suggestible. Clinical observations point to the idea that suggestibility may emerge only in the context of idealized, romanticized, and clingingly dependent relations, and that it may easily change to suspiciousness, distrust, pouting, or stubbornness under conditions of intense competitiveness with men or women. Another characteristic classically attributed to the hysterical personality is excessive dependency. As already mentioned, however, dependency characterizes only a few, very intense relations. A third assumed characteristic of hysterical patients is egocentricity—a self-centered, self-indulgent, vain quality conveyed by the exhibitionistic, attention-seeking behavior of these patients and their excessive sensitivity to other people's reaction. But such a characteristic does not correspond to their actual capacity for deep involvements with others, their stability in engagements, loyalty, and commitment. Other attributes that imply a lack of the capacity for emotional investment coupled with a deficiency in moral functioning are equally not characteristic of this personality disorder—for example, emotional shallowness, fraudulent affects, mendacity, and pseudologia fantastica, all mentioned in the early literature.

Shapiro (1965) and Horowitz (1977) have described a cognitive style in hysterical patients characterized by a tendency toward global (in contrast to detailed) perception, selective inattentions, and impressionistic rather than accurate representations. These characteristics may reflect a generally repressive organization of defensive functions, which, together with inhibition of competitiveness (because of an unconscious sense of inferiority as a woman), may contribute to intellectual inhibition.

The Hysterical Personality in Men

Blacker and Tupin (1977) have summarized the characteristics of male patients with hysterical and histrionic personality disorders. Their descriptions utilized the model of a continuum of character pathology ranging in severity under the heading "hysterical structures." Men with hysterical personality reveal the same tendency toward emotional dramatization and affective lability seen in hysterical women. They also present outbursts of emotion or temper tantrums and impulsive and infantile behavior under conditions of intimate emotional involvements while maintaining the capacity for differentiated behavior under ordinary social circumstances.

Men with hysterical personality manifest several patterns of disturbances in their sexual adaptation. One pattern is characterized by a pseudohypermasculine quality, a histrionic accentuation of culturally accepted masculine behavior, usually a stress on independence, and an attitude of dominance and superiority over women, combined with childlike sulkiness when these aspirations cannot be fulfilled.

A related pattern, though it superficially appears to be contrasting, is that of a seductive, subtly effeminate, infantile sexual behavior that combines flirtatiousness and heterosexual promiscuity with a dependent, childlike attitude toward women. Or a childlike Don Juan type combines a stress on masculine attire and manners with subtly dependent and childlike behavior and is prone to engage in dependent though transitory relations with dominant women.

In treatment, both the effeminate and hypermasculine types reveal underlying conscious or unconscious guilt over sexual relations in depth with women and a surprising inability to identify with an adult male sexual role in approaching women that is in sharp contrast to their surface behavior. These characteristics, particularly as presented by the pseudohypermasculine type, correspond to what Reich (1933) called the "phallic-narcissistic character." These cases need to be differentiated from the more severe histrionic personality disorder in men and from sexual promiscuity as a symptom of the narcissistic personality disorder in men with the corresponding severe pathology of object relations.

The Histrionic Personality in Women

These patients present self-centered, self-indulgent behavior that may still be accompanied by intense dependency upon others, but their clinging dependency needs do not show the mutuality of the relationships of the hysterical personality disorder. At the same time, histrionic patients have a higher capacity for emotional involvement than the emotionally aloof and distant narcissistic personality disorder. Their very clinginess and the stability of their highly immature involvements contrast with the absence of this feature in the narcissistic personality.

Unlike the hysterical personality disorder, histrionic personalities present diffuse emotional lability, undifferentiated relations with significant others, and immature, self-centered emotional investments. In contrast to the socially appropriate extroversion of the hysterical personality, the histrionic personality overidentifies with others and projects unrealistic, fantasied intentions onto them. Her dramatization of affects, emotionally volatile and labile behavior, general excitability, and inconsistency of reactions convey an underlying emotional shallowness and incapacity for differentiated object relations. Histrionic personalities have difficulty understanding others as well as themselves in depth, and the childlike, clinging nature of all their object relationships contrasts with the hysterical personality in this respect. Their selection of marital or sexual partners is often highly inappropriate.

Dependent and exhibitionistic traits are less sexualized in the histrionic personality disorder than in the hysterical personality disorder. The histrionic personality may use sexualized behavior crudely and inappropriately to express exhibitionistic and dependent needs, tends to have fewer sexual inhibitions, and is more frequently promiscuous than the hysterical personality. There are fewer repressive features in the histrionic personality's sexual life and more generalized dissociative features, such as the alternation of contradictory sexual fantasies and engagements (expressed in polymorphous infantile sexual behavior). The degree of pathology in any particular interpersonal relationship is in proportion to the intensity of involvement or intimacy with the other person.

The histrionic personality disorder may present masochistic tendencies, but these are not closely linked to sexual behaviors. She is diffusely impulsive, which makes for an unpredictability that reinforces the instability and intensity of relations with others, and she shows inappropriate, intense anger or uncontrolled anger and sharp mood swings. She is prone to making suicide gestures and attempts and to utilizing suicide fantasies and wishes to attract attention and reassurance. Manipulative suicide threats are only one aspect of generally manipulative interpersonal relations. These patients frequently lie and manifest antisocial behavior and pseudologia fantastica. Such cases must be differentiated from the antisocial, in addition to the narcissistic personality disorders: the prognosis, with or without treatment, is much poorer for the antisocial personality.

Histrionic patients are prone to develop feelings of depersonalization and, under extreme stress, transitory psychotic symptoms of insufficient severity or duration to warrant an additional diagnosis. These characteristics, in addition to their identity disturbances and the general characteristics already described, also correspond to those listed for the borderline personality disorder in DSM-III-R. With these reservations, the diagnostic criteria for the histrionic personality disorder outlined in DSM-III-R adequately cover the significant characteristics of female patients with this personality disorder.

The Histrionic Personality in Men

Histrionic personalities in men usually present identity diffusion, severe disturbances in object relations, and lack of impulse control. They also evince promiscuous, often bisexual, and polymorphous perverse sexual behavior, antisocial tendencies, and, with surprising frequency, conscious or unconscious exploitation of organically determined or psychogenically determined physical symptoms. Male patients with "compensation neurosis" and/or hypochondriasis often present the generalized emotional immaturity, dramatization, affective shallowness, and impulsiveness characteristic of the histrionic personality disorder, together with antisocial features and exploitative tendencies in their relation to the helping professions. The so-called chaotic or impulse-ridden personality disorders of earlier descriptions that did not correspond to the antisocial personality proper reflected what today would be diagnosed as histrionic and narcissistic personality disorders functioning on an overt borderline level. In fact, in all cases of male patients with histrionic features, the differential diagnosis with the narcissistic personality and the antisocial personality disorders is important for its prognostic and therapeutic considerations.

CLINICAL COURSE AND PROGNOSIS

Although there are as yet no empirical studies providing solid evidence regarding the prognosis for the hysterical and histrionic personality disorders, women with hysterical personality disorder have been observed to improve their functioning in later adulthood and old age, raising the question to what extent their good ego strength, their capacity for engagement with others in work and professions, and the gradual compensation of sexual inhibitions and conflicts throughout life may facilitate a better social and intrapsychic adaptation in later years. The histrionic personality disorder, in contrast, appears to decompensate in later adulthood and old age. The cumulative effects of the incapacity to pursue personal, professional, cultural, and social values, the frequent disruption of and failure in intimate relations, and the identity diffusion typical of these patients' personality may interfere with ordinary social learning and create a circular reaction that worsens their functioning with the years.

The hysterical personality disorder has excellent prognosis with psychoanalytic treatment. The histrionic personality disorder has only a moderately favorable prognosis within modified psychoanalytic treatment, but a better prognosis with psychoanalytic or exploratory psychotherapy. The development of psychoanalytic psychotherapy for the borderline personality disorders in recent years has improved the prognosis for these patients.

ETIOLOGY

Freud stressed the importance of the genital stage of development and of the Oedipus complex in hysteria. Abraham complemented this idea with his study of the female castration complex, specifically the development of a "wish-fulfillment type" and a "revenge type" of hysterical personality in women (1920, p. 348). Abraham elaborated on aspects of penis envy as an unconscious conflict reflected in descriptive aspects of the hysterical personality. Wittels (1931), Reich (1972), and Fenichel (1945) further developed an understanding of the relation of unconscious intrapsychic conflicts to the phenomenological characteristics of the hysterical personality. They all stressed the Oedipus complex and castration anxiety and penis envy as its dynamics and proposed that pregenital conflicts, particularly oral fantasies and character traits, represented a defensive regression against the oedipal. And they all stressed the prevalence of repression and related defenses—such as displacement, affect storms, reversal of affects, and hysterical types of identification—

and pointed to the manifestations of instinctual conflicts and defenses in the transference neurosis of hysterical patients.

Marmor (1953), in sharp contrast, proposed that oral fixations are of basic importance in the hysterical character, that they give the subsequent Oedipus complex of these patients a strong pregenital cast, and that the greater frequency of hysteria in women might reflect in part the cultural facilitation of "oral aggressivity, dependency, and passivity" as feminine traits, more acceptable in women than in men. Subsequent discussions in the psychoanalytic literature, stimulated by Marmor's paper, gradually led to the realization that there were indeed patients with predominantly oral conflicts centering around pathological dependency, passivity, and above all, evidence of deep disturbances in preoedipal mother-infant relations, but that these cases corresponded to what we are now calling the histrionic, infantile, or hysteroid personality disorder, whereas the psychodynamics of castration anxiety and the Oedipus complex correspond to the hysterical personality proper as now defined.

Easser and Lesser (1965, 1966), Zetzel (1968; see also Kernberg 1975) focused on the relation between levels of severity within the hysterical spectrum and corresponding differences in prevalent unconscious conflicts, defensive operations, ego structure, and transference characteristics. According to these writers, the predominant conflicts of the hysterical personality proper are oedipal and relate to the genital phase of psychosexual development. The ego structure of these patients is organized around repression and is characterized by solid ego identity, as reflected in the typical manifestations of neurotic transference developments. Oral regressions in these patients are temporary and defensive and may be interpretively resolved, thus leading to the central oedipal conflicts. Histrionic, infantile, hysteroid, or Zetzel type 3 and 4 personality disorders, in contrast, typically present a condensation of preoedipal and oedipal features under the predominance or preoedipal (especially oral) aggression and an ego organization centering around primitive dissociation or splitting and related defensive mechanisms; these are expressed in treatment in the primitive "part-object" transferences typical for borderline patients.

Family Dynamics and Cultural Factors

While most information in this area stems from reviewing patients' records and psychoanalytic exploration of patients' past experiences, this literature conveys a growing consensus that women with hysterical personality disorder come from rather stable families having common characteristics. Their fathers are described as seductive, often combining sexually seductive and overstimulating behavior toward their daughters with abrupt, authoritarian, and sometimes sexually puritanical attitudes toward them: seductiveness during the daughter's childhood typically shifts into prohibition against sexual and romantic involvements in her adolescence. These patients' mothers are described as domineering and controlling of their daughters' lives, often conveying the impression that they were attempting to realize their unfilled aspirations through their daughters. At the same time, these mothers were effective and responsible at home and in their community functions.

There is less information available regarding the family background of the histrionic personality disorder. In general, it appears that these patients come from more disturbed families, with profound and chronic conflicts involving mother-child relations and severe personality disturbances in the mothers.

A consensus seems to be growing that cultural factors play a fundamental role in determining the organization of pathological character traits that mediate the relations between unconscious intrapsychic conflict and social adaptation. Cultural stereotypes regarding gender roles, the power relation between the sexes, and the boundaries of encouraged and permitted sexual behavior are considered of crucial importance in the dynamic organization of pathological character traits. The literature in this area is still mostly speculative, but perhaps empirical studies will help clarify these issues and thus reduce the temptation to decide them on the basis of theoretical bias or ideological commitment.

DIAGNOSIS AND DIFFERENTIAL DIAGNOSIS

The most important differential diagnosis of the hysterical and histrionic personality disorders is first distinguishing them from each other. Only secondarily need they be differentiated from other personality disorders. The importance of this differential diagnosis lies in the significant differences between these disorders in their prognosis and treatment. The clinical description presented earlier should permit making this differential diagnosis.

Regarding the differential diagnosis with other personality disorders, the hysterical personality needs to be differentiated first from the narcissistic personality disorder, with which it tends to be confused. Both entail attention-seeking and exhibitionistic behavior; the chief difference is in the patient's capacity for object relations. Narcissistic personalities characteristically show a lack of this capacity, are unstable in their sexual involvements, and display a coldness that contrasts with the warmth and commitment of the hysterical personality.

In women with high intelligence and a rich cultural background, the hysterical personality disorder tends to be confused with the obsessive-compulsive personality (the Compulsive Personality Disorder in DSM-III-R). These women's competitiveness with men and women may take a predominantly intellectual form, giving a pseudo-obsessive quality to their rationalizations and use of intellectualization.

In hysterical women with strong masochistic features reflecting unconscious prohibitions against sexual freedom and enjoyment, the differential diagnosis with the depressive-masochistic personality disorder (see chap. 3) is of interest. This category is not found in DSM-III-R, although it pretty much overlaps with the Self-Defeating Personality Disorder tentatively outlined there. It has been described by Laughlin (1967), who classifies the character traits of the depressive-masochistic personality disorder as reflecting (1) excessively harsh superego functioning, (2) overdependence on support, love, and acceptance from others, and (3) difficulties in expressing aggression. In many ways, all three categories have the faulty "metabolism" of dependency needs as a predominant issue. These patients feel guilty because of intense ambivalence toward loved and needed objects, and they are easily frustrated if their dependent longings are not gratified. In contrast to the hysterical personality disorder, however, they do not have marked sexual conflicts and specifically sexual inhibitions.

The sexual promiscuity present in the hysterical, histrionic, and narcissistic personality disorders often leads to the exploration of the differential diagnosis of these conditions. Sexual promiscuity in the depressive-masochistic and hysterical personality disorders stems from unconscious guilt. These patients typically give evidence of stability only in sexual relations that have a masochistic quality. The hysterical personality, in particular, may tolerate a satisfactory sexual experience only when it is carried out under objective or symbolic suffering. These patients' capacity to understand, differentiate, and empathize with their love objects is remarkably high, in contrast to the corresponding incapacity on the part of the narcissistic personality disorder. Sexual promiscuity in the narcissistic personality disorder goes hand in hand with severe pathology of object relations. In addition, narcissistic personality disorders characteristically present the dominance of the defense mechanisms of grandiosity and omnipotence, projective identification, idealization, and devaluation, whereas the hysterical personality disorder presents higher-level defenses. The sexual promiscuity of the histrionic personality disorder is part of a generally polymorphous perverse quality of sexual life, with little repression of sexual fantasy and uninhibited, often chaotic, sexual behavior.

All personality disorders may present depression as a prevalent symptom. The depressive-masochistic, hysterical, histrionic, and narcissistic personality disorders frequently present acute or chronic depressive reactions, jointly constituting so-called characterological depression. The term *hysteroid dysphoria* (Liebowitz and Klein 1981) refers precisely to histrionic patients with such chronic dispositions to depression, and the question has been raised to what extent some of these patients may have a genetic predisposition to major affective illness that colors or codetermines their character pathology. The mechanisms by which depression is triggered in all these cases vary.

Although DSM-III-R stresses the exhibitionistic and histrionic qualities of the histrionic personality disorder, a careful analysis reveals that DSM-III-R is describing the borderline personality disorder as presenting traits similar to those presented by the former. Patients with either disorder are described as impulsive or unpredictable, presenting patterns of unstable and intense interpersonal relations, inappropriate, intense anger or lack of control of anger, affective instability, proneness to suicide gestures and attempts, and incessant efforts to attract attention and reassurance. The manual explicitly describes the borderline personality disorder as presenting an identity disturbance, but the characteristic histrionic personality also manifests identity disturbance. And both histrionic and borderline personality disorders are described as prone to developing brief psychotic episodes. In practice, therefore, the histrionic and the borderline personality disorders in DSM-III-R largely overlap or coincide; this area of the manual would seem to need revision.

TREATMENT

The treatment of the hysterical personality disorder is essentially psychotherapeutic, with psychoanalysis the treatment of choice. It needs to be emphasized, however, that the hysterical personality disorder, like the obsessive-compulsive and depressive-masochistic personality disorders, has an excellent prognosis for the entire spectrum of psychoanalytically oriented psychotherapies, although psychoanalysis appears to be the treatment with broadest psychotherapeutic results (Kernberg et al. 1972). Patients who consult for relatively mild or minor neurotic symptoms that complicate a hysterical personality disorder may not require more than the treatment of their symptoms. Milder forms of psychosexual dysfunctions (such as inhibited female orgasm) may respond satisfactorily to sex therapy. To what extent the hysterical personality disorder is of sufficient severity to warrant treatment beyond the symptomatic resolution is still open to question. Many patients consulting a psychiatrist for relatively time-limited interpersonal conflicts linked to conversion symptoms, phobic reactions, or dissociative experiences may benefit from expressive or exploratory psychotherapy. When the patient complains about only minor symptoms, however, and the diagnostician sees that the hysterical personality disorder might have serious effects on the patient's marriage, work, or profession, a major psychotherapeutic intervention such as psychoanalysis may be warranted.

The specific technical difficulties in the psychoanalytic treatment of the hysterical personality disorder include early, intense transference developments with pseudoerotic defenses against aggressive impulses, regressive transference developments as a defense against the activation of more directly expressed oedipal conflicts, affect storms as a form of acting out, and dissociation of affects from their unconscious meanings. These patients may make it difficult for the therapist to detect negative transference elements because of their eroticized transference.

The treatment for the histrionic personality disorder is not psychoanalysis; it is essentially psychotherapeutic, with expressive or exploratory psychoanalytic psychotherapy usually the treatment of choice. Supportive psychotherapy is indicated when the patient presents contraindications for exploratory psychotherapy, including marked antisocial features, unusually severe pathology of object relations, and acting out that offers the patient secondary gain. Histrionic personality disorders with secondary depressive symptoms or characterologically determined depression may respond to MAO inhibitors or tricyclic or tetracyclic antidepressants. I believe, however, that medication should be reserved for patients with severe depression and discontinued if no clear and definite improvement of the depression occurs within a few months.

All cases of histrionic personality disorder should be treated psychotherapeutically and as early as possible after the diagnosis is made. Whereas the hysterical personality disorder may gradually improve in internal and interpersonal adjustment over the years, the usual course of the untreated patient with histrionic personality disorder is precarious at best, with the danger of gradual worsening as life opportunities are missed or destroyed.

Patients falling into an intermediate range between the hysterical and the histrionic personality present a difficult therapeutic problem. I think such cases should tentatively be treated with psychoanalysis and shifted into psychoanalytic psychotherapy only if psychoanalysis is contraindicated for such individual reasons as secondary gain of illness, lack of motivation, and/or conspicuous inability for emotional introspection. There is a growing tendency, however, to start out with exploratory or psychoanalytic psychotherapy in cases with dubious indication for psychoanalysis and shift to psychoanalysis later on.

The principal difficulties in the psychotherapeutic treatment of histrionic personality disorders are the patient's tendency toward massive acting out, secondary gain with the treatment situation itself serving as a refuge from life, the development of apparently "chaotic" treatment situations as an expression of primitive transferences, and deep regression in the communicative process in the treatment so that nonverbal behaviors predominate over verbal communication. These difficulties coincide to all intents and purposes with the general technical problems in the psychotherapy of the borderline spectrum of personality disorders.

Chapter 5 ANTISOCIAL AND NARCISSISTIC PERSONALITY DISORDERS

In this chapter the focus is on the intimate relationship between the narcissistic personality disorder and the antisocial personality disorder. In essence, I propose that all patients with an antisocial personality disorder present features typical of the narcissistic personality disorder plus a specific pathology of their internalized systems of morality (their superego functions) and a particular deterioration of their world of internalized object relations. The only significant exception to this rule is the relatively infrequent and prognostically grave clinical syndrome of "pseudopsychopathic schizophrenia" typically found in chronic schizophrenic patients with periodic improvement (with or without treatment) and antisocial behavior during such periods of "improvement," which disappears only when the patient again becomes psychotic. There is also a group of patients who stand somewhere between the narcissistic personality disorder and the antisocial personality disorder, characterized by what I have called the syndrome of malignant narcissism (1984). This syndrome is defined by the combination of (1) a narcissistic personality disorder, (2) antisocial behavior, (3) ego-syntonic aggression or sadism directed against others or expressed in a particular type of triumphant self-mutilation or attempts at suicide, and (4) a strong paranoid orientation.

I am thus describing a dimension of antisocial behavior that links the narcissistic personality disorder with the antisocial personality disorder and malignant narcissism. This dimensional characteristic linking these three disorders is similar to other dimensional links connecting other personality disorders with each other, such as the relationship of the schizoid personality disorders to the schizotypal personality disorder and that of the hysterical personality disorder to the histrionic (or hysteroid, or infantile) and borderline personality disorders (Kernberg 1984; and chap. 4 above).

My interest in the subject of the antisocial personality disorder derives from what I see as the shortcomings of the DSM-III-R (American Psychiatric Association 1987) description of this disorder. The manual's criteria are certainly broad enough to include practically all antisocial personality disorders who present predominantly aggressive interactional patterns and criminal behavior. In its stress on childhood antecedents, DSM-III-R appropriately directs the clinician to the childhood origins of this character pathology. Unfortunately, however, in its emphasis on the criminal aspect, it includes delinquents with very different personality makeup and blurs the distinction between sociocultural and economic determinants of delinquency, on the one hand, and psychopathology of the personality, on the other. Thus, DSM criteria contribute to what Rutter and Giller (1983) have described as the indiscriminate lumping together of delinquent behavior, which they believe interferes with the attempt to find predisposing factors for those with a specific personality disorder. The DSM-III-R criteria also neglect the nonaggressive passive type of antisocial personality disorder, in which chronically parasitic and/or exploitative rather than aggressive behaviors predominate. But what I find most disconcerting about the DSM-III-R description of the antisocial personality disorder is the absence of focus on personality traits as opposed to antisocial behaviors, a criticism that Millon (1981) cogently formulated a decade ago.

Diagnosis of the antisocial personality disorder is further complicated by the vicissitudes of terminology used. In 1952, DSM-I (American Psychiatric Association 1952) shifted from the traditional term *sociopathic personality*, which stressed the socially maladaptive aspects of these patients and the interplay of personality and social determinants, to *sociopathic personality disturbance*. It also differentiated the *antisocial reaction*, referring to the psychopath as classically defined in the English-language literature (Henderson 1939), from the *dissocial reaction*, referring to patients who disregard social codes, grow up in an abnormal social environment, but are still able to display strong personal loyalties.

Cleckley's *The Mask of Sanity* (first published in 1941 and issued in its fourth edition in 1964) remains, in my view, the basic text describing what we now call the antisocial personality disorder. In an effort to circumscribe the diagnosis of psychopathy, DSM-II (American Psychiatric Association 1968, p. 43) shifted the terminology to *antisocial personality* and proposed a capsule definition that, in essence, derived from Henderson's (1939) and Cleckley's (1941) work:

> This term is reserved for individuals who are basically unsocialized and whose behavior pattern brings them repeatedly into conflict with society. They are incapable of significant loyalty to individuals, groups or social values. They are grossly selfish, callous, irresponsible, impulsive and unable to feel guilt or to learn from experience and punishment. Frustration tolerance is low. They tend to blame others or offer plausible rationalizations for their behavior. A mere history of repeated legal or social offenses is not sufficient to justify this diagnosis.

From a clinical viewpoint, this is a remarkably relevant and meaningful definition; though brief, it includes references to the narcissistic personality features of these patients. Then DSM-III (American Psychiatric Association 1980) kept the term *antisocial personality*, adding *disorder* at the end, but shifted to a broader, criminal-behavior-oriented focus. The epidemiological research carried out by O'Neal and his colleagues (1962), Guze (1964a, 1964b), and particularly Robins (1966) was responsible for this approach.

It seems to me that psychoanalysis has contributed to both confusing the diagnostic issues and clarifying the structural characteristics of the antisocial personality. Alexander (1930; Alexander and Healy 1935) developed the concept of the "neurotic character" to refer to marked character pathology, including character pathology with antisocial features; thereby he implicitly blurred the distinction between the antisocial personality disorder proper and the other personality disorders. Eissler (1950), in employing the term *alloplastic defenses* in contrast to *autoplastic defenses*, also contributed to a homogenized approach to character pathology that blurred the differential diagnosis of the antisocial personality. The emphasis in the psychoanalytic literature of the 1940s and 1950s on Freud's (1916) description of "criminals from [an unconscious] sense of guilt" interpreted antisocial behavior (naively, I now think) as a reaction formation against unconscious guilt rather than an expression of deficits in superego development.

It was only with Johnson and Szurek's (Johnson 1949; Johnson and Szurek 1952) description of superego lacunae that psychoanalytic thinking began to focus on the structural rather than the dynamic aspects of antisocial personalities. Their relatively simple formulation was rapidly overtaken by the more sophisticated description of pronounced superego pathology linked to the narcissistic personality by Rosenfeld (1964) and Jacobson (1964, 1971b), whose work has influenced my own views.

Rutter and Giller's *Juvenile Delinquency: Trends and Perspectives* (1983) reviews comprehensively the epidemiological studies dealing with the relationship between juvenile delinquent behavior and abnormal personality functioning, in the process reevaluating our present knowledge regarding the etiology of these conditions. From the viewpoint of the ongoing debate regarding biological, psychological, and sociological factors influencing the development of antisocial behavior, they point to a clear relation between specific constellations of early childhood development in the family and the individual's later degree of social compliance, but state that the mechanisms by which the familial factors are associated with delinquency are still unclear. They also point to a relation between social change and an increase in delinquency, again stressing the lack of available knowledge regarding the corresponding mechanisms. They conclude that multiple causes appear to be active in juvenile delinquency, including peer-group influence, social control and social learning, biological factors influencing extreme types of antisocial behavior, and situational factors. In their view, it is absurd to look for a single explanation for juvenile delinquency, and they emphasize that no clear strategy of prevention is yet available.

Lewis and her colleagues' study (1985) of the early histories of children who later commit murder points to the prevalence of psychotic symptoms, major neurological impairment, psychotic first-degree relatives, the witnessing of violent acts during childhood, and severe physical abuse, thus strongly highlighting biological and psychosocial factors.

Dicks (1972) investigated the background and personality development of a series of German SS mass murderers before and after they functioned in concentration camps. He provides dramatic evidence that these criminals, though suffering from severe personality disorders with a predominance of narcissistic, paranoid, and antisocial features from early childhood on, engaged in repugnant criminal behavior only when the SS training and death camps provided social facilitation for the behavior; they reverted to their previously nondelinquent personality functioning during and after their prison terms. This illustrates what almost amounts to an empirical study of social facilitators of criminality. (Obviously, the burn-out tendencies of middle-aged delinquents also need to be taken into consideration here.)

Ideally antisocial behavior should be defined in terms of its psychological meanings rather than in behavioral or legal terms. For example, "ran away from home overnight at least twice while living in parental or parental surrogate home (or once without returning)"—one of the criteria for antisocial personality disorder in DSM-III-R—is a purely descriptive phrase that fails to consider whether the child ran away from an impossible home with physically abusive parents or from a well-constituted home. Again, "has never sustained a totally monogamous relationship for more than one year," another DSM-III-R criterion, applies to a vast number of late adolescents and early adults whose dating behavior may be influenced by a variety of neurotic inhibitions, culturally determined patterns, and almost any of the personality disorders. Sexual promiscuity has different meanings depending on the social setting and personality structure in which it is manifest. To use promiscuity as a criterion again shifts the diagnostic focus to the behavior rather than keeping it on what is responsible for that behavior.

A PROPOSED DIAGNOSTIC FRAME

I have found that, regardless of the degree of delinquent behavior, or even if it is absent, from a clinical perspective the first indication of the possible existence of an antisocial personality disorder is the presence of a narcissistic personality disorder. In fact, the clinical profile of the antisocial personality described by Cleckley falls naturally into three categories: (1) certain basic characteristics that differentiate the antisocial personality from psychosis and organic brain syndromes: "absence of delusions and other signs of irrational thinking" and "inadequately motivated antisocial behavior" (the dominant immediate symptom); (2) a series of characteristics found in severe narcissistic character pathology: "sex life impersonal, trivial, and poorly integrated," "unresponsiveness in general interpersonal relations," "general poverty in major affective reactions," "pathological egocentricity and incapacity for love"; (3) what amounts to manifestations of deep superego pathology: "unreliability," "untruthfulness and insincerity," "lack of remorse or shame," "poor judgment and failure to learn by experience," and "failure to follow any life plan."

I find only four of Cleckley's clinical profile listings questionable: "absence of 'nervousness' or psychoneurotic manifestations," "fantastic and uninviting behavior with drink and sometimes without," "suicide rarely carried out," and "superficial charm and good intelligence." Many antisocial personalities do present psychoneurotic symptoms; impulsive suicide occurs in these patients as well as in patients with the syndrome of malignant narcissism; and "fantastic and uninviting behavior with drink and sometimes without" seems to me too nonspecific. Many patients with the antisocial personality disorder, particularly those within the criminal population, do not show superficial charm, and the disorder is found at all levels of intelligence.

But antisocial behavior linked with a narcissistic personality disorder is not a sufficient basis for the diagnosis of an antisocial personality disorder. As I mentioned before, there is a group intermediate between the narcissistic personality disorder and the antisocial personality disorder: malignant narcissism. Antisocial behavior may also emerge in the context of other personality disorders; differential diagnosis becomes highly relevant in evaluating this symptom, for it has both prognostic and therapeutic importance. Antisocial behavior in a nonnarcissistic personality structure is prognostically favorable, in contrast to the extremely poor prognosis of antisocial behavior in the antisocial personality proper.

Antisocial behavior may also be a consequence of a normal or pathological adaptation to a highly pathological social environment, such as the "culture of the gang"; though this is a clinically infrequent condition, the "dissocial reaction" of DSM-I was a useful reminder of this group of patients. Sometimes antisocial behavior may be the equivalent of a neurotic symptom: neurotic adolescent rebelliousness, for example, may occasionally take the form of antisocial behavior.

Antisocial behavior should be explored in the light of the patient's general level of organization of superego functions, which brings us to reexamine the question of the "criminal out of an unconscious sense of guilt." Antisocial behavior that derives from an unconscious sense of guilt and a corresponding unconscious search for punishment has to be differentiated from the vast majority of cases in which self-destructiveness and self-provoked punishment are a consequence of the antisocial behavior but do not reflect such an unconscious motivation. In fact, the psychoanalytic hypothesis of an unconscious sense of guilt can be demonstrated to be valid only if the guilt becomes conscious as a result of psychoanalytic exploration. This definitely does not occur in intensive, long-term psychoanalytic psychotherapy with most patients presenting serious antisocial behavior. In addition, on purely theoretical grounds, given all the other evidence of extreme deterioration or unavailability of basic superego functions in most patients with antisocial behavior, the assumption that they operate out of an unconscious sense of guilt is highly questionable.

In clinical practice, there are patients with neurotic personality organization (in contrast to borderline personality organization) who may present antisocial behavior unconsciously aimed at self-punishment or at obtaining punishment from external sources. The type of the dominant personality disorder (hysterical, obsessive-compulsive, depressive-masochistic) points to this rather infrequent etiology.

In this connection, a relatively rare symptom, pseudologia fantastica, should also be explored in the light of the personality disorder within which it emerges. Pseudologia fantastica may be found in hysteroid, histrionic, or infantile personalities, and prognostically it is less dismal than either chronic lying or pseudologia fantastica in narcissistic and antisocial personality disorders. Once again, it is crucial to pinpoint the dominant character pathology in the differential diagnosis of antisocial behavior.

An issue that very frequently complicates the differential diagnosis of antisocial behavior is the presence of alcoholism and/or drug abuse and its secondary symptoms. Another related and often complexly interwoven psychopathology is that of antisocial behavior and a well-structured perversion or sexual deviation—"paraphilia" in DSM-III and DSM-III-R terminology. For practical purposes, the main issue here is the extent to which ego-syntonic aggression is built into the deviant sexual pattern: the more the personality structure shifts from the narcissistic to the antisocial, the more such aggressive behavior may become life-threatening, and a subgroup of aggressive antisocial personalities may center their criminal behavior on sexual assaults and murder (chaps. 15, 17).

CLASSIFICATION AND DIFFERENTIAL DIAGNOSIS

What follows is a classification of personality disorders in which antisocial features are prominent, according to severity. In all patients presenting antisocial behavior, it is helpful first to rule out the diagnosis of an antisocial personality proper. For this reason, I systematically investigate the potential presence of antisocial behavior in all patients with narcissistic personality disorder.

The Antisocial Personality Disorder

These patients typically present a narcissistic personality disorder. The typical symptoms of the narcissistic personality in the area of *pathological self-love* are excessive self-reference and self-centeredness; grandiosity and the derived characteristics of exhibitionism, an attitude of superiority, recklessness, and overambitiousness; overdependency on admiration; emotional shallowness; and bouts of excessive insecurity alternating with grandiosity. In the area of *pathological object relations*, these patients' predominant symptoms are inordinate envy (both conscious and unconscious); devaluation of others as a defense against the envy; exploitativeness manifested by greediness, appropriation of others' ideas or property, and an attitude of entitlement; an incapacity to truly depend on others in a mutual relationship; and a remarkable incapacity for empathy with and commitment to others. The *basic ego state* of these patients is characterized by a chronic sense of emptiness, evidence of an incapacity to learn, a sense of isolation, stimulus hunger, and a diffuse sense of the meaninglessness of life.

In addition, these narcissistic patients present some degree of *superego pathology*, including the incapacity to experience self-reflective sadness, deep mood swings, a predominance of shame as contrasted to guilt in their intrapsychic regulation of social behavior, and a value system more childlike than adult; that is, they value physical beauty, power, wealth, and the admiration of others as against capabilities, achievements, responsibility, and relation to ideals.

The antisocial personality disorder proper presents even more serious superego pathology. These patients' antisocial behavior includes lying, stealing, forgery, swindling, and prostitution—all of a predominantly "passive-parasitic" type; assault, murder, and armed robbery are characteristic of the "aggressive" type (Henderson 1939; Henderson and Gillespie 1969). In other words, one may differentiate clinically the behaviorally aggressive, sadistic, and usually also paranoid orientation of some patients with antisocial personality disorder from the passive, exploitative, parasitic type of others.

It should be stressed that, with intelligent patients from a favorable socioeconomic and cultural background who present a predominantly passive-parasitic type of antisocial behavior, the childhood antecedents of such behavior may appear to be apparently mild or even go unnoticed, particularly in some highly pathological yet socially adaptive families. For example, one patient was a brilliant student through elementary school, high school, and college and socially successful and well liked as a young man. His occasional stealing was generously forgiven by his parents, and his lack of a sense of responsibility was attributed to his having been spoiled and overprotected by an admiring mother and grandparents. He obtained a postgraduate degree, married a woman with whom he maintained an apparently normal marital relationship for over fifteen years, and was kind to his children. At the same time, he was embezzling funds from associates and from his family business. While running up inordinate debts, he also gave expensive gifts to friends and associates, appeared to be a year-round "Santa Claus," and was brought to consultation by his family only when he was threatened with a jail sentence because of tax evasion.

The crucial differentiation of both passive and aggressive antisocial behavior as part of a narcissistic personality disorder from an antisocial personality disorder proper depends on the absence in the latter of the capacity for feeling guilt and remorse. Thus, even after being confronted with the consequences of their antisocial behaviors and in spite of their profuse protestations of regret, there is no change in their behavior toward those they have attacked or exploited or any spontaneous concern over this failure to change their behavior.

Although the differential diagnosis of the capacity for experiencing guilt and concern requires the inferential step of evaluating a patient's reaction to confrontation and the breakdown of his omnipotence, other characteristics reflecting this incapacity for guilt and concern may become directly evident in the interviews. For example, such patients are unable to imagine an ethical quality in others. After insisting to the diagnostician that he is telling the truth and subsequently being caught in a flagrant lie, the patient may react sheepishly. But when asked to empathize with the therapist's reaction to him, he cannot; he can only sense that the therapist must be angry with him for his having made a fool of him. Or the antisocial patient may "confess" his guilt but only in regard to those actions in which he has been caught, thus entering into a flagrant contradiction of his simultaneously professed remorsefulness over his past behavior.

The inability to invest in nonexploitative relationships with others may be reflected in transient, superficial, indifferent relationships, inability to invest emotionally even in pets, and the absence of any internalized moral values, let alone the capacity to empathize with such values in others. The deterioration of these patients' affective experience is expressed in their intolerance of any increase in anxiety without developing additional symptoms or pathological behaviors, their incapacity for depression with reflective sorrow, and their inability to fall in love or experience any tenderness in their sexual relations.

These patients have no sense of the passage of time, of planning for the future, of contrasting present experience and behavior with aspired ideal ones; they can plan only to improve present discomforts and reduce tension by achieving immediately desired goals. Their failure to learn from experience is an expression of the same incapacity to conceive of their life beyond the immediate moment. Their manipulativeness, pathological lying, and flimsy rationalizations are well known. Paulina Kernberg (personal communication) has coined the term *hologram man* to refer to patients who create a vague, ethereal image of themselves in the diagnostic sessions that seems strangely disconnected from their current reality or their actual past, an image that changes from moment to moment in the light of different angles of inquiry and leaves the diagnostician with a disturbing sense of unreality.

Again, once the diagnosis of a narcissistic personality structure is obvious, the crucial diagnostic task is to evaluate the severity of any presenting antisocial features, their past history and childhood origins, and the patient's remaining capacity for object relations and superego functioning. The virtually total absence of the capacity for nonexploitative object relations and of any moral dimension in personality functioning is the key element in differentiating the antisocial personality proper from the less severe syndromes of malignant narcissism and narcissistic personality disorder. This diagnosis may be arrived at by taking a complete history, carefully exploring the patient's narrative, tactfully confronting him with contradictory and obscure areas in this narrative, evaluating his interaction with the diagnostician, and exploring his reactions to being confronted with contradictions among objective information from his past, his current narrative, and his behavior.

It may be very helpful to explore the patient's reactions to inquiry about potential antisocial behavior that might follow from what he has said but has not acknowledged. For example, to ask a patient whose history shows a natural tendency to engage in prostitution "What prevented you from engaging in prostitution?" or, similarly, with a drug abuser, to ask "Why would you not be dealing?" may test the patient's superego functions as well as his honesty vis-à-vis the therapist. Obviously, detecting patients who are lying to the therapist without acknowledging that they are lying (many antisocial personalities may acknowledge that they are lying but continue doing so) requires that we take history from the relatives, sophisticated social-work interventions, and reports from institutional settings with which the patient has been involved.

Considering the patient's reasons for consulting a psychiatrist—they may include a manipulative effort to obtain a certificate of health for reinstatement in school or to avoid facing legal procedures—may serve diagnostic as well as prognostic purposes. The investigation of all these factors usually requires several interviews; it may be necessary to return again and again to areas of uncertainty and confusion and to evaluate repeatedly the patient's reaction to confrontation with his deceptive maneuvers or contradictions.

Countertransference to patients with pronounced antisocial behavior may provide a second line of information: the therapist may react with a sense of confusion, tempted either to accept the patient's statements uncritically or to reject them with a paranoid stance in the countertransference, a protective "pseudoneutrality" that conceals an underlying devaluation of the patient or the wish to escape from an intolerable relationship with a patient who implicitly attacks the most basic values of human relations. In my view, a therapist's oscillation between a paranoid stance and moments of concern—in other words, a true ambivalence in his reaction to these patients—constitutes a healthy response. It is helpful for the therapist to be able to present himself as moral but not moralizing, fair but not naive, confronting but not aggressive. Confrontation as a technical device means the tactful bringing together of contradictory or confusing aspects of the patient's narrative, behavior, and/or past; it is not an aggressive display of criticism or disagreement with the patient.

Usually, the possibility that a major affective disorder exists can be eliminated by careful history-taking and mental-status examinations; psychological tests may provide additional help in ruling out an organic mental disorder, such as temporal-lobe epilepsy or a limbic-lobe syndrome, disorders that may present with explosive aggressive behavior. They may also help to rule out an atypical schizophrenic disorder, such as "pseudopsychopathic schizophrenia." When antisocial behavior develops in middle or late adulthood together with a loss of memory and higher abstract reasoning, many possible chronic organic mental disorders may have to be investigated, requiring, in addition to psychological testing, neurological, EEG, and radiological studies.

If an antisocial personality proper can be ruled out, the next diagnostic category to be considered is a narcissistic personality disorder with the syndrome of malignant narcissism, or narcissistic personality with predominantly passive-parasitic antisocial trends.

Malignant Narcissism

These patients, characterized by a typical narcissistic personality disorder, antisocial behavior, ego-syntonic sadism or characterologically anchored aggression, and a paranoid orientation, in contrast to the antisocial personality proper, still have the capacity for loyalty to and concern for others or for feeling guilty; they are able to conceive of other people as having moral concerns and convictions, and they may have a realistic attitude toward their own past and in planning for the future.

Their ego-syntonic sadism may be expressed in a conscious "ideology" of aggressive self-affirmation but also, quite frequently, in chronic, ego-syntonic suicidal tendencies. These suicidal tendencies emerge not as part of a depressive syndrome but rather in emotional crises or even out of the blue, with the underlying (conscious or unconscious) fantasy that to be able to take one's life reflects superiority and a triumph over the usual fear of pain and death. To commit suicide, in these patients' fantasy, is to exercise sadistic control over others or to "walk out" of a world they feel they cannot control.

The paranoid orientation of these patients (which psychodynamically reflects the projection onto others of unintegrated sadistic superego precursors) is manifest in their experience of others as idols, enemies, or fools in an exaggerated way. These patients have a propensity for regressing into paranoid micropsychotic episodes in the course of intensive psychotherapy; thus they illustrate most dramatically the complementary functions of paranoid and antisocial interactions in the interpersonal realm (Jacobson 1971b; Kernberg 1984). Some of them may present rationalized antisocial behavior—for example, as leaders of sadistic gangs or terrorist groups. An idealized self-image and an ego-syntonic sadistic, self-serving ideology rationalizes the antisocial behavior and may coexist with the capacity of loyalty to their own comrades.

Narcissistic Personality Disorders with Antisocial Behavior

These patients present a variety of antisocial behaviors, mostly of the passive-parasitic type, and show remnants of autonomous moral behavior in some areas and ruthless exploitativeness in others. They do not evince the ego-syntonic sadism, self-directed aggression, or overt paranoid orientation typical of malignant narcissism. They have a capacity for experiencing guilt, concern, and loyalty to others and an appropriate perception of their past, and they may realistically conceive of and plan for the future; in some cases, what appears to be antisocial behavior is simply a manifestation of incapacity for commitment in depth to long-range relationships. Narcissistic types of sexual promiscuity, irresponsibility in work, and emotional or financial exploitation of others are prevalent here, although these patients are still able to care for others in some areas and maintain ordinary social responsibility in more distant interpersonal interactions.

Other Severe Personality Disorders
with Antisocial Features

The next level of pathology, with less negative prognostic and therapeutic implications, is antisocial behavior in personality disorders other than the narcissistic personality. These are patients with borderline personality organization and nonpathological narcissism. Typical examples are the infantile, histrionic, hysteroid, or Zetzel type 3 and 4 personality disorder (not to be confused with a hysterical personality proper; see chap. 4), and the paranoid personality disorder: these are the two most frequent personality disorders of this group that present with antisocial behavior. In the infantile personality, pseudologia fantastica is not uncommon; the "paranoid urge to betray" (Jacobson 1971a) illustrates treacherousness in a paranoid context. In my experience, most patients with factitious disorder with psychological and/or physical symptoms, pathological gambling, kleptomania, pyromania, and malingering, if they do not present a typical narcissistic personality disorder, form part of this group of personality disorders with antisocial features.

Neurotic Personality Disorders with Antisocial Features

Here we find Freud's (1916) criminals from (an unconscious) sense of guilt. These patients are of great clinical interest because their sometimes dramatic antisocial behavior occurs in the context of a neurotic personality organization and has an excellent prognosis for psychotherapeutic and psychoanalytic treatment.

A patient with an obsessive-compulsive personality disorder stole minor objects from public places where he worked, exposing himself to the humiliating possibility of being caught and threatened with dismissal. Fortunately, a sophisticated psychiatric evaluation by a colleague provided the information that protected this patient's future while treatment was initiated. Although such cases are relatively rare, the enormous difference between their prognosis and that of the groups previously mentioned warrants a careful assessment of the personality structure in each case of antisocial behavior.

Antisocial Behavior as Part of a Symptomatic Neurosis

This category refers to occasional antisocial behavior as part of adolescent rebelliousness, in adjustment disorders, and/or in the presence, in many cases, of a facilitating social environment that fosters channeling psychic conflicts into antisocial behavior.

Dissocial Reaction

This clinically relatively rare syndrome refers to the normal and/or neurotic adjustment to an abnormal social environment or subgroup. In clinical practice, most of these patients present some type of personality disorder that facilitates their uncritical adaptation to a social subgroup with antisocial behaviors.

PROGNOSTIC AND THERAPEUTIC CONSIDERATIONS

The treatment of antisocial behavior is essentially psychotherapeutic, except, of course, when the behavior occurs in the context of organic mental disorder or a psychotic illness. The levels of severity of antisocial behavior I have described correspond to the prognosis for psychotherapeutic treatment. The first level, the antisocial personality disorder proper, has the poorest prognosis to the extent that almost none of these patients responds to ordinary psychotherapeutic approaches. Treatment of the antisocial personality disorder in childhood, however—the "conduct disorder" in DSM-III-R—has a more favorable prognosis, and encouraging results with treatment of these children in specialized residential settings (Diatkine 1983) have been reported. "Unsocialized aggressive conduct disorder" seems to have the least favorable prognosis. This diagnosis corresponds to what is called "solitary aggressive type" in DSM-III-R.

Regarding adult patients, outpatient psychotherapy with antisocial personality disorders has been very discouraging. I believe it is too early to know whether specialized therapeutic community settings for such patients can be effective in the long run. Extended inpatient treatment in specialized closed hospitals or prison systems would seem to be effective in some cases, particularly if firm and incorruptible environmental control is combined with the opportunity for therapy in groups constituted by delinquent patient-prisoners (Reid 1981).

The first task in evaluating patients with antisocial behavior under ordinary outpatient conditions is to establish carefully the differential diagnosis elaborated above, and then to separate out the prognostically more favorable personality disorders from the antisocial personality proper. The second task is to protect the patient's immediate social environment from the consequences of his behavior, help members of his family protect themselves, and tactfully but openly provide the family with full information and counsel regarding the nature of this psychopathology and its prognosis. The fact that, as many researchers and clinicians have pointed out, the antisocial personality disorder tends to burn out in middle and later adult years may provide some long-range hope or at least some consolation to the family (Glueck and Glueck 1943).

The third task is to create realistic conditions for whatever treatment is attempted, eliminating all secondary gains of treatment—escaping from the law, for example, or ongoing parasitic dependency on parents or other social-support systems.

The prognosis for the treatment of malignant narcissism, though reserved, is significantly better than for that of the antisocial personality proper; in the course of intensive, long-term psychoanalytic psychotherapy some of these patients can achieve a gradual transformation of their antisocial behavior and the corresponding manipulative, exploitative behavior in the transference into predominantly paranoid resistances. Such paranoid resistances may even lead to a paranoid transference psychosis but also, if and when such regression can be contained and managed in the psychotherapy, to further gradual transformation into more ordinary transferences characteristic of severe narcissistic personality disorders. One possible limitation to such treatment efforts is presented by patients whose aggressive behavior is potentially threatening to others, including the psychotherapist; the possibility of dangerous violence connected with pronounced paranoid transference reactions should be evaluated before intensive psychotherapy is undertaken.

The treatment of patients with narcissistic personality and antisocial features may follow the customary stages of intensive psychotherapy with this personality disorder. These patients usually have an indication for psychoanalytic psychotherapy rather than psychoanalysis proper, which is also true for other severe personality disorders with antisocial features. For patients with antisocial behavior as an expression of unconscious guilt—that is, in neurotic personality organization—psychoanalytic treatment is indicated.

THE PSYCHODYNAMICS OF MALIGNANT NARCISSISM AND OF THE ANTISOCIAL PERSONALITY

In my view, the psychodynamic findings about patients with malignant narcissism open the way for a psychoanalytic understanding of the intrapsychic structure and internal world of object relations of the antisocial personality disorder proper.

The transferences of patients with malignant narcissism reflect both faulty early superego formation and the failure to consolidate total object relations in the context of integration of ego identity. In essence, these patients are so dominated by the earliest sadistic superego precursors that the subsequently idealized superego precursors cannot neutralize them; hence superego integration is blocked, and the more realistic superego introjects of the oedipal period are largely unavailable. Realistic expectations or prohibitions from the parental objects have been either devalued or transformed into persecutory threats. These patients convey the impression that their world of object relations has experienced a malignant transformation, leading to the devaluation and sadistic enslavement of potentially good internalized object relations on the part of an integrated, yet cruel, omnipotent, and "mad" self (Rosenfeld 1971). This pathological grandiose and sadistic self supplants the sadistic precursors of the superego, absorbs all aggression, and transforms what would otherwise be sadistic superego components into an abnormal self-structure, which then militates against the internalization of later, more realistic superego components.

These patients experience external objects as omnipotent and cruel. They feel that loving, mutually gratifying object relations not only can easily be destroyed but contain the seeds for an attack by the omnipotent, cruel object. One way to survive is by total submission. A subsequent route is to identify with the object, which gives the subject a sense of power, freedom from fear, and the feeling that the only way to relate to others is by gratifying one's aggression. An alternative route is to adopt a false, cynical way of communication, totally denying the importance of object relations, becoming an innocent bystander rather than identifying with the cruel tyrant or submitting masochistically to him.

My limited experiences in attempting a psychodynamic exploration of patients with antisocial personality proper together with the findings derived from intensive psychotherapy and psychoanalysis of patients with malignant narcissism lead me to propose the following tentative considerations.

These patients convey having had experiences of savage aggression from their parental objects and frequently report having both observed and experienced violence in their early childhood. They also convey that they are totally convinced of the impotence of any good object relation: the good are, by definition, weak and unreliable, and the patient shows contempt for those vaguely perceived as potentially good objects. The powerful, in contrast, are needed to survive but are also unreliable, and they are invariably sadistic. The pain of having to depend upon powerful, desperately needed, but sadistic parental objects is transformed into rage and is expressed as rage—for the most part projected—thus further exaggerating the sadistic image of powerful bad objects who become towering sadistic tyrants. In this world, which is reminiscent of George Orwell's *1984* (1949), aggression is prevalent but unpredictable, and this unpredictability precludes submission to the sadistic tyrant and prevents the patient from idealizing the sadistic value system of the aggressor.

This failure to achieve any idealization of objects differentiates the antisocial personality proper from the "self-righteous" aggression of the patient with malignant narcissism, who has at least found some possibility of condensing sadism and idealization by identifying himself with an idealized, cruel tyrant. The failure of idealization also prevents the antisocial patient from attempting masochistic submission to a predictable although sadistic authority. The patient is deeply and totally convinced that only his own power is reliable and that the pleasure of sadistic control is the only alternative to the suffering and destruction of the weak. In such a world, there is a need (to paraphrase Paul Parin [1971]) to "fear thy neighbor as thou fearest thyself" and to devalue all weakening linkages with others.

So far, I have focused on the predominantly aggressive antisocial personality disorder. The passive-parasitic antisocial personality disorder, in contrast, has found a way out of gratification via sadistic power by denying the importance of all object relations and regressively idealizing the gratification of receptive-dependent needs—food, objects, money, sex, privileges—and the symbolic power exerted over others by extracting such gratifications from them. To get the needed supplies while ignoring others as persons and protecting oneself from revengeful punishment is the meaning of life. To eat, to defecate, to sleep, to have sex, to feel secure, to take revenge, to feel powerful, to be excited, all without being discovered by the surrounding dangerous though anonymous world—this constitutes a sort of adaptation to life, even if it is the adaptation of a wolf disguised to live among the sheep, with the real danger coming from other wolves similarly disguised, against whom the protective "sheepishness" has been erected. This psychological structure permits the denial of aggression and its transformation into ruthless exploitation.

In patients with malignant narcissism, some idealized superego precursors have been drawn into the aggressively infiltrated, pathological grandiose self, facilitating at least a consolidated sense of self, of self-continuity throughout time, and, by means of projection, a sense of stability and predictability of the world of powerful and dangerous others as well. The pathological narcissism, ego-syntonic grandiosity, antisocial behavior, and paranoid alertness of these patients allow them to control their internal world of object relations. This same pathological grandiose self simultaneously protects them from the unbearable conflicts around primitive envy that torment the less protected narcissistic personality. The antisocial personality proper, in contrast, is protected from rageful envy only by aggressive, violent appropriation or passive-parasitic exploitation of others.

Zinoviev (1984) has made a study of social groups and institutions in totalitarian political regimes whose moral authority images are projected onto the supreme hierarchy of the system as external "persecutory" figures. Zinoviev stresses the generalized social corruption that is a consequence of such a social structure and that may affect the public behavior of large segments of the population. His dramatic description of the general corruption of public life under such circumstances illustrates the dependency of the individual's moral behavior upon the surrounding social structure. Milgram's (1963) famous experiments indicate how uncritical obedience to authority may easily bring about guiltless participation in sadistic behavior even at high levels of psychological organization and in an atmosphere of social freedom. The antisocial personality's reality is the normal person's nightmare; the normal person's reality is the nightmare of the psychopath.

Part III CLINICAL APPLICATIONS OF OBJECT RELATIONS THEORY

Chapter **6** OBJECT RELATIONS THEORY IN CLINICAL PRACTICE

Let me say at the outset that psychoanalytic technique based on ego psychology–object relations theory is grounded on the assumption that affects are central to the psychoanalytic situation.

Following Fenichel (1941), I believe that economic, dynamic, and structural factors provide the optimal criteria for deciding when, what, and how to interpret the patient's unconscious conflicts, their defensive and impulsive aspects, and, I would add, the unconscious internalized object relations in which they are embedded. The economic criterion for the material to be interpreted within any psychoanalytic session or any segment of a session is that the material be linked to the patient's dominant affect disposition. This disposition or affect state is not necessarily conscious and may have to be inferred from the patient's free associations, his or her nonverbal behavior, and the general atmosphere created by the confluence of the patient's transference and the analyst's countertransference.

This affect state always signals the activation of an unconscious object relation between an aspect of the patient's self representation and a corresponding object representation. And the conflict between impulse and defense is reflected in a conflict between a defensively activated and an impulsively dominated, rejected internalized object relation. Unconscious fantasy, the unconscious wishes and fears activated in the session, reflects these internalized object relations.

I believe that a self representation, an object representation, and an affect state linking them are the essential units of psychic structure relevant for psychoanalytic exploration. Sexual and aggressive drives always emerge in the context of internalized object relations organized by affect states that, at the same time, signal these (hierarchically supraordinate) drives. To put this differently, if, as Freud (1915a) said, the only knowledge we have of drives is through their mental representations and affects, these representations are of the self and an object linked by a dominant affect state.

In practice, my approach requires at the start of each session a willingness to wait to intervene until the patient's verbal communications and nonverbal behavior, the overall emotional atmosphere, and my countertransference guide me to the affectively dominant theme. There are, of course, times when the analyst experiences strong internal pressures to intervene interpretively on the basis of what has happened in an earlier session or in response to a subject that seems to have current urgency for the patient or following some information from external sources. The analyst's willingness to explore these pressures internally as well as the new information provided by the patient in this session should permit a gradual sorting out of what is affectively dominant at the time.

In this regard, Bion's (1967) recommendation that the analyst proceed "without memory nor desire" has to be questioned. The analyst's "memory" at the beginning of the hour may be what he needs to consider rather than eliminate from his awareness; and strong wishes to influence the patient in a certain direction ("desire") may reflect the analyst's countertransference. All these considerations help us determine what is economically—that is, affectively—dominant in the session.

THE DOMINANT OBJECT RELATION, AFFECTIVE CONTENT, AND TRANSFERENCE ANALYSIS

The psychoanalytic "frame" (the regularity of the sessions, the temporal and physical arrangements, the rule of free association for the patient and of abstinence and technical neutrality for the analyst) sets the stage for a potential "real," "objective," or "normal" object relationship. This relationship includes the analyst as an interested, objective, but concerned and sympathetic listener who respects the patient's autonomy, and the patient as one who expects to be helped to a greater understanding of his unconscious conflicts. This realistic relationship, based on the patient's awareness of the analyst as knowledgeable, benign, concerned, and nonjudgmental, facilitates the development of a psychoanalytic process. It certainly includes the patient's realistic awareness of the analyst's personality features as these emerge in their interaction.

In this process the patient is able to regress as a consequence of the interpretation of defenses that would ordinarily protect him against such regression. The regressive process changes the nature of the object relationship from a "realistic" one into one controlled by the dominant transference-countertransference constellation within which the defensive and impulsive aspects of the patient's unconscious conflicts are embedded. This unconscious object relation in the transference is under the control of an affect disposition that differs from the initial "objective" sense of safety and security that stems from the "real" object relation defined by the psychoanalytic frame.

Any particular psychoanalytic situation may thus include (1) the residues of the "objective" object relation determined by the psychoanalytic frame, (2) an object relation corresponding to the prevalent transference, and (3) an object relation corresponding to a theme affectively dominant in the hour. In practice, the object relation reflected in the dominant affect usually coincides with the object relation dominant in the transference; this facilitates the analyst's decision to interpret the affectively dominant material as it emerges in the transference. Sometimes, however, the affectively dominant object relation is related to a situation outside the transference, communicated via the content of what the patient says or does. Or perhaps, against the background of a certain habitual transference disposition, an acute conflict in the patient's life activates another affectively charged object relation that may become temporarily dominant in a session. Here, affective dominance takes precedence over transference dominance in determining the analyst's interpretation.

Sometimes the patient may present material concerning his relationship with somebody else, and the analyst, in trying to clarify this relationship, may find that an aspect of the transference is significantly intruding into the communicative process. Now a transference resistance emerges as a barrier to the full exploration of what initially seemed an issue external to the transference. The affective dominance has shifted from another theme to the transference itself, and this requires the analyst to focus interpretively on the transference before proceeding with the other theme. In patients with severe character pathology, particularly those with strong narcissistic, paranoid, or schizoid personality features, the infiltration of transference resistances reflecting the prevalent character pathology can be so pervasive that, for practical purposes, all material immediately resonates with dominant transference issues.

And then there are patients, particularly those with narcissistic character pathology, in whom the pervasive resistances against a dominant transference pattern also weaken the initial "objective" object relation; it is as if the relationship between two people in the same room were impersonal. No signs of an affectively charged relationship are evident;

all communication seems mechanical, deanimated, even dehumanized. These conditions, I believe, were implicit in Winnicott's (1971, p. 103) description of a psychic "space" between patient and analyst, a space in which affect-laden fantasies may emerge, a space of fantasied emotional relations that we take for granted in the psychoanalysis of the neurotic patient. (For a more extensive discussion of this subject, see chapter 9.) The analyst's intuitive assessment of this space by means of his countertransference constitutes a "third channel" of communication for the transference. (The "first channel" refers to the patient's communication of his subjective experience, and the "second channel" is the analyst's observation of the patient's nonverbal behavior.) If the obliteration of this psychic space persists, it may require systematic analysis. With disappearance of the analytic space, the dominant affective theme becomes conspicuous by its absence. What is "absent" is in fact a very much present defense (an implicit, fantasied object relation) against an impulse directed toward the analyst, and this is what must be interpreted.

Ordinarily in the treatment of patients with neurotic personality organization, the verbal and nonverbal channels of communication override by far the importance of the analysis of the analytic space and the countertransference. Although when any patient temporarily regresses, deeply strong countertransference reactions may be activated in the treatment, it is only with severe character pathology and borderline personality organization that countertransference becomes a truly essential source of information about the developments in the transference and acquires a central role in determining affective dominance and the investigation of the object relation linked to this affect disposition.

TRANSFERENCE AND TRANSFERENCE INTERPRETATION

The basic contribution of object relations theory to the analysis of the transference is to expand the frame of reference within which transference manifestations are explored, so that the increasing complexities of transference regression in patients with deep levels of psychopathology may be understood and interpreted. In practice, the transference of patients with classical psychoneurosis and patients with character pathology in a neurotic personality organization can still be understood as the unconscious repetition in the here-and-now of pathogenic relations from the past—more concretely, the enactment of an aspect of the patient's unconscious infantile self in relating to (also unconscious) infantile representations of the parental objects.

The fact that neurotic patients regress to a relatively integrated although repressed unconscious infantile self that relates to relatively integrated although unconscious representations of the parental objects makes such transferences fairly easy to understand and to interpret: it is the unconscious relation to the parents of the past, including realistic and fantasied aspects of such relations and the defenses against them, that is activated in the transference. The unconscious aspect of the infantile self carries with it a concrete wish reflecting a drive derivative directed to such parental objects and a fantasied fear about the dangers involved in expressing this wish. What ego psychology–object relations theory stresses is that even in these comparatively simple transference enactments, the activation is always of basic dyadic units of a self representation and an object representation linked by a certain affect, and these units reflect either the defensive or the impulsive aspects of the conflict. More precisely, an unconscious fantasy that reflects an impulse-defense organization is typically activated first in the form of the object relation representing the defensive side of the conflict and only later by the object relation reflecting the impulsive side of the conflict.

For example, a neurotic patient with masochistic personality structure misinterpreted my comments as devastating criticism at precisely those moments when she felt our working relationship was good. She then became enraged with me, challenging, defiant, accusing me of trying to control her as her mother had done. I understood her behavior to mean that our working together had activated in her the unconscious fantasy that I as her father was sexually seducing her (derived, in turn, from her projection onto me of underlying positive oedipal wishes). She defended herself masochistically by experiencing me as her nagging mother and herself as an impotent child.

My interpretation focused on her view of me as her critical mother after she felt I had helped her and she had expressed her appreciation; this gradually permitted the emergence of more direct positive feelings with a mixture of erotic excitement and the fear of my becoming a seductive father. Now I interpreted this fear as an expression of her projection onto me of sexual impulses that she did not dare to experience directly. A more direct expression of positive oedipal fantasies about me followed.

What does an object relations approach add to these formulations regarding the transference? First, it highlights the consistent set of dyadic units (a self representation interacting with an object representation under the dominance of a certain affect), and it frames the experience of concrete unconscious fantasies, wishes, and fears. Second, it sees each defense-impulse organization as reflected in two opposed units, so that both defense and impulse are reflected in a fantasied relation between self and object. Third, even at the neurotic level of pathology, a process may be observed that becomes prevalent with deeper psychopathology: the rapid reversal or alternation between the activation of the patient's self representation with the object representation projected onto the analyst and other moments when the patient enacts an identification with that object representation while projecting the self representation onto the analyst. When the masochistic patient was experiencing me as aggressively scolding her, which resulted in her feeling hurt and mistreated, she lashed out at me angrily in ways that clearly echoed her description of her mother's behavior. I, temporarily paralyzed by her onslaught, found it very difficult to interpret the situation to her. In other words, when patients temporarily regress, there is both an intensification and a primitivization of the affect reflecting the corresponding drive derivative and a proclivity to rapid reversals of identifications with self or object, which may be understood and interpreted more easily within the organizing frame of internalized object relations.

In thus examining afresh the nature of identifications in the transference, I am suggesting that all identifications are with a relation to an object, not with an object. I am further suggesting that in the relation the patient identifies with both self and object, with the possibility of reenacting the roles of either. I believe this conceptualization throws new light on Freud's (1915a) observation that an instinct may undergo, among other things, the vicissitudes of reversal into its opposite and finding the object in the subject's self. Freud also emphasized that mental life generally is governed by dichotomies—of subject (ego) and object (external world), of pleasure and unpleasure, of active and passive. In the light of object relations theory, the expression of an "active" impulse— aggression, for example—that was first experienced passively may be understood as either the activation of a self representation under a subjectively experienced attack from the object or as the activation of an identification with the object representation of that interaction. "Identification with the aggressor," also illustrated in my example and now conceptualized as a consequence of identifying with both self and object, exemplifies the transformation of passive into active impulse expression.

The expression of an impulse against the self as opposed to the expression of that impulse against an object also may be understood as identification with an attacking object. For example, the masochistic patient's attacking me when she felt erotically stimulated in the transference represented her enactment of her mother's punitive behavior (reflected in her superego identification with mother), while she projected onto me her self representation—masochistically submitting to mother. The structural conflict between superego and ego was enacted in an object relation "with reversed functions" in the transference. She was enacting a defensive masochistic object relation that derived from her having internalized the aggressive-submissive interaction with mother. She correspondingly internalized the attacking mother as part of the superego (giving rise to the masochistic behavior), and in a secondary characterological distortion of her ego as well (in the patient's characterological identification with mother's hostile behavior). At other times she enacted, in other ego identifications, her identification with the masochistically submissive daughter.

For practical purposes, then, instead of interpreting the vicissitudes of a "pure" impulse-defense configuration, we interpret the transference in terms of the activation of an internalized object relation that gives rise to alternating activations of the same conflict in what may look like contradictory experiences and behavior. This approach enriches the interpretation with clarifying nuances and details. Thus I was able to point out to my masochistic patient that, in treating me as aggressively as she felt herself treated by her mother, she was identifying with mother and simultaneously implicitly submitting to mother's internalized image and becoming like mother as an expression of unconscious guilt over the feared sexualized relation with me as father. I am proposing that the time-honored clinical observation that one affect may be employed as a defense against another repressed or dissociated affect should be reformulated as the defensive use of one internalized object relation and its corresponding affect against another internalized object relation and its affect.

What makes the analysis of internalized object relations in the transference more complex (but also permits the clarification of such complexity) is the development, in patients with severe character pathology, of a defensive primitive dissociation or splitting of internalized object relations. This splitting occurs in patients functioning at a borderline level, in narcissistic personalities, and even in analytically approachable psychoses. In these patients, the tolerance of ambivalence characteristic of higher-level neurotic object relations is replaced by a defensive disintegration of the representations of self and objects into libidinally and aggressively invested part-object relations. The more realistic or more easily understandable past object relations of neurotic personalities are replaced by highly unrealistic, sharply idealized, or sharply aggressivized or persecutory self and object representations that cannot immediately be traced to actual or fantasied relationships of the past.

What is activated here are either highly idealized part-object relations under the impact of intense, diffuse, overwhelming affect states of an ecstatic nature or equally intense but painful and frightening primitive affect states that signal the activation of aggressive or persecutory relations between self and object. We can recognize the nonintegrated nature of the internalized object relations by the patient's disposition to rapid reversals of the enactment of the role of self and object representations. Simultaneously, the patient may project a complementary self or object representation onto the analyst; this, together with the intensity of affect activation, leads to apparently chaotic transference developments. These rapid oscillations, as well as the sharp dissociation between loving and hating aspects of the relation to the same object, may be further complicated by defensive condensations of several object relations under the impact of the same primitive affect, so that combined father-mother images confusingly condense the aggressively perceived aspects of father and mother. Idealized or devalued aspects of the self similarly condense various levels of past experiences.

An object relations frame of reference permits the analyst to understand and organize what looks like complete chaos so that he can clarify the various condensed part-object relations in the transference, bringing about an integration of self and object representations, which leads to the more advanced neurotic type of transference.

The general principles of transference interpretation in the treatment of borderline personality organization include the following tasks (see Kernberg 1984): (1) to diagnose the dominant object relation within the overall chaotic transference situation; (2) to clarify which is the self representation and which is the object representation of this internalized object relation and the dominant affect linking them; and (3) to interpretively connect this primitive dominant object relation with its split-off opposite.

CLINICAL EXAMPLES

Ms A, in her midthirties, with a predominantly narcissistic personality functioning on an overt borderline level, became enraged at the end of every session, experiencing my saying that we had to stop as a narcissistic blow. And it was always at the end of the session that she remembered crucial issues that she felt an urgent need to discuss then and there. During the sessions, she treated me with contempt and found innumerable grounds for criticizing me. In each session, she offered a different complaint about me, which was never mentioned again. Her rage and contempt for me certainly had the effect of preventing her from discussing her real-life problems.

She demanded that I respond precisely and fully to all her questions rather than ask her to reflect about what she was saying and that I comply with her requests for changes in the hours without her having to tell me why she was requesting the change. But she left each session with an air of having been cruelly treated and profoundly hurt. Later, overwhelmed with despair, she would telephone me and beg me to talk with her.

I was gradually able to point out to Ms A how, during the sessions, she was identifying with a controlling and sadistic person who insisted on forcing me into total obedience, and, at the end of the sessions, she experienced me as a controlling and sadistic object who was treating her as worthless. Slowly she was able to understand that this series of enactments was an aspect of a relationship with her mother activated with role reversals. Eventually she was able to realize that this "mad" relationship reflected not reality, present or past, but an exacerbation of all the hostile aspects of her relationship with mother under the impact of her fantasies created by her rage at mother. As her primitive, persecutory object relation was clarified, Ms A became more able to reflect upon and less obliged to enact this relationship.

Indeed, she progressed far enough for me to explore with her the implications of her reluctance to end her sessions and her need to telephone me afterward. When I asked how she would feel if I were in fact totally available to her in every respect, she said she would like nothing better, but the idea made her anxious because it was so unrealistic—such greedy demandingness was bound to make me feel resentful. And yet it was exactly what she wanted.

I then suggested that she seemed to want a relationship with me that was like the relationship between a loved only infant child and a totally dedicated mother. Ms A interrupted me to say that any mother would grow to terribly resent such an expectation from her baby. I said that was precisely the fear connected with her wish. If I represented a mother totally committed to her infant baby girl, then she, in identifying with such a baby, could relax, relent, and be happy. Ms A agreed, with a smile, and said that then the world would be all right.

My interpretation had uncovered the split-off, idealized aspect of the patient's relationship with mother, one fraught with danger because of Ms A's greedy demandingness and her intolerance of her own rage resulting from any frustration from this ideal mother. After months of working through this transference paradigm, a new aspect of Ms A's relation to mother developed—namely, an intense resentment of mother because of the patient's inordinate sense of dependency on her. Resentment and envy unconsciously caused her to poison mother's image in her own mind. She expressed this clinically in a negative therapeutic reaction following precisely the activation of the split-off, idealized transference.

Ms B, a schizophrenic professional woman in her early twenties, was in psychoanalytic psychotherapy and on a low-maintenance dose of a neuroleptic that permitted her to continue to function but did not eliminate her psychotic thinking. She had the delusion that people, particularly dominant women, were stealing her physical energy, draining her so that she would be left exhausted and weakened, unable to think clearly. In one session, while I was discussing her fear of sexual intimacy with her boyfriend, Ms B suddenly looked anxious and suspicious and asked why I had just made a gesture with my hand. I told her that I was not aware of having made any particular gesture but wondered if she felt that I, like others, was trying to steal her energy.

In a sudden burst of anger, Ms B accused me of knowing perfectly well that I had just been stealing her energy; why did I need to engage in such a despicable game of pretending? I told her I believed she was convinced that I had been stealing her energy, but I was equally convinced that I had not; I had been concentrating totally on what we had been talking about. I wondered whether she could accept my statement as the truth. My emphasis on our mutually incompatible realities and, therefore, on the differences and separation between us represented an effort to signal my view of her experience as possibly psychotic, as well as my tolerance ("containment") of the discrepancy. I also wanted to reduce the blurring of boundaries between self and object that she was obviously experiencing. I was, in addition, implying that I thought she could tolerate this separation from me.

Ms B said she could believe that this was my conviction, but it upset her that I thought she was crazy. I told her I was not making any judgment except to acknowledge that we had momentarily incompatible perceptions of reality and that she was experiencing me as having tried to weaken and damage her, which must have been very frightening and upsetting. She agreed that it was very upsetting and immediately spoke of how her mother used to steal her energy and never admit it while trying to control and dominate her.

I said I realized that she was now perceiving me as if I were a replica of her mother, and if this were so, it impressed me that I had become like her mother precisely when I was trying to help her become less afraid of sexual intimacy with her boyfriend. Ms B said she was afraid that I was trying to push her into a sexual relationship; she felt I was so convinced that she should go to bed with a man that I was trying to influence her thoughts directly, to the extent that she could no longer tell whether these were my thoughts or hers. She added, as an afterthought, that her father used to behave quite seductively with her at times, although she was not sure whether she had behaved seductively toward him. Anyhow, she added, her mother hated the closeness of her relationship with father.

I said I wondered whether she had perceived my inquiry about her fears of sexual intimacy with her boyfriend as an indirect suggestion that she go to bed with him, which made me a sexually seductive man whom she perceived as similar to her father. If that were so, I added, it would be only natural that the image of her mother would impress itself upon her as a dangerous enemy, jealous of that sexual closeness with father, so that now I had become mother trying to punish her by robbing her of her energy. Ms B, looking much more relaxed, said she felt that this was exactly what had happened.

I then said it seemed to me that behind the feeling of loss of energy, her fear of my penetrating her mind, and her concern about interchange of energy at a physical level was the fear of sexual seduction and penetration and the fear of punishment for that, and these fears were so closely linked to her parents that she found them unbearable. For this reason, I said, she might have transformed the fear of dangerous relationships with both parents into the fear of exchange of physical energy, which was more painful and mysterious but less disturbingly threatening than the fantasied interactions with her parents.

Ms B asked me whether all mental functioning was not connected with physical energy. I said it seemed to me that the direct translation of a psychological experience into a sense of gain or loss of physical energy was a protective operation that could become frightening in its own right because of the mysterious and magical ways in which ordinary relationships between people were thus transmuted. The patient seemed satisfied with my remarks and said that she felt fine now. She gave no further indication that her fears were persisting or that she was being compliant.

The situation here is again different from that with borderline patients. If a central problem with borderlines is the activation of primitive, overwhelming, part-object relations that continuously alternate in their role distribution in the transference and require a long time to trace back to infantile reality, the problem with psychoses is the blurring of boundaries between self and object representations. Under these circumstances, the activation of a certain object relation in the transference may induce an immediate confusion between self and object and, therefore, confusion regarding the origin of an intolerable impulse. This activates a defensive object relation within which self and object become further confused and the protective quality of the defensive object relation fails.

Thus Ms B understood my comment about her fear of intimacy with her boyfriend as a sexual assault from me as father, equivalent to her own sexual desire for father. But she was not able to place the origin of this sexual desire. As a result, she experienced immediate punishment by mother's attack on her. And again it was impossible for her to distinguish attacker from attacked; secondarily, she was unable to differentiate sexual from aggressive affects. Hence a primitive transformation of the fear of losing the boundaries of the self into a sense that physical energy was being extracted from her body (that is, a regressive blurring of mind-body boundaries) provided her with a delusional escape from the conflict. Again, my interpreting the situation not in terms of impulses alone (or impersonal impulse-defense configurations) but in terms of the activated object relations permitted clarification of the immediate situation and temporary reduction of the psychotic regression.

Object relations theory also enlarges our understanding of the transference resistances of patients with narcissistic personality structure. The emergence in the transference of various characteristics of the pathological grandiose self and the corresponding admiring, devalued, or suspiciously feared object representations often permit clarification of the component internalized object relations that have led to condensation of the pathological grandiose self.

For example, a mathematician in his early thirties with a narcissistic personality structure was unable to maintain sexual interest in any woman with whom he was emotionally involved. Impatient at the slow pace of his psychoanalytic treatment, he suspected that my interest in him was venal, just as he suspected the motives of the women in his life. He offered to pay me a large amount of money if I would significantly shorten his treatment "by really putting effort into it." Basically he was resentful because he thought I was exploiting him.

It took me some time to sort out, within this transference, his projection onto me (and onto women) of his own greediness, the enactment of various aspects of his mother—particularly her constant warning that women would always try to exploit him—and his identification with his father's sense of entitlement, expressed by father in crudely aggressive acts. This patient's dominant self-concept, in short, could be clarified as constituted by identifications with selective aspects of both parents that fed into his grandiosity, demandingness, suspiciousness, and fear of dependent relations.

In general, gradual analysis of the components of the pathological grandiose self usually permits the emergence of the underlying primitive
object relations characteristic of borderline personality organization and,
eventually, the development of the patient's normal infantile self and the
capacity to establish authentically dependent relationships with others.

What I have said so far about the structure of internalized object relations in patients with varying degrees of psychopathology in effect modi-
fies Fenichel's (1941) structural criteria of interpretation, mentioned at
the opening of this chapter. Patients who present a neurotic personality
organization have unconscious conflicts that are predominantly *inter*-
systemic; in these cases the classic dictum holds that one should always
interpret from the side of the ego and clarify, over a period of time, the
agencies involved in the conflict and how they are participating in it. But
with patients presenting severe psychopathology and predominantly
*intra*systemic conflicts, the focus is on the currently dominant internalized object relation as part of the defense function of the transference
and on the internalized object relation currently functioning as a dissociated impulse structure. This conceptualization facilitates applying
structural in addition to economic and dynamic criteria to our interpretive work.

GENETIC CONSTRUCTIONS AND RECONSTRUCTIONS

My view differs from those of other proponents of object relations theories such as Klein (1945, 1946, 1957), Segal (1967), Fairbairn (1954), and
Mahler (Mahler, Pine, and Bergman 1975) in that I focus less on any
particular time in the patient's past at which the currently dominant
pathogenic conflicts and structural organization of the personality may
have originated. I believe it is crucial that the analyst not have preconceived ideas about the source of the current unconscious conflict and
allow the patient's free associations to serve as a guide to the genetic
origin of the "here-and-now" in the "there-and-then."

I agree with Jacobson (1964) and Mahler (Mahler and Furer 1968) that the
predominant organization of psychic structures (neurotic, borderline,
narcissistic, or psychotic) points to certain key periods in development.
But subsequent events make one-to-one connections risky. Similarly, the
traditional Kleinian tendency to focus on what is assumed to occur in the
first year of life does not, I believe, do justice to the complexity of psychosexual development.

Hence, I try to follow the dynamic principle of interpretation by proceeding from the surface downward and to help the patient understand

the unconscious meaning in the here-and-now in a relatively ahistorical way, in an "as if" mode: "It is as if such-and-such a kind of child were relating to such-and-such a kind of parent." The patient's associations may transform this into a concrete memory or fantasy that relates the present unconscious with the past genetic origin (Sandler and Sandler 1987).

In my view the question of whether conflicts related to a particular kind of psychopathology are typically oedipal or preoedipal is spurious. I have never seen a patient whose problems were "either/or" or one in whom oedipal problems were not central. The principal difference between neurotic as opposed to severe psychopathology is that in the latter the condensations of oedipal and preoedipal issues are more complex. Anal or oral conflicts, for example, may be observed along the entire spectrum of psychopathology but never in isolation from other conflicts; and the same holds true for conflicts originating at all other levels of psychosexual development.

At the same time, we must acknowledge that some crucial early traumatic experiences are beyond reconstruction by evoked memory. In such cases, reconstruction of an early past that was never fully conscious has to be attempted with the help of constructions derived from currently dominant unconscious object relations. With the patient who could not leave my office at the end of the session, the desperate search for a perfect mother was clearly a construction suggested by me. A Mahlerian, Winnicottian, Kleinian, or Kohutian approach might attempt to fix the most reasonable time for the construction of a past experience (real or fantasied). I feel comfortable if such a construction is placed in context, as the "timeless hinterland" around which more concrete, time-specific reconstructions from the past may or may not eventually be achieved.

Concrete knowledge of the patient's past is of course extremely helpful in the systematic analysis of the unconscious meanings in the here-and-now. To establish a hypothesis that links the unconscious here-and-now with known aspects of the patient's history not previously incorporated into the fabric of genetic reconstructions may provide helpful bridges to the past. We have to be very cautious, however, in introducing "objective facts" from the past, particularly with patients with severe psychopathology, in whom the distance between objective facts and subjective experience, between developmental data and genetic development, is enormous.

We are left, therefore, with a paradox: in better-functioning patients, with whom reconstructions are easier, they are less necessary because the patients' associations lead easily into the unconscious past. But with serious psychopathology, genetic reconstructions are very difficult, and whatever objective history is obtained is of little help because of the patients' limited capacity for consciously penetrating the past. Therefore, I question, for example, Rosenfeld's (1987) tendency to link such objective data directly with the findings in the transference of psychotic and borderline patients.

COUNTERTRANSFERENCE

I have found Racker's (1957) observations about the analyst's identifications and countertransference most helpful. Racker distinguished two types of such identifications: concordant identification, when the analyst identifies with what is activated in the patient, and complementary identification, when the analyst identifies with the agency that is in conflict with the agency the patient is identifying with. The latter is usually one the patient cannot tolerate and hence projects. In object relations terms, we might say that in concordant identification the analyst identifies with the same representation activated in the patient, self with self, object with object. Concordant identification in the countertransference is of central importance as the source of ordinary empathy when the patient is in a reflective mood, but also under conditions in which the analyst, by overidentifying with the patient, may be tempted to share, by proxy, his acting out.

In complementary identification, the patient and the analyst temporarily enact the self and object representations of a certain internalized object relation. If the transference is sexualized, for example, the analyst may respond seductively to the patient's fear of and temptation toward an oedipal acting out. More frequently, when a particularly negative transference predominates, the analyst becomes the patient's aggressive and threatening object, and the patient becomes his own frightened self. Or a reversal takes place: the analyst may feel paralyzed by the patient's aggression, reacting with fear and impotent hatred as he identifies with the patient's threatened self representation; at the same time the patient is identifying with his threatening object.

In general, under complementary countertransference, the analyst is identified with an internal imago that the patient at that point cannot tolerate and has to dissociate and project. In fact, complementary countertransference reactions are usually evoked by the patient's defensive use of projective identification: the analyst now feels empathic with what the patient cannot tolerate in himself. By the same process, the analyst may acquire significant information regarding the total object relation that has been activated in the transference. Here lies a potentially most rewarding use of the countertransference on the part of the psychoanalyst. The danger, of course, is the temptation to act out this complementary identification rather than use it as material to be integrated into the interpretive process.

If the analyst tolerates his countertransference, he can use it to clarify the dominant object relation in the transference, provided, of course, that professional boundaries are maintained. It is important that, should countertransference acting out occur, the analyst refrain from offering explanations beyond acknowledging what the patient has observed.

DREAM ANALYSIS

Fairbairn (1954) opened the road to a new frame of reference for dream analysis by applying an object relations theory model to it. He thought that various aspects of a patient's identifications might be represented by different persons in the dream and that significant objects in the patient's psychic life also were represented several times in the dream as functions of various aspects of the patient's internal relations and identifications with them.

Meltzer (1984) and Rosenfeld (1987) have applied a Kleinian object relations approach to dream analysis, Meltzer in a systematic way and Rosenfeld indirectly by means of clinical material illustrating the centrality of dream analysis in their approaches. Although I disagree with the tendency of both these writers to interpret directly the manifest content of dreams as symbolically reflecting aspects of the first year of life, I have found helpful their integration of the formal aspects of the dream with what is currently dominant in the transference. This approach, it seems to me, is not unrelated to Erikson's (1954) focus on the formal aspects of the patient's relating of a dream and points to the increasing importance of the expressive and interactional—in contrast to the directly symbolic—aspects of dream analysis.

I try to elicit associations to the manifest content of the dream without interpreting directly in terms of unconscious symbolic meanings. I pay attention to (1) the dominant emotional qualities of the content of the dream, (2) how the dream is told, (3) the relation of the content of the dream in terms of its dominant object relations to the object relation activated during the communication of the dream, (4) the general transference background against which the narrating of the dream occurs, and finally (5) the day residues.

Chapter 7 AN EGO PSYCHOLOGY— OBJECT RELATIONS THEORY APPROACH TO THE TRANSFERENCE

The analysis of the transference is a central concern in my general technical approach. Transference analysis consists in analyzing the reactivations in the here-and-now of past internalized object relations. This process constitutes, at the same time, the analysis of the constituent structures of ego, superego, and id and their intra- and interstructural conflicts. In contrast to the interpersonal object relations theoreticians such as Sullivan (1953, 1962) and Guntrip (1961, 1968, 1971), and in contrast to Kohut's (1971, 1977) self psychology, I conceive of internalized object relations as reflecting not actual object relations from the past but rather a combination of realistic and fantasied—and often highly distorted— internalizations of such past object relations and defenses against them under the effects of instinctual drive derivatives. In other words, I see a dynamic tension between the here-and-now, which reflects intrapsychic structure, and the there-and-then unconscious genetic determinants derived from the patient's past developmental history.

Transference interpretation differs according to the nature of the patient's psychopathology. Patients with neurotic personality organization present well-integrated superego, ego, and id structures. Within the psychoanalytic situation, the analysis of resistances brings about the activation in the transference, first, of relatively global characteristics of these structures and, later, of the internalized object relations of which these are composed. The analysis of drive derivatives occurs in the context of the analysis of the relation of the patient's infantile self to significant parental objects as projected onto the analyst.

The patient with borderline personality organization, in contrast, shows a predominance of preoedipal conflicts and psychic representations of preoedipal conflicts condensed with representations of the oedipal phase. Conflicts are not so much repressed as expressed in mutually dissociated ego states reflecting the primitive defense of splitting. The activation of primitive object relations that predate the consolidation of ego, superego, and id is manifest in the transference as apparently chaotic affect states; these have to be analyzed in sequential steps, which I have described elsewhere (Kernberg 1984). The interpretation of primitive transferences of borderline patients brings about a transformation of part object relations into total object relations, of primitive transferences (largely reflecting stages of development that predate object constancy) into the advanced transferences of the oedipal phase.

At severe levels of psychopathology, splitting mechanisms permit the contradictory aspects of intrapsychic conflicts to remain at least partially conscious in the form of primitive transferences. Patients with neurotic personality organization, in contrast, present impulse-defense configurations that contain specific unconscious wishes reflecting sexual and aggressive drive derivatives embedded in unconscious fantasies relating to the oedipal objects. In these patients we find relatively less distortion of both the self representations relating to these objects and the representations of the oedipal objects themselves. Therefore the difference between past pathogenic experiences and their transformation into currently structured unconscious dispositions is not as great as in the primitive transferences found in patients with borderline personality organization.

My emphasis is on the internalized object relation rather than on the impulse-defense configuration per se: the unconscious wishful fantasy expresses such an object relation. The two ways in which, according to Freud (1915c), unconscious wishes may become conscious (in the form of ideational representatives and as affects) are, in my view, evident in the relation between a self representation and an object representation under the impact of a certain affect. Glover's (1955) comments on the need to identify both libidinal drive derivatives and ego- and superego-derived identifications in the transference I believe point in the same direction. If the transference neurosis is manifested in instinctual impulses expressed as affects and in identifications reflecting internalized object relations, then the object relations frame of reference I propose may be considered a direct clinical application of the metapsychological concept of the dynamic unconscious and the conditions under which it appears in consciousness.

I assume that in all cases the transference is dynamically unconscious in the sense that, because of either repression or splitting, the patient unconsciously distorts the current experience owing to his fixation to pathogenic conflicts with a significant internalized object of the past. The major task is to bring the unconscious transference meanings in the here-and-now into full consciousness by means of interpretation. This is the first stage in analyzing the relation between the unconscious present and the unconscious past.

Rather than make a direct connection between currently conscious or preconscious experiences in relation to the therapist and the conscious past, or to an assumed unconscious past, I expect the patient's free associations to the uncovered unconscious transference meanings in the here-and-now to lead us into the unconscious past. I therefore suggest reconstructions in tentative and open-ended formulations that should permit the patient to proceed in any of several directions.

My theoretical framework is expressed clinically in the way I listen to patients. My only expectation is that the patient's free associations will lead to the emergence in the transference of past internalized object relations superimposed on the actual interactions of patient and analyst.

I wish to stress again that I leave as open-ended as I can the question of assumed genetic origins in the process of uncovering the unconscious meaning in the here-and-now. Although it is true that the nature of the activated object relation itself points to its probable genetic and developmental origins, I think it premature to pin down this hypothetical origin before the patient's free associations and exploration of unconscious meanings of his behavior in the here-and-now have given access to new evidence. I am always acutely aware of the danger that the analyst's preconceived notions may close this investigative field prematurely. A theoretical frame that locates the patient's dominant conflicts in a pre-determined area or time seems to me to restrict both the analyst's and the patient's freedom to explore the origins of the unconscious present in the unconscious past.

The traditional Kleinian tendency to relate primitive defensive operations and object relations to the first year of life (Klein 1945, 1946, 1952b, 1957), Kohut's assumption that an ever-present fragility of the self is the primary determinant (Reed 1987), or, for that matter, the analyst's consistent search for the oedipal determinants or for separation-individuation pathology, and so on result in narrowing the interpretive frame and limit the analyst's capacity for discovering and investigating the unknown.

CHANNELS OF COMMUNICATION OF THE TRANSFERENCE

The unconscious object relations that superimpose themselves on the actual one—the patient and the analyst working together within the jointly agreed-upon boundaries of the psychoanalytic situation—might be either a variety of unconscious object relations in conflict with each other or a defensively functioning object relation activated against an underlying contrasting one with impulsive functions. These unconscious object relations may emerge through the channels mentioned in the preceding chapter. With patients presenting neurotic personality organization, and in the advanced stages of treatment of patients with severe character pathology and borderline pathology, they emerge mostly from the patient's free associations.

Let me illustrate with a clinical vignette. Mrs. C, an architect in her early thirties, consulted because of chronic interpersonal difficulties in her work and a severe depression related to the breakup of an extramarital relationship with a senior business associate she described as being sadistic. Diagnostic evaluation revealed a hysterical personality with strong masochistic features. A happy early childhood relationship with her father had turned into bitter struggles with him during her adolescence, when he was having serious marital difficulties. Mrs. C saw her mother as an innocent victim. A sexually intolerant, suppressive atmosphere in the home had become internalized in Mrs. C's own rigid repression of all sexual impulses until only a few years before starting her analysis: she was frigid with her husband and was able to achieve orgasm only in extramarital affairs.

A few weeks after she began her analysis her mood improved; she no longer seemed depressed; she now conveyed the impression of an agreeable, submissive little girl who seemed eager to please the analyst. She was obviously trying hard to say whatever came into her mind, and the content of her early free associations related mostly to her work, particularly to her superiors, whom she described as narrow-minded, biased, uninformed professionals, lacking an original, creative approach to design. She was so obviously dismissive of these men that she herself raised the question during a session whether she might be risking losing her job. She had indeed lost a job with another firm in the not-so-distant past because of her interpersonal difficulties.

When I said I was puzzled by the cheerful way in which she expressed her concern over the prospect of being thrown out, Mrs. C acknowledged a dare-devil attitude in herself, adding that her behavior might indeed be dangerous, but it was gratifyingly exciting, too. Further associations revealed her fantasies of meeting her boss, who would sternly notify her that she would have to leave, and to whom she would then convey by means of subtle insinuations that she was sexually interested in him. In her fantasy, this might lead to a sexual relationship with him at the very time he was dismissing her from her job. She found it exciting to be sexually involved with a man who was throwing her out.

This vignette illustrates the early emergence of a "nice little girl" attitude in the transference as a defense against the underlying temptation of a pseudorebellious, provocatively aggressive attitude toward a male authority aimed at bringing about an underlying, desired self-punitive sexual relationship (presumably, with a sadistic father image). The fact that the apparently positive early transference relationship permitted the emergence of the underlying negative transference dispositions in the content of the patient's free associations rather than directly in the transference relationship itself actually gave us lead time to elaborate this unconscious conflict before its full actualization in reality or in the transference. The focus on the contents of free association, on Mrs. C's subjective experience, was the predominant communicative channel through which the unconscious pathogenic object relation emerged in the transference.

In patients with severe character pathology and borderline personality organization, dominant unconscious object relations in the transference typically emerge by means of nonverbal communication. This does not mean that what is verbally communicated through free association is not relevant or important; rather, the nonverbal communication acquires economic (that is, affective) predominance in conveying information to the analyst.

A mental health professional in his late twenties, Mr. D, consulted because of difficulties in relationships with women, uncertainty about his professional interests and future, and extreme passivity in his work and daily life. In his early analytic sessions Mr. D dwelt on detailed descriptions of the altercations he was having with his girlfriend. My efforts to clarify the issues in what appeared to me confusing descriptions of these arguments elicited his ironic comment that I was slow and pedestrian and did not grasp the subtlety of what he was telling me. He also expected me to approve immediately the statements he had made and actions he had taken regarding his girlfriend. I asked why he felt the need for me to support his actions or agree with his evaluation of her. He then angrily accused me of not being sympathetic to him and of being a traditional, poker-faced psychoanalyst.

Soon Mr. D also complained that I was not providing him with any new understanding that would permit him to deal more effectively with his girlfriend. But when, after getting a better feel for what was actually going on in their interactions, I questioned his interpretations of her behavior and wondered about the reasons for some of his behaviors, he accused me of taking her part, of being unfairly biased against him, and, in fact, of making his relations with her worse by undermining his sense of security. He also offered various psychoanalytic theories to account for his girlfriend's sadistic behavior toward him, pointed out to me that he himself was obviously a masochistic character, and, with growing anger, charged that I was not doing my job—I was not making a connection between what was happening to him now and his childhood experiences.

Although my initial diagnosis of Mr. D had been severe character pathology with paranoid, narcissistic, and infantile features—and I was prepared for stormy transference developments—I was taken aback by the intensity of his complaints and accusations and became increasingly cautious in my comments to him. He immediately perceived my caution and angrily accused me of treating him like a "sickie" rather than being direct with him. I then focused on his difficulty in accepting anything I said that differed from his own thinking, pointing to the internal conflict he experienced in his relation with me: he very much wanted me to help him and to be on his side, while at the same time he experienced everything that came from me as either hostile and damaging or absurd and worthless. Mr. D agreed (for the first time) with my assessment of the situation. He said that he found himself very much in need of help but faced with an incompetent and hostile analyst. I then asked whether he was indeed convinced that this was a reality because, if it was, it would naturally lead him to ask why he had selected me as his therapist, and he was not raising that question. His response was to accuse me of trying to throw him out. I told him I was trying to understand how he felt and not necessarily confirming his views of me.

He then reviewed the circumstances that had led him to consult with me and to select me as an analyst after several unhappy experiences with other psychotherapists. In the course of this review, it emerged that Mr. D had been very pleased when I accepted him as a patient but had also felt very unhappy about what he experienced as the enormous difference in our status. He talked about how painful it was for him to have to consult professionals he considered representative of a most conservative psychiatric and psychoanalytic establishment. He had consulted me because I had been highly recommended to him, but now he was wondering whether brief treatment by a therapist from one of the "antipsychiatry" schools might help him much more. I suggested that he might find it congenial to perceive me as incompetent and hostile because this permitted him to preserve his own self-esteem, although this perception of me was also frustrating his wish to be helped. In other words, I began to interpret the acting out of his needs to devalue and disparage me, needs that reflected dissociated envy of me.

From the beginning of the treatment the principal channel of communication for unconscious object relations activated in the transference was in Mr. D's attitude toward me rather than in the content of his free associations. Certainly the content of his verbal communication was important in clarifying what went on in the relation to me, but the nature of Mr. D's behavior was the dominant focus of communication.

On the surface, he was devaluing me as an admired yet enviously resented parental authority, with himself a grandiose and sadistic child. At a deeper level, he was enacting unconsciously the relationship of a frustrated and enraged child with a parental image that he much needed but also deeply resented because he perceived it as controlling and devaluating. This view of the parental object triggered intense rage, expressed in the wish to devalue and destroy the object while, at a still deeper level, unconsciously hoping that it might survive. In fact, it took many weeks to unravel these unconscious meanings in the here-and-now. Months later, we learned that this object relation reflected Mr. D's unconscious relationship with his mother and that his repeated failure in relationships with women followed a pattern strikingly similar to the one described in his relationship with me. All these women represented mother, as did I in the transference enactment.

There is still a third channel of communication, which might be considered an outgrowth of the second one, except that the nonverbal communication is expressed in the apparent absence of any specific object relation in the transference. It sometimes happens that over a period of many months or even years, the patient shows only minimal signs of transference regression and an almost total absence of aggression or libidinal investment in the transference. I have stressed elsewhere (1984) that such patients present subtle, pervasive, and highly effective transference resistances against being dependent on the analyst and against the related regression in the transference, a condition I described in the preceding chapter as an obliteration of the analytic space. To put it concretely, an absence of emotional depth, of emotional reality, and of fantasy in the analytic encounter becomes the dominant resistance in the treatment.

Mr. E, in his late twenties, consulted because of his dissatisfaction with his bisexual style of life and growing sexual inhibition. Mr. E's personality had strong narcissistic features and an "as if" quality. His mother died when he was nine years old, and an older sister took over her household duties while his father took over many of mother's other functions. His description of both parents was vague and contradictory. The patient conveyed a quality of unreality about his entire history. He had an adequate surface social adaptation, but there was something artificial in his appearance. He was one of those patients whose "perfect free association" effectively mimics an authentic analytic process. There was something mechanical about him, but I found it extremely difficult to link this impression to any concrete manifestations in the transference. He showed a similar lack of involvement with his girlfriend, toward whom, in spite of ample provocation, he showed absolutely no signs of jealousy.

By the third year of his analysis, although I was able to maintain interest in him, I felt that I was being seduced into a strange inactivity, that I was watching a theatrical display that had the quality of a film and no depth. The patient seemed unable to acknowledge me as a person different from himself yet available to him or to acknowledge his own presence in the room beyond that of recorder of external reality. I finally decided to focus on the nature and symptoms of his consistent unavailability to me and my unavailability to him as conveyed in his attitude in the sessions. I used the technique I have described elsewhere (1984) of imagining how a "normal" patient might behave in a particular session in order to sharpen my focus on the concrete manifestations of the artificiality in this man's relationship with me.

The effect of my focus on this "absence" in the transference was striking: Mr. E began to experience anxiety in the sessions. Over a period of several weeks, his anxiety increased and his associations changed significantly. He developed an intense fear of me, seeing me as someone totally unreal. In his experience, I presented a façade of a friendly psychoanalyst that covered an underlying frightening empty space. He was alone in the middle of a devastating experience of himself as damaged, disintegrating. It was as if only dead objects surrounded him.

In a few weeks this man changed from an almost inanimate robot to an abandoned, terrified child. An intense primitive object relation was activated in the transference and, as part of my countertransference reaction, a concordant identification (Racker 1957) with that self representation. Following this development an intensely ambivalent relationship to a powerful father emerged in the transference, with projection onto me of the image of a sadistic, controlling, savage father who would be disgusted by the patient's sexual fantasies and wishes. In short, elements that had previously been presented in a flat mosaic now acquired depth in the transference. Mr. E dramatically illustrates the predominance, in the communication of the transference, of the third channel represented by the constant yet latent space of the analytic encounter.

TRANSFERENCE, UNCONSCIOUS PRESENT, AND UNCONSCIOUS PAST

I have stressed that it is crucial to uncover the unconscious meanings of the transference in the here-and-now and to make the expression of this object relation in the transference fully conscious before attempting reconstructions of the past. In the course of this process, the previously unacknowledged, denied, repressed, projected, or dissociated object relation may now be fully acknowledged and become ego-dystonic. Only then do we consider questions about the genetic determinants of the currently activated unconscious intrapsychic conflict and how to interpret them to the patient (Sandler and Sandler 1987).

Our first case, Mrs. C, provided dynamic information that would seem quite naturally to reflect a masochistic transformation of a positive oedipal relationship. As is characteristic of neurotic patients, the links between the consciously known history from the past and the unconscious activation of repressed object relations in the here-and-now were apparently direct. I nevertheless avoided any reference to the relationship with her father until Mrs. C herself, wondering about her needs to first transform a good relationship with a man into a bad one in order to sexualize it, started to associate about her adolescent interactions with father.

With Mr. D, the mental health professional, I could not link a very chaotic and complex acting out in the transference directly with any known aspects of the patient's history: the information he had conveyed about his past was itself so contradictory and chaotic that it would have been difficult to accept any of it at face value. It took a long time to clarify the unconscious meanings in the here-and-now; only when that had been accomplished could I begin to raise the question of what should be explored in terms of genetic and developmental antecedents.

The dynamics of Mr. D's desperate search for dependency upon a dangerously and cruelly controlling object might lead theoreticians of different persuasions to different conclusions. A Mahlerian might conclude that it related to the rapprochement subphase of separation-individuation; a Kleinian might relate it to an envied good (and/or) bad breast; a traditional ego psychologist might think in terms of the guilt-determined anal regression from a positive oedipal conflict. But because I had no information as to what developmental stage this conflict had originated in or regressed to, I avoided speculating about it before the unconscious here-and-now developments had become completely conscious and ego-dystonic.

Mr. E really highlights the danger of making premature genetic reconstructions. Here, even at the time of a breakthrough from a long analytic stalemate, I refrained from linking the activated primitive object relation with any aspect of the past before further evidence emerged in the transference and in the patient's free associations.

In summary, then, I first attempt to carry out atemporal constructions of the unconscious meanings in the here-and-now and only later, when the conditions warrant it, cautiously try to transform these constructions into reconstructions of the unconscious past. Similarly, I try to avoid the genetic fallacy of equating the most primitive material with the earliest, as well as any mechanical linking of certain types of psychopathology with fixed stages of development.

These three cases also illustrate another aspect of my technique: namely, the importance of carefully exploring developments both in the patient's experiences outside the analytic hours and in the analytic relationship itself. I spent considerable time with Mrs. C exploring her relationship with colleagues and superiors at work before attempting to link that material to the relationship with me—in spite of my very early observation of her "nice little girl" attitude in the analytic hours.

My first efforts with Mr. D were focused on clarification of his chaotic relationship with his girlfriend. Only when, in the course of the failure of all my efforts to help him gain further understanding, it became obvious that the transference issues had acquired highest interpretive priority did I focus consistently on his relationship with me. I had to wait a long time before I could link the relationships with his girlfriend and with me.

In the third case, of course, a long history of failed efforts to explore both his extra-analytic and his analytic relationships led to the diagnosis of what I have referred to as obliteration of the analytic space. In metapsychological terms, economic criteria (that is, the search for areas of dominant affective activation, whether conscious or unconscious) should dictate whether the intervention focuses predominantly on an interaction with the patient in the hour or on the patient's external reality (Kernberg 1984).

It must be apparent by now that though I strongly emphasize the analysis of the unconscious meanings of the transference in the here-and-now I do not neglect the importance of the analysis of genetic antecedents, the there-and-then. In my emphasis on the here-and-now I am in agreement with Gill's proposals. I believe, however, that overextending the concept of the transference as "an amalgam of past and present" (Gill 1982, p. 177) blurs the differentiation of what is inappropriate in the here-and-now and needs to be explained by its origin elsewhere.

I think the actual aspects of the analyst's behavior that trigger and/or serve to rationalize the patient's transference should not be included as part of the transference itself. For the analyst to phobically avoid acknowledging the reality of an aspect of his behavior that has been noticed by the patient and that sets off a certain reaction in the patient is a technical error; even further, the analyst's failure to be aware of what in his own behavior may have unconsciously triggered aspects of the transference is also a technical error. I think it is a distortion of the classical concept of transference to assume that what the analyst is really contributing to the interaction with a patient should be ignored or denied; to do so implies that the analyst is perfectly adjusted and 100 percent normal. As I pointed out in earlier work:

> Patients rapidly become expert in detecting the analyst's personality characteristics, and transference reactions often first emerge in this context. But to conclude that all transference reactions are at bottom, at least in part, unconscious or conscious reactions to the reality of the analyst is to misunderstand the nature of the transference. The transference is the inappropriate aspect of the patient's reaction to the analyst. The analysis of the transference may begin by the analyst's "leaving open" the reality of the patient's observations and exploring why particular observations are important at any particular time.

If the analyst is aware of realistic features of his personality and is able to accept them without narcissistic defensiveness or denial, his emotional attitude will permit him to convey to the patient: "So, if you are responding to something in me, how do we understand the intensity of your reaction?" But the analyst's character pathology may be such that the patient's transference reaction to him results in the erosion of technical neutrality. When the analyst is incapable of discriminating between the patient's realistic and unrealistic perceptions of him, countertransference is operating. (Kernberg 1984, p. 266)

What is enacted in the transference is never a simple repetition of the patient's actual past experiences. I agree with Melanie Klein's (1952b) proposal that the transference derives from a combination of real and fantasied experiences of the past and defenses against both. This is another way of saying that the relation between psychic reality and objective reality always remains ambiguous: the more severe the patient's psychopathology and the more distorted his intrapsychic structural organization, the more indirect is the relationship of current structure, genetic reconstruction, and the developmental origins. But to conclude that reconstruction of the past is impossible because it is difficult and to use the difficulty of connecting past with present to question the possibility of uncovering the past are really evasions and are unwarranted.

COUNTERTRANSFERENCE, EMPATHY, MEMORY, AND DESIRE

My views of countertransference have been spelled out in earlier work (1975, 1984). Here I wish to stress the advantage of a global or broad concept of countertransference that includes, in addition to the analyst's unconscious reactions to the patient or to the transference (in other words, the analyst's transference), the analyst's realistic reactions to the reality of the patient's life, to his own life as it may become affected by the patient, and to the transference. For practical purposes, all these components except the last should remain rather subdued under ordinary psychoanalytic circumstances.

Obviously, if the analyst has retained serious nonanalyzed character pathology or if there is an unfortunate mutual "resonance" between the patient's and the analyst's character pathology, the analyst's transferences to the patient may be accentuated. The greater the patient's psychopathology and the more regressive the transference, the more intense the therapist's realistic emotional responses to the patient. It is this area, the realistic responses to the patient and their link with the analyst's deeper transference dispositions, that presents both potential dangers for countertransference acting out and potential assets in the form of clinical material to be explored by the analyst and integrated in his understanding of the transference.

In chapter 6, I described Racker's (1957) concepts of concordant and complementary identifications in the countertransference. In my view, complementary identification in the countertransference is of particular importance in the analysis of patients with severe character pathology and regressive transference developments. By means of unconscious defensive operations, particularly projective identification, patients are able, through subtle behavioral communications, to induce emotional attitudes in the analyst that reflect aspects of the patients' own dissociated self or object representations.

The psychoanalyst's introspective analysis of his complementary countertransference reaction permits him to diagnose projected aspects of the patient's activated internalized object relations, particularly those communicated nonverbally and by changes in the quality of the analytic space—that habitual, silent relationship between patient and analyst. Under optimal circumstances, the analyst's understanding of his own affective pressure deriving from the patient's unconscious communications in the transference may lead to a fuller understanding of the object relation activated in the transference.

My attitude regarding the activation in the analyst of intense emotional dispositions toward the patient, particularly at times of transference regression, is to tolerate my own feelings and fantasies about the patient, and attempt to use them to better understand what is going on in the transference. I remain alert to the need to protect the patient from any temptation I might have to act on these feelings or to communicate them to him. Not communicating countertransference reactions to the patient allows the analyst freedom to work with them and use them in his interpretations.

A related issue is to determine the nature of what is projected onto the analyst and activated in his countertransference. Patients may project a self representation while enacting the object representation of an object relation activated in the transference; or, vice versa, they may project an object representation while enacting the corresponding self representation. These projections tend to be relatively stable in patients with neurotic personality organization, but they are unstable and rapidly alternating in patients with severe character pathology and borderline personality organization.

For example, Mrs. C unconsciously tried to ingratiate herself with me as an object representation of her father in order to protect herself against her impulses to defy me (as father) and to seduce me into an aggressive— and sexualized—counterattack. Several relatively stable self representations under the impact of different affective states were activated in the patient, as well as a relatively stable projection onto me of object representations unconsciously representing father under different affective states. In other words, we did not "exchange personalities."

But Mr. D showed a rapid and almost chaotic alternation of self and object representations in his identifications and in his projections onto me, reflecting different affective states as well. For instance, at one point, he projected onto me a withholding, indifferent, and rejecting parental image, perceiving me as dominant, self-centered, unable to tolerate any view different from my own, and ready to angrily dismiss him (my child), who dared to think differently. Only minutes before or after such an experience, Mr. D would identify himself with the image of such a parental figure and dismiss me (his child), declaring that he had just decided to stop his analysis because he could not tolerate such a totally misguided and obstinate analyst. His attitude implied that such a sudden termination of his relationship with me would come most naturally and without any risk of his missing me. In other words, activated in the transference between us was a rapid exchange of the roles of the sadistic, neglecting parent and the neglected, mistreated child.

I think it is of crucial importance that the analyst tolerate the rapidly alternating, at times completely contradictory, emotional experiences that signal the activation of complementary self and object representations of a primitive internalized object relation. The analyst's capacity to tolerate such rapid changes in his emotional responses to the patient without denial or acting out includes several preconditions.

First, the analyst must maintain strict boundaries of space and time in the analytic situation, privacy outside the treatment hours, and a sense of his own physical security during the sessions.

Second, the analyst must be able to tolerate, as part of his empathic response to the patient, the activation of primitively aggressive, sexual, and dependent affect states in himself. The analyst must, for example, accept his own aggression in the countertransference (Winnicott 1949), such as the gratifying experience of sadistic control; this experience may be much more of a problem for the analyst than tolerating, for example, sexual arousal.

Third, the analyst must maintain sufficient confidence in his creativity as part of his analytic work that he may tolerate the patient's need to destroy his efforts without a reactive counterattack, devaluation of the patient, or withdrawal from him. Only if the analyst can feel comfortable with his own aggression will he be able to interpret aggression in the patient without fearing that this is an attack on the patient or submission to the patient's accusation that he is being attacked (a manifestation of the patient's intolerance of his own aggression).

The impression I have gained from studying the clinical material presented by self psychologists is that they implicitly or explicitly accept the
view that the analyst's interpretation of aggression in the patient corresponds to an attack on the patient, as if all aggression were "bad." Such a
view of aggression obviously cannot but reinforce the patient's own conviction that aggression *is* bad and that he must defend himself against
this "accusation" by whatever means at his disposal.

As I have stressed in earlier work (1975), empathy must therefore include not only concordant identification with the patient's ego-syntonic,
central subjective experience but also complementary identification
with the dissociated, repressed, or projected aspects of the patient's self
concept or object representations.

Bion, in a paper called "Notes on Memory and Desire" (1967), stressed
the importance of facing the patient's material in each session without
preconceived notions about the patient's dynamics ("memory") and
without any particular wishes regarding the patient's material, functioning, and experience, and without any wishes of his own that are not
related to the patient ("desire"). Insofar as Bion's contribution marks an
indirect criticism of the formulations traditionally prevalent in the Kleinian school and a plea for openness to new material with a minimum of
analytic preconceptions, his point is well taken. I think, however, that
Bion neglects the importance of the analyst's long-range experience with
the patient's material, the understanding of an analytic process that develops over a period of weeks and months, an understanding that may
become a frame of reference the analyst can use without becoming en-
slaved by it.

My point is that the analyst needs to maintain a sense of the continuity of
the analytic process and, particularly, a view of the patient, his behavior,
and his reality that transcends the subjective view of the patient at any
particular moment in any particular hour, as well as the patient's own
"myths" or preconceived organization of his past. Such a frame of reference ("memory") is the counterpart to the analyst's tolerating periods of
not understanding in the expectation that new knowledge will emerge
eventually. Similarly, regarding the analyst's "desire," his tolerance of
impulses, wishes, and fears about the patient that evolve throughout time
may provide the analyst with important information that may enter his
awareness in the sessions, again, without necessarily enslaving him.

Although much of what I have said may apply to psychoanalytic psychotherapy with nonanalyzable borderline and narcissistic patients, my
intention has been to spell out my basic approach to the transference in
the context of standard psychoanalysis with a broad spectrum of pa-

tients. It has been my experience that when I apply this approach to patients with neurotic personality organization (see chap. 11), it differs little from the traditional ego psychology approach or from other object relations approaches. In contrast, the differences between my approach and that of self psychology are obviously profound and global. With regressed patients, however, important differences between my approach and traditional ego psychology, the British object relations schools, and the object relations techniques of interpersonal psychoanalysts in the United States seem to emerge.

Chapter **8** AN EGO PSYCHOLOGY—
OBJECT RELATIONS THEORY
OF STRUCTURAL CHANGE

One of our assumptions is that psychoanalytic treatment results in structural change. Although the precise definition of structural change has not achieved consensus, it is generally agreed that the symptomatic and character changes achieved have depth and stability and are based upon a significant restructuring of the patient's personality. Such change is assumed to transcend changes resulting from behavioral manipulation, "transference cures," suggestion and placebo effects, and other techniques used in psychotherapy.

Structural change is traditionally defined as a significant modification of the unconscious intrapsychic conflicts underlying symptom formation. Change in the underlying unconscious psychic structures is usually reflected by significant shifts in the equilibrium of ego, superego, and id, with a significant expansion of the system ego and a corresponding reduction of the pressures of the unconscious superego and id. Another way of formulating this concept is to say that a significant shift occurs in impulse/defense configurations, with a reduction of the defenses that restrict the ego, a shift from repression to sublimation, and the incorporation of previously repressed drive derivatives into ego-syntonic behavior. The concept of structural change refers, therefore, not only to the stability or endurance of behavioral change but also to a significant shift in the unconscious dynamics linked to such change. I see this concept as raising important theoretical, clinical, and research problems.

The traditional definition of structural change, just given, implies that a well-differentiated tripartite structure is characteristic of mental functioning. My own understanding differs from this assumption in that, on the basis of findings regarding the psychopathology of borderline conditions (Kernberg 1976, 1984), I believe that impulses and defenses must be explored in terms of patterns of internalized object relations—the building blocks of the tripartite structure. The dissociation or integration of these building blocks is reflected in the patient's character, in his interpersonal relations, and in transference developments.

According to my understanding of the psychopathology and treatment of severe character disorders, changes in the internal organization of self representations and object representations should be incorporated in the psychoanalytic concept of structural change. In addition, the possibility that structural change may be induced by the psychoanalytic psychotherapy of borderline personality organization—and not only by psychoanalysis—needs to be explored within a theoretical frame that does justice to a broad spectrum of psychopathology. Also, if one characteristic of severe character pathology is the expression of primitive impulses that have been dissociated rather than repressed, ego expansion in the course of therapeutic improvement of borderline patients may be characterized by modification through integrating (and partially suppressing) such impulses rather than by lifting them from repression. These changes may in fact emerge in intimate relations with a few significant others as well as in the transference. What we see is an integration of the patient's self-concept and an increase in his capacity for both realistic understanding and emotional investment of these others.

Another problem regarding the psychoanalytic theory of structural change is the confusion between change reflecting a reorganization of intrapsychic structures (whether we are referring to ego, superego, and id or to internalized object relations) and change reflected in actual behavior patterns. Rapaport's (1960) definition of psychic structures as processes with a slow rate of change seems to have led to a concept of structural change that includes manifestations of modification of behavior patterns. Wallerstein (1986), in agreement with Schwartz (1981), points to the ambiguity around the issue of what constitutes true structural change as distinct from "only" adaptive or behavioral change.

On the strength of empirical evidence accumulated over many years (Kernberg et al. 1972; Wallerstein 1986), I believe that enduring change in a vast area of psychic functioning may be obtained by psychoanalytic psychotherapy and even by treatments that traditional psychoanalytic theorists would see as "supportive" or "ego strengthening" as well as by psychoanalysis. Enduring behavioral changes may in turn profoundly affect the individual's conflictual equilibrium and therefore the relations within the tripartite structure and the world of internalized object relations in general. In earlier work (Kernberg 1975, 1984), I spelled out the specific indications and technical characteristics of a particular type of psychoanalytic psychotherapy aimed at the treatment of borderline personality organization, an application of psychoanalytic theory to a patient population that usually does not respond well to standard psychoanalysis. In addition, I believe that there has been an unwarranted implicit devaluation within the field of psychoanalytic psychotherapy of the profound changes that may be obtained by the provision of an ongoing, specific therapeutic environment, such as the skillful psychotherapeutic management of some chronic schizophrenic patients.

If lasting change that profoundly affects an individual's relations with himself, with others, with work and life in general, can be obtained in so many ways, is there any *specific* mechanism of stable change derived from psychoanalysis and psychoanalytic psychotherapy?

One might argue that what matters to the patient in terms of outcome is symptom relief and character change, so that if research shows that psychoanalytic treatment produces such changes, questions concerning the concept of structural change can be avoided. After all, the evaluation of the effectiveness of psychoanalytic technique in producing patient improvement may be carried out regardless of psychoanalytic assumptions about what produces it. To thus evade the problem is, however, unsatisfactory.

Insofar as the basic instrument of psychoanalytic technique—interpretation—focuses precisely on the dynamic relation between impulse and defense—and, I would add, on the activation of unconscious conflicting internalized object relations represented in such impulse-defense constellations—the concept and testing of changes in conflictual equilibrium is central to psychoanalytic technique as well as to its theory of outcome. Then, too, testing the effectiveness of interpretations involves evaluating the expansion of the patient's insight—that is, his affective and cognitive awareness of his conflict, his concern over it, and his utilization of that awareness and concern for active work on the conflict.

Furthermore, the investigation of the extent to which the patient's improvement is a product of the therapist's conceptual "indoctrination" as opposed to the emergence of the patient's new knowledge about himself through introspection is crucial to the evaluation of psychoanalytic technique as against suggestive or supportive approaches. In short, the concept we hold of structural change will influence the choice of treatment modality and technique. And our concept of structural change depends on our concept of psychic structure.

In borderline personality organization, the principal analytic task consists in bringing together, by means of integrating interpretations, the mutually dissociated or split-off part-object relations that reflect the unconscious intrapsychic conflicts as they are activated in the transference, clarifying, in the process, their corresponding self and object representations and dominant affects.

As I hope the preceding chapters have made clear, I see the principal analytic task with neurotic patients as bringing repressed, unconscious transference meanings in the here-and-now into full consciousness, using the patient's free associations, with interpretation as the essential therapeutic tool. I expect the patient's free associations to the uncovered unconscious transference meanings in the here-and-now to lead us into the unconscious past.

Within this theoretical framework, structural change resulting from psychoanalytic treatment is reflected in the development of significant shifts in predominant transference patterns and definite and enduring changes in the therapeutic relationship as these shifting transference patterns are resolved. We find an expansion of the patient's awareness of the nature of these transference developments, their unconscious past origins, and their effects on the patient's experiences and behavior outside the sessions as well as in the treatment situation itself. Clinically, therefore, the general concept of change is reflected not in an assessment of the patient's defensive operations or the adequacy or appropriateness of his impulse expression (such as the integration of aggressive and sexual drives) but primarily in the shifts in the nature of the object relations activated in the transference. Two clinical examples will illustrate my formulation of structural intrapsychic change.

CLINICAL ILLUSTRATIONS

Ms F, in her late twenties, entered psychoanalytic psychotherapy, three sessions per week, because of severe self-mutilating behavior, chronic manipulation of others, and sporadic multiple drug abuse over the previous twelve years. Her practice of burning herself extensively with cigarettes and her suicidal attempts were such that hospitalization was seen as indispensable. The treatment was based upon the diagnostic conclusion that Ms F presented a borderline personality organization with narcissistic, infantile, and antisocial features.

Over a period of four years, the following behavior patterns were frequently repeated. Ms F would engage in self-mutilating behavior, including suicide attempts, whenever her lying and manipulative efforts to
control others failed. The lying and manipulation of others usually followed failure to control them by provocation and making them feel
guilty. Her provocative behavior emerged when her envy and resentment
of others became intolerable. She was particularly envious of other people's capacity to maintain autonomy and to have meaningful and satisfactory relationships, which she felt herself unable to have. These sequences
were played out repeatedly in the patient's relationships with her family
and friends as well as with the therapist.

Exploration of Ms F's conflicts between intense aggression and un-
fulfilled longings for dependency gradually resulted in a shift in her communicative style from direct expression in action to verbalization of her
underlying pain, rage, and despair. After several months of hospital treatment it was possible to put her on an outpatient basis. But although her
self-destructive impulses became less life-threatening (the cigarette
burning became more superficial and the suicide attempts less frequent
and less severe), her tendency to lie and manipulate others persisted
unabated; they were also expressed in revengeful and gleeful rejection of
all understanding from the therapist. Later, when Ms F became able to
verbalize her wishes to discard everything coming from the therapist, her
lying and other distortions of information about her life became less
marked in the sessions. Simultaneously, she displayed a certain capacity
to carry out studies and work, with less dependence on her family.

Her cycles of behavior, which originally consumed several weeks or
months, gradually accelerated, so that they could be diagnosed and discussed fully in less and less time, sometimes within four to five sessions.
Over the third and fourth years of treatment, further condensation and
acceleration of these cycles occurred. At the same time, new contents
began to emerge in the sessions, so subtly at first that the therapist was
able to recognize their appearance only after retrospective analysis of the
material covering several months of treatment. Ms F began to express
primitive aggressive wishes of an almost savage kind: she dreamed, for
example, that she was gassing elderly patients in a nursing home in
collusion with the director of the institution and that, though these
patients were being killed, she was having friendly and animated conver-
sations with their relatives at another location, gleefully thinking about
the mass murder taking place.

Simultaneously, Ms F started to express concern about whether the
therapist would still be able to accept her, given these monstrous dreams

and fantasies. Former friends whom she had lost over the years and toward whom she had felt completely indifferent reemerged in her memory, and she had reawakened feelings for them. For the first time, she experienced sorrow over the destruction of past relationships, longings for closeness, and moments of intense dread at her own hostility toward people.

In one session, Ms F began to talk at length about a woman friend who had been very understanding and encouraging and whom she had seriously neglected. Now she had decided to write to her friend, acknowledge her coldness, and ask for forgiveness. The psychotherapist was startled by this development. Because of Ms F's exploitative patterns and her long-standing callousness toward others, he was suspicious at first and relaxed his suspicions only after the end of the session. He decided to take up this issue at the first opportunity and did so the following week, commenting that only retrospectively had he realized how deeply she had changed in her attitude toward her former friend. Ms F then said thoughtfully that she had also wondered whether he was so conditioned by her habitual way of reacting to people that he had lost all hope in her. She also warned the therapist that her change might be "true only for this moment," thus expressing both her awareness of change in herself and her anxiety over the frailty of this change.

It was as if the patient had discovered a new split between a basic humanity that had been lying dormant in her and a sadistic, tyrannical aspect of her personality that had dominated most of her life. Now, in the sixth year of treatment, her relationships with people changed in parallel to the development of concern and loving feelings for the therapist. The patient's dishonesty in the transference disappeared, and the self-destructive tendencies faded away as she recognized that she had been forced to destroy any potential for good relationships with others, including her own survival, by that sadistic internal enemy.

The second case is Mr. G, a businessman in his early thirties, an obsessive-compulsive personality with a mixed neurosis including symptoms of depression, anxiety, and suppressed homosexuality. Mr. G entered psychoanalytic treatment because of long-standing dissatisfaction with his daily life and work, problems in his relationships with his wife and two small children, and chronic feelings of depression. His family, friends, and colleagues all saw him as cold and aloof, and he knew that, in spite of his efforts to be more outgoing, he was inhibited, awkward, rigid, and perfectionistic. Mr. G's masturbation was accompanied by homosexual fantasies, and the manifest content of his dreams was also often homosexual. But he had never had any actual homosexual experience and was terrified at the thought that he might be homosexual. It gradually emerged that his wishes to be helped to overcome his homosexual conflicts and to improve his sexual functioning with his wife were his true motives for entering treatment. Holding an administrative position in a large business, Mr. G was afraid of asserting himself with his subordinates and also very afraid of criticism from his superiors.

Mr. G was the only child of rigid, pious, hardworking parents, both of whom had expected him to do small chores and to keep his things in order, as they did, with a place for everything and everything in its place. Mother was clearly the dominant figure in the household. At her insistence he had undertaken the study of the violin when he was still very young. He had hated practicing and still had some ambivalence about music. But he enjoyed his capacity to express himself musically, and although he had been playing less and less, he was now a fairly accomplished musician. I noticed that he became more animated when he talked about his music.

He was a good student but felt he was not liked by his classmates and had only a few friends with whom he felt comfortable. He began dating occasionally during high school in connection with musical events. He started to date the woman he married during his last year of college. Although his uncertainty about his sexual response to her and corresponding feelings of guilt troubled him from the beginning, her willingness to stick with him in spite of his aloofness finally persuaded him to marry her. Homosexual masturbation fantasies started in early adolescence, and he was very concerned about maintaining absolute secrecy regarding these fantasies. He had hoped that his marriage would help him overcome his sexual interest in men, but this had not happened.

When the treatment started, Mr. G's behavior in the sessions reflected a surface submission to, and underlying rebellion against, powerful authority figures, eventually traced to his father. He began almost every session with a monotonous description of the various tasks he was performing in his woodworking workshop, recitals that were slowly revealed to be an unconscious mockery of free association. The interpretation of the unconscious meanings of this pattern gradually resolved it and shifted the transference into the development of strong dependent wishes toward me as father image.

The strong homosexual wishes with which he had struggled since adolescence also became apparent in the transference, along with an intensification of masturbation fantasies of homosexual relations with kind, protective men. The interpretation of his fear of homosexual wishes toward me, which made it possible for him to talk more freely about these issues, also triggered the development of intense fears of me as a sadistic parental image that condensed both father's angry, imposing attitudes and mother's rigid, demanding perfectionism.

Repeated cycles of dependent longing for an all-giving and protective motherly father and fear of this threatening father-mother image changed again after his submissive sexual fantasies were interpreted as a defense against underlying rage against this sadistic father-mother image.

Now the relationship in the transference became predominantly maternal: he experienced me as cold and demanding, with characteristics that were related to his mother's demands in regard to cleanliness and work and her suspiciousness and prohibition of his sexual impulses. It became apparent that a stalemate that had developed over several months during the second year of treatment reflected masochistic traits that also were evident in Mr. G's work situation and social life. These masochistic tendencies were a defense against deep-seated oral aggression toward mother, condensed, at a still deeper level, with oedipal rivalry toward father.

In a renewed cycle of dread of his sexual impulses, it emerged that his homosexual feelings included both heterosexual impulses that were unacceptable to his mother and displaced sexual feelings from her toward his father that, in turn, had to be rejected because of the fantasied implication that to become a homosexual meant to be castrated. In his relationship with me, he now shifted from the passive resistance that had been his usual weapon over the years in relation to his superiors at work, to outspoken criticism and barely controlled outbursts of anger.

Three consecutive sessions after two and a half years of treatment give evidence of a crucial change that took place at that point in his psychoanalysis.

In the first of these sessions, the patient came in looking aloof and self-absorbed. After lying down on the couch, he was silent for a short while and then said, "Nothing comes to my mind." He saw himself in his workshop at home, fixing the divisions of a bookshelf he was working on, and he desultorily described technical aspects of this project. He repeated several times that this was not getting anywhere, that this was useless talk, and, after some further silence, that I must be fed up with him, and he couldn't blame me for that. His wife was taking the children out to dinner at a local fast-food restaurant. She had come down to the basement to ask whether he wanted to join them, and he said that he wanted to finish his work. After she took the children out, he was relieved to be alone, although he felt guilty because he wasn't spending sufficient time with them. He also felt relieved because he did not feel like talking with anyone anyhow. Mr. G then resumed talking about his workshop, his tools, again repeating that he was not getting anywhere and that the analysis was a useless exercise. This treatment was not getting him any-where.

I said that he was afraid I might get fed up with him because he was not giving me any useful material, just as his wife and children might get fed up with him because he was not showing any interest in them. I went on to say that his feeling that he was not giving anything to me was painful to him, and he thought the treatment was worthless because this allevi-ated his guilt feelings toward me. I also wondered whether his feeling that it was a relief not to go out with his children and his wife alleviated his guilt feelings toward them.

After a brief silence, Mr. G said that he knew all this, but, so what! A longer silence. Then, "You are not helping me in any way." And another silence. After two or three minutes, he said that I was punishing him with my silence.

He remained silent again for a few minutes and then said that he had masturbated again before the mirror. He had planned to tie himself up and masturbate while watching himself tied up, but he had not found this as satisfactory as it used to be. With some hesitation, he went on to tell me that he had fantasied, while masturbating, that he was the leader of a group of gangsters who broke into a nightclub, smashing lamps and furni-ture and glasses and dishes until the entire dance floor was covered with glass splinters. His gang then forced at gunpoint all the couples on the dance floor to strip naked and dance over the broken glass, and he was able to ejaculate with great pleasure.

Mr. G lapsed into another silence. He looked considerably upset, and I asked him what he was thinking. He said he felt very ashamed of what he had just told me. He thought that my silence indicated that I was dis-gusted with him; he was himself disgusted with this fantasy. I said that he was attributing to me his own self-criticism and that in the harshness of his self-condemnation I sensed the attitude of his mother, who had not only forbidden him to masturbate when he was a child but had constantly reminded him of her loathing of everything sexual. Mr. G repeated that he was no longer satisfied with tying himself up as a prerequisite for enjoying watching himself masturbating before a mirror and that he had experienced a sense of freedom and of intense excitement with his fan-tasy of power, of being in control of all the naked couples on the nightclub dance floor.

I said that this fantasy seemed different from his usual masturbation fantasy that a powerful man with strong muscles was holding him in his arms while he stroked the man's penis and his own penis at the same time. Now, I went on, he seemed to be excited by a sense of power residing in himself and with the fantasy of powerfully intruding into sexual contacts between couples of men and women. Mr. G immediately added that he had also had the fantasy that, with all these couples having to dance barefoot on a floor covered with glass splinters, their pain would interfere with their sexual excitement, and none of the men would be able to maintain an erection. The men would feel ashamed of this failure and humiliation, and while dancing together, the couples would be ashamed to be in each other's arms. After a brief silence he added that he was not afraid now that I would be either critical or disgusted with him. He said he had often felt insecure and resentful when faced with an open display of sexual intimacy between a man and a woman. He then referred to a couple he and his wife knew; he had in earlier sessions mentioned how much he admired the man and found him sexually attractive. He now added that this friend's natural and secure attitude toward his wife often made him feel insecure, exposed, or inadequate in relating to his own wife. Another brief silence, and that was the end of the session.

The following day began with silence and Mr. G's activities at his workbench. His monotonous voice was in striking contrast to the intensity with which he had spoken at the end of the previous session. After a few minutes, I asked whether he might again feel afraid that I was critical of him because of his monotonous repetition of the standard theme that he considered typical of empty or wasted sessions. After a brief silence, Mr. G said he had his usual fantasy of being in the arms of a strong, masculine man. He said he now thought that I was sexually unattractive: small, bald, totally asexual. But, he added, in a way he was asexual too. But he felt he would respond sexually to a powerful, muscular man.

He returned to his workshop activities and then shifted to talk about problems at the office. He had the distinct sense that two of his subordinates were being very friendly with him in a way that he experienced as a mockery. To ensure that they showed respect he felt he had to keep his distance from them. Eventually he would get back at them and show them who was in charge.

I said that his monotonous descriptions of his woodworking were efforts to stay away from me. I reminded him of his sense of excitement and relief when he had shared his sexual fantasies with me toward the end of the last session. I suggested that he was afraid that an open relationship with me meant a potential sexual submission to me. Therefore he had to keep his distance and to assure himself that he would be attracted sexually only by a physically powerful man who looked totally unlike me. By fantasizing that he was protected by a warm and powerful man he was protecting himself from sexual seduction by me and from the danger of being under my control as a sadistic authority.

Mr. G remained silent, his tension visibly increasing. After a while I added that he might be experiencing me as keeping my distance from him because I suspected him of being defiant, in the same way that he had to keep his distance from his subordinates. And I also wondered whether he was again afraid that I might despise him for talking about his sexual fantasies.

Mr. G said that he felt ashamed after his last session, like a little boy talking about fantasies of being superman, the big gangster. He thought it was laughable; the painful truth was that he envied couples who could enjoy sex. After a short silence, he said that he hated his boss, a pompous, self-congratulatory fool. He described in some detail a meeting at work at which he, for once, stood up to his boss and proved him to be wrong.

Another silence was followed by a reversion to his workbench, his tools, and a mechanism for building a hidden compartment into the bookcase. He said how much he enjoyed his control over his little world in the basement. Even the children were now aware that they had to stay away from there. He was silent for a few minutes; then he said he had been withholding from me some associations he had after telling me about the masturbation fantasy of the nightclub. His threatening the dancing couples at gunpoint had reminded him of a dream he had had several weeks earlier, of being the commander of a Nazi concentration camp while I was one of the prisoners trying to escape, and he was ready to shoot me.

He also had had a dream the previous night of having sex with a big man who was holding him while he was stroking the man's big penis; as he looked up into the man's face it turned into the face of his boss. In his dream he felt very much afraid of being caught as a homosexual and expelled from work or of being forced to submit to his boss forever, now that his boss was in on the secret of his homosexuality.

I said he might have been afraid to tell me his association to his nightclub fantasy of that dream because it was a direct expression of his wish to control me at gunpoint and sadistically force me into submission. The fantasy was the reversal of the experience in the dream in which he was being blackmailed by his boss, who had uncovered his homosexuality. I said that it was as if he would either establish control over me at gunpoint or be threatened by my doing the same to him. He might feel very anxious, I added, because it was no longer clear whether a homosexual relationship with a powerful man would protect him against such violent interactions with male authority; to be sexually seduced meant to fall into the trap of a powerful authority.

Mr. G responded by saying that he suddenly had an intense headache and palpitations—a sense of pressure on his chest and difficulty in breathing. I told him to try to continue to tell me what was on his mind, and he remembered a movie he had seen in which a sadistic killer was torturing a detective he had caught while the detective was trying to free a woman the killer had imprisoned. The patient then had the fantasy of beating and kicking a powerless old man on the ground. He then grew silent and looked very tense.

I said that he was afraid of being destroyed if he dared to challenge a powerful male authority, and that he was identifying himself with the detective of the movie who in trying to free a woman was tortured by a sadistic killer. Both in the nightclub fantasy and in his memory of the movie he was trying to become a powerful man himself, disrupting other men's control over women, but he dared not experience any sexual wishes for a woman directly; he could only do so by proxy, in the form of the men dancing with women and the detective attempting to free the woman victim. He was afraid, I said, of his own fantasy of beating and kicking an old man, which represented the destruction of dangerous male authority.

Mr. G remembered incidents he had already recalled on previous occasions. He remembered how, before he was five years old, his father, enraged at him because he had been naughty, left him locked in a closed car, and he broke the car window with his toy shovel. He remembered that once his finger got caught as his father slammed the car door shut, and he had the fantasy that his father had done it on purpose to cut off his fingers. And he remembered his fear of fighting with boys in school because his mother had warned him that if he broke a finger he would not be able to play the violin.

Mr. G said he wanted to stop the session and asked whether he could leave early. He had not had time to tell me, he added, that he had initiated sex with his wife during the past weekend and had enjoyed having sex with her while having sadistic fantasies of disrupting other sexual couples. It was an intensely enjoyable experience, although of course his wife did not know the nature of his fantasies. He added that he was feeling very anxious, and that was the end of the session.

Mr. G looked strained as he came in the following day. He said he had felt very anxious after the last session and throughout the evening, although he did not know what he was afraid of.

He remained silent for a few minutes, looking very tense. He said he was thinking of his boss and described a staff meeting the previous afternoon directed by his boss. He was on edge when he arrived there and started to feel much worse during the meeting as his boss "hammered in" his views of the business. Mr. G went into great detail as he criticized the dictatorial ways in which his boss was imposing his views, acting with a heartiness that was totally artificial and convinced nobody. It was clear that underneath he was sadistically enjoying asserting his dominance over the assembled staff. His boss, Mr. G went on, was really a very disagreeable character, and Mr. G could sense weakness and uncertainty beneath his haughty and controlling manner at the meeting. Mr. G was certain that his boss was weak, insecure, nasty, and impulsive in his private life.

Mr. G had mentioned in an earlier session that he disliked his boss's wife but was curious about how she got along with her husband. Now he again described her in detail as a loud-mouth, vulgar, domineering woman who exploited her husband's prominent position to give herself importance. No wonder his boss was such a domineering and sadistic man in the office: at home he had to be meek and subservient to his wife, though deeply resentful of her. As Mr. G talked, his anger and disgust seemed to mount. He finally exclaimed that he did not know whether he was enraged at her or simply afraid of her. His own wife, Mr. G added thoughtfully, was so much nicer. But then again, he would never be able to stand up to a woman like his boss's wife. Perhaps his boss's ability to be married to such an obviously tyrannical wife required strength. Perhaps he underestimated his boss's strength.

I reminded him of the dream he had reported the day before, of having sex with a man with a big penis who turned out to be his boss. I reminded him that he had started to feel anxious when he expressed his fear that, having caught him in a homosexual act, his boss would use this to control him and blackmail him into submission. I added that it seemed to me he became even more anxious after my comments about his dream, particularly my suggestion that he was feeling anxious because he could no longer decide whether a homosexual relationship with a powerful man would protect him or, to the contrary, would throw him into an extremely dangerous position vis-à-vis a male authority.

Mr. G said that the memory of that dream disgusted him, the image of this huge penis being his boss's penis. He said he was afraid that he might not be able to control his anger with his boss, might get outraged with him and attack him in public, which would threaten his future at the firm. But he did not know whether he felt more enraged with his boss or disgusted with himself for having, even in dreams, sexual thoughts about him. He repeated how disgusted he now felt by the image of the penis that had been sexually attractive to him in the dream.

Mr. G suddenly looked shaken and upset. Gesturing as if he were suddenly remembering something, he said that he had thought that I had lined myself up with his boss in my interpretation of the dream. My putting myself into the same category as a man in authority frightened him. He had never felt so afraid of me. He actually had felt that I talked in an authoritarian voice, a voice he now associated with that of his boss, and after the end of the last session he had fleetingly thought that I might use my knowledge of his homosexuality against him. But he immediately reassured himself that I would never do that and that he could be totally certain of me. But then again, was I really so benign? And last night, on going to bed, he had felt very anxious, he could not fall asleep; he felt out of control and really dependent on me. Would I be able to help him get rid of this anxiety? Could he really trust me?

I finally broke the long silence that followed by asking what he was thinking about. He said he had been thinking that I had never seemed attractive to him as a man. Now, however, he saw me as if I were in some strange alliance with his boss, and although he was aware that this was absurd, he did not feel safe. He also felt that what I had said in the last session was taking away his security, his fantasy of lying in the arms of a strong man who would soothe him. That was the essential ingredient of his sexual excitement with strong men; if he could not rely on that, he was completely unprotected.

Mr. G repeated his fear that his boss was a potentially cruel man and that if he ever provoked him he would lose his job and have to leave town. It would be the end of his analysis and a disaster for his family. I would be completely impotent; I would not be able to protect him or do anything at all for him. His anxiety, which had seemed somewhat less in the last few minutes, now seemed to increase.

I said that he seemed to be oscillating between two equally frightening alternatives: either I was aligned with his boss, dangerous and powerful like him, and would sadistically exploit my knowledge of his homosexuality and harm him in some way, or else I was as weak and impotent as he experienced himself at this moment.

Mr. G then said that the previous night he had thought I was a nice man but very weak, and that the problem was the conflict on his job, his powerful boss, and I could not help him with that. But it was true that he had become anxious before that, when he experienced me as an ally of his boss. In fact, at one point, he had almost confused my manners with those of his boss: that was really frightening. And now he was afraid that I might misunderstand what he was saying as an attack on me because I was like his boss, and he really did not want to attack me at all.

After a short silence he said that his wife did not know anything about all this. It would be so good if he could trust her and tell her about his problems, but he did not dare tell her because it would be a terrible shock for her. What was most frightening was not to know what somebody else thought: he remembered his father's angry outbursts and the outbursts of his boss. If you knew what was coming, it was less frightening. He added that he often anxiously watched his boss's face with a feeling of disgust and fear. Perhaps his boss might feel insecure at moments when he, Mr. G, was watching him so intently. This was the end of the session.

These sessions initiated a series of sadistic fantasies of controlling and torturing me. Fantasies of intruding into my sexual relations with my wife evolved into more direct expression of primal-scene incidents. During the fourth year of his analysis, fears of triumphing over rivals at work were connected with the fear of his own sadistic impulses. Transference resistances, which had largely disappeared in the second part of the third year of his analysis, now reemerged. The patient again showed "passive resistance," refusing to free associate or to listen to interpretations.

The gradual working through of these resistances brought about the emergence of numerous memories and fantasies about his father's efforts to make him submit to work he hated, as well as strong conscious feelings of anger and open triumph because he had escaped from his father's control. His homosexual fantasies were now completely oriented toward control and efforts to subjugate other men. At the same time, his sexual life improved, and he could for the first time be more aggressive sexually with his wife without sadistic fantasies during intercourse. His insecurity with women because they represented the sexually desired mother and because of the fear of revengeful destruction by father became the final principal subject of the analysis. It brought about a major revision of the patient's attitude not only toward his sexual experiences with his wife but also toward women in general and toward morality. This change in turn led to a gradual acceptance of an internal sexual freedom.

During the last half year of analysis his homosexual fantasies disappeared almost completely, and his sexual interest and capacity to obtain gratification with his wife acquired normal characteristics. For the first time, he also began to function well in his work and to actually enjoy it. His long-standing projection onto his wife of his mother's prohibitive attitudes in regard to all manifestations of sexuality had disappeared.

DISCUSSION

I have selected two cases, a borderline patient and a neurotic one, to illustrate the different ways in which unconscious intrapsychic conflicts can be played out. In Ms F, there was a gradual development of a conflict between a sadistic, grandiose, primitive self and a fragmented, originally unavailable, normal, dependent self, in the context of almost total destruction of her capacity for object relations that were not exploitative and destructive. In Mr. G, the activation of intersystemic conflicts (the struggle between a restrictive, prohibitive superego and repressed sexual and oral-dependent drive derivatives) gradually emerged in the context of specific internalized object relations reactivated in the transference.

Both cases illustrate the gradual clarification, confrontation, and interpretation of dominant transference patterns, the value of these patterns for clarifying the internal structure of the illness, the development of change in the patterns, and the dependence of both symptomatic and behavioral changes in the patient's life on changes in these transference patterns. The clinical material also illustrates the time that might be needed for achieving the diagnosis of dominant transferences and their dynamic implications and, most important, how intrapsychic change may first be detected as part of the psychotherapeutic process in the patient's relationship to the analyst. In addition, these cases illustrate the importance of measuring significant pathology case by case rather than relying on standardized lists of symptoms; they also suggest the possibility of operationalizing for each individual case a few predominant patterns of interactions in the transference and their relation to the appearance of structural change, and the possibility of testing the development of insight at points of shift in these predominant transference patterns.

In my view, the structural change that is specific for psychoanalytic treatment emerges first in the transference, and its relation to insight can be evaluated by focusing on the relationship between introspection and behavioral change. Both cases illustrate the relationship between the repetition of past internalized object relations in the transference and the capacity for establishing new types of relationships with the analyst and others in the patient's external life. Patients with severe psychopathology suffer not simply from a lack of available good object relations but from unconscious, conflictual, pervasive past object relations, which they need to understand through their controlled activation of these in the transference, and which they may become able to abandon by acquiring cognitive and emotional understanding of them as they are reactivated in the transference.

These considerations also point to the illusory nature of "dynamic formulations" at the initial stage of psychoanalysis or long-term psychotherapy of patients with severe character problems. Such initial hypotheses usually relate current psychopathology to assumed unconscious intrapsychic conflicts, and those, in turn, to their assumed antecedents—pathogenic infantile conflicts with parental objects. The case material illustrates, however, the problem with such initial dynamic hypotheses; not only does it take time for significant transference patterns to develop fully, but with severe psychopathology, the current internal relations of dominant transference patterns must be clarified before the connections of each pattern to the past can be established in a meaningful way. Only at advanced stages of the treatment can the significant unconscious pathogenic object relations from the past be fully clarified. As I have suggested in the preceding chapters, the more severe and regressive the patient's psychopathology, the more indirect and complex are the connections among current personality structure, genetic history, and actual past developments.

The interpretation of patterns of behavior enacted in the transference should gradually lead to the patient's growing curiosity about the rigid, repetitive, obligatory aspects of his behavior and to his providing new understanding of the shifts in the transference patterns in the context of jointly examining with the analyst their interaction in the sessions. The patient's learning about himself emerges in the context of the systematic examination of transference paradigms, and at some point the new understanding should lead to a change in the obligatory nature of the repetition of a certain pattern, to an actual disruption of the rigidity of the pattern, and to the emergence of new, unexpected behavior followed by further exploration regarding the unconscious meaning of this new behavior and a shift away from the previously obligatory behavioral sequence. Insight and shifts in the transference are thus intimately linked, and the patient's transfer to his behavior outside the sessions of the knowledge acquired in this context would be an important additional confirmation that structural change is occurring.

But how does such behavioral change, first in the treatment hours and then in the patient's external life, differ from behaviorally induced change in supportive psychotherapy or even in behavior modification techniques? After all, new cognitive formulations shared by the therapist with a patient could emerge in many treatments other than in one psychoanalytically oriented. In my view, the specific aspect of the relationship between interpretation and structural change is the emergence of new information spontaneously provided by the patient in the context of exploring the transference, information that indicates new understanding of his current behavior as well as its links to his other experiences, both present and past. The patient will experience a change in his self-awareness and in his internal relations to others and will be surprised by the nature of what he is experiencing—unexpected by him and by his analyst. This new, unexpected information is illustrated by the first patient's dream in which she was gassing the inmates of a nursing home in collusion with the nursing home director, and by the second patient's masturbation fantasy of the gang disruption of a nightclub.

The unpredictability, the spontaneous emergence of new information, the expansion of understanding as a precondition for changes in the transference, and the extension of such change and understanding into other areas of the patient's behavior are what differentiate insights derived from interpretation from other, cognitively induced changes in the patient's understanding and from the patient's compliance with direct instructions from the therapist for behavioral change. The reconstruction of significant parts of a patient's past may be an important consequence of the patients spontaneously and unpredictably acquiring and developing new knowledge about himself through introspection. But early in the treatment, this would hold true mostly for patients with neurotic personality structure rather than for patients with severe character pathology.

Eventually, all significant insight should be expressed in the patient's concern for his current conflicts, in motivation for change, and in further self-exploration. In contrast, purely intellectual speculations, with the patient playing his own analyst (in narcissistic structures) or compliantly submitting to the psychoanalyst's theories, or a transference characterized by strong identification with certain conceptions of the therapist do not conform to the criteria I have described (that is, first an exploration of the meaning of a characteristic sequence of behaviors in the transference, a subsequent shift in the behavioral sequence, a development of new knowledge based upon that shift, an expansion of the behavioral change, and an understanding of and transfer to other areas of the patient's life). The enjoyment of primitive fantasies and primary-process associations or of diffuse, intense affects dissociated from any concern about himself on the patient's part also fail to conform to these criteria.

Wallerstein (personal communication), in discussing an earlier version of this chapter, stressed the importance of "disarticulating" the outcome criteria for achieved structural change from the process criteria of how the changes have been brought about. Only then will we be able to assess whether there are indeed specific changes brought about by psychoanalysis and psychoanalytic psychotherapy that differ quantitatively and/or qualitatively from the changes brought about by other procedures. What I have stressed are process criteria in the sense that they evaluate structural change by the predominant patterns of the transference. I believe that the changes seen in the therapeutic process should bring about structural change in outcome and suggest the following outcome criteria.

In patients with neurotic personality organization, structural change should become evident in a broadened self concept, the inclusion in the self experience of previously dissociated or repressed instinctual impulses, an increased tolerance for previously rejected emotional experiences in self and others, a broadened awareness of previously automatic character patterns, and a reduction of the rigidity of these patterns. In patients with borderline personality organization, structural change should become evident in the integration of the self concept and the concepts of significant others, a corresponding integration of previously dissociated or split-off affect states (so that affective experience and expression become enriched and modulated), increased capacity for empathy with self and others and for establishing discriminating relationships in depth with others.

Current opinion is divided on the question of whether the uncovering of intrapsychic conflict leads to reconstruction of the patient's unconscious past or to a structural reorganization of the unconscious perception of the past with which the patient came into treatment. The transformation of one myth about the patient's past into another one induced by the analyst versus the spontaneous organization and reorganization of information regarding the patient's past that emerge at crucial disruptions of rigid transference patterns in the context of interpretation and insight might be explored experimentally as part of research efforts linking process evaluation to outcome studies. The stability of change might be explored by comparing the stability of change induced by supportive means with that derived from spontaneous transformations in the transference.

Another implication of what I have said about structural change is that its evaluation ideally should be derived from individualized process evaluation and only secondarily from the evaluation of change in such relatively nonspecific "structural variables" as "ego functions," "object relations," and nonspecific aspects of ego strength (anxiety tolerance, impulse control, and so on). A major problem with ego functions and structures is their tendency to co-vary to such a degree that they tend to get collapsed into one big factor, "ego strength" (Kernberg et al. 1972); and ego strength, in turn, is intimately related to the severity of symptoms. It may well be that severity of symptoms and of character pathology influence ego functions to such an extent that symptomatic improvement and behavioral change may be nonspecifically reflected in improved ego functioning as well. This problem has haunted research in psychoanalytic psychotherapy; it points to the importance of linking outcome research to process research.

In contrast, focus on process, on significant changes in the transference, may permit more specific delineation of structural change and may answer such concrete questions as, is the patient experiencing a "transference cure" (that is, presenting symptom and behavior change as a consequence of transference gratification) or structural change? Whether structural change via psychoanalysis is more enduring than change effected otherwise could be tested in this context.

I think these considerations point to some important developments in psychotherapy research on structural change. I am referring here to the studies by Luborsky and Horowitz. Luborsky (1977) devised a method designated "the core-conflictual-relationship-theme method," which evaluates comparatively by means of content analysis a patient's interactions with significant people in earlier sessions and in later sessions of the treatment. He demonstrated that the patients who improved, in contrast to those who did not, showed evidence of some mastery of these themes. Although this is only an early, albeit exciting, approach to grappling with the concept of structural change in terms of change in predominant transference patterns, it acquires additional significance in view of Luborsky's observations that in each psychotherapeutic treatment only a few predominant relationships are activated that reflect the patient's core conflictual themes (CCRT), so that the evaluation of personality structure and personality change in terms of transference developments may be less difficult than might be anticipated.

Horowitz (1979), describing significant change (in brief psychotherapy) in terms of shifts in a patient's specific sequence of affective and cognitive states that imply activation of self and object representations and mutual roles and conflicts among them, has linked—for the first time, I think—a sophisticated contemporary object relations model with the experimental analysis of intrapsychic change. Although the application of that methodology to long-term-psychotherapy research may still present major difficulties, Horowitz's research, in addition to its methodological contributions, is conceptually and clinically an important step in the right direction.

I strongly believe in the importance of differentiating the specific type of change attempted and/or induced by psychoanalysis and psychoanalytic psychotherapy from lasting change brought about by other technical approaches. Wallerstein (1986) has convincingly pointed to the fact that not all the changes obtained in psychoanalytic treatment are related to insight and conflict resolution. Although structural change may occur in the context of these developments, other changes also occur as part of supportive elements that may have characterized the treatment and are certainly an aspect of a vast majority of expressive and supportive psychotherapies. Structural change, it would seem, is obtained in many ways, through many mechanisms. Structural change specific to psychoanalysis and psychotherapy needs to be evaluated by means of process research focused on the developments in the transference.

Chapter 9 TRANSFERENCE REGRESSION AND PSYCHOANALYTIC TECHNIQUE WITH INFANTILE PERSONALITIES

The category of patients described in this chapter is within the spectrum of borderline personality organization who may be treated with psychoanalysis but present particular technical problems for therapeutic success. Ernst Ticho (1966) once described undertaking to treat narcissistic personalities by psychoanalysis as "heroic." I am adding the infantile personality to this category. Until about twenty years ago, these patients were usually considered hysterical personalities. Easser and Lesser (1965), Zetzel (1968), and I (1975) saw them as regressive forms of the hysterical personality and referred to them as infantile, histrionic, hysteroid, or Zetzel type 3 and 4. I have dealt with the differential diagnosis of these personalities in chapter 4; here I shall only summarize their salient characteristics before examining some typical developments they present in the course of psychoanalytic treatment.

Patients with an infantile personality present the three characteristics dominant in all borderline patients: identity diffusion, primitive defense mechanisms, and good reality testing. Identity diffusion reduces their capacity for empathy with others and for realistic evaluation and prediction of their own and other people's behavior. In consequence, they present highly conflictual object relations, although they can engage in depth in the sense of lasting—though chaotic and clinging—relations with significant others. This capacity for deep involvement with others, even if highly neurotic in nature, differentiates them from other patients with borderline personality organization, such as the narcissistic, schizoid, and paranoid personalities.

Because these patients present a predominance of defensive operations centering around splitting, they evince fewer repressive mechanisms than are typical of the hysterical personality proper. Thus, the latter's sexual inhibition may be replaced by the persistence of polymorphous perverse infantile trends, even in patients who definitely do not present evidence of sexual perversion. Splitting operations underlie these patients' contradictory, discontinuous, chaotic interpersonal behavior.

Infantile personalities present the emotional lability and histrionic quality characteristic of hysterical patients, but in all their object relations rather than specifically linked to their sexual relationships. They also show the extroverted, exhibitionistic behavior of the hysterical personality, except that their behavior has a childlike, clinging, rather than erotic quality. Infantile patients convey the impression that erotic seductiveness is a means to gratify clinging and dependent rather than sexual needs.

From a psychodynamic viewpoint, infantile patients present the typical condensation of oedipal and preoedipal conflicts characteristic of borderline personality organization, but with an accentuation of later or advanced types of oedipal conflicts, which brings them much closer to the hysterical personality than is true of all other borderline patients.

One might indeed describe a continuum from the hysterical personality proper to the infantile personality proper, a point of view already implicit in Zetzel's (1968) classification of this syndrome into four types (see chap. 4). In light of my more recent experience, most of these patients can be treated with psychoanalysis; thus they constitute, together with the narcissistic personality, the important exceptions to the dictum that psychoanalysis is not appropriate for patients with borderline personality organization. In order for psychoanalysis to be indicated for an infantile personality, however, it is important that the patient present at least some motivation for treatment, some capacity for emotional introspection or insight, and for impulse control, anxiety tolerance, and sublimatory functioning (nonspecific aspects of ego strength). These requirements exclude from consideration for psychoanalysis the typical Zetzel type 4 patient, with nonspecific manifestations of ego weakness, apparently uncontrollable acting out, and limited capacity for realistic self-reflection.

Some of the treatment failures of the psychotherapy research project of the Menninger Foundation (Kernberg et al. 1972) included patients of this kind. I have wondered whether what has since been discovered about the psychoanalytic treatment of borderline cases might explain those failures. I have therefore given considerable thought and attention to more recent and more successful psychoanalytic treatment of patients who might be characterized as occupying the intermediate zone between the hysterical personality and the most regressed infantile patients. In what follows I present the salient aspects of two such cases to illustrate their technical management.

MS H

Ms H, in her early thirties, was a skilled professional in an industrial research laboratory. She had entered the hospital because of a deep and acute depression, which responded rapidly to antidepressive medication; subsequently she entered treatment because she was dissatisfied with her obesity and her relations with men. She abused drugs and had phobic fears of driving on highways and bridges. She was not unattractive but dressed in a way that exaggerated her (moderate) obesity. She explained that she could be interested only in men who were unavailable. She was nonetheless interested in people and had close friends.

After great hesitation, she confessed to what she considered her most serious symptom: she deliberately falsified the results of her laboratory work and then performed certain experiments that would demonstrate the error of the false findings she herself had presented earlier. Her actual contributions to her field were slowed down dramatically because she worked very hard, staying until late at night, to undo the effects of her own falsifications. Careful evaluation of her superego functioning in other areas of antisocial tendencies revealed only a brief period of shoplifting in early adolescence; she was otherwise scrupulously honest.

She provided contradictory, even chaotic, descriptions of her closest friends and relatives and of herself. She presented identity diffusion, a predominance of primitive defensive operations, chaos in intimate sexual relations, and a multiplicity of neurotic symptoms—a typical borderline personality organization. I diagnosed her as an infantile personality with masochistic features, but her capacity for object relations in depth and the absence of antisocial features other than the specific symptom at work and of nonspecific manifestations of ego weakness seemed to justify attempting psychoanalytic treatment.

Ms H had enormous difficulties in conveying a realistic picture of her parents and her two sisters. She described her father as distant and unavailable, cold and withdrawn, and yet warm and engaged with her—in fact, almost openly seductive. In the course of the treatment she remembered her own sexually seductive behavior with her father. In fact, it became apparent quite soon after the analysis started that it was not clear to her whether he had been seductive with her or she with him.

It was almost impossible for me to obtain an image of her mother, who remained an almost mythical presence during the several years of analysis. In contrast, the image of a much older aunt who carried out the functions of a maternal figure became prominent from early treatment on. Ms H expressed a longing for the childhood relationship with this warm, understanding, and giving relative.

In the transference, there were long stretches during which she presented oedipal material, fears of and wishes for being seduced by me that gradually shifted into wishes to seduce me as a father figure, with a parallel uncovering of deep, dissociated unconscious guilt over this seductiveness, expressed in self-defeating patterns in her relationships with other men in her life. In fact, one might say that her oedipal conflicts showed up not in a dynamic equilibrium involving unconscious, repressed positive oedipal longings and guilt feelings over them but in simultaneous, mutually dissociated, or split-off acting out of unconscious guilt over good relations with men outside the analysis, and direct expression of conflicts around sexual seductiveness and fear of being rejected in the analytic situation itself.

After several months a new theme emerged that gradually took over significant periods in the transference. Ms H mentioned a colleague, X, who was carrying out work somewhat related to hers in the laboratory, a woman the patient found extremely attractive and, at the same time, a potential serious professional rival. She gradually developed strong homosexual feelings toward X, together with intense fear that X was trying to steal her ideas in order to advance her career.

Ms H's fears of X impressed me as having a paranoid quality: X was a horrible witch with unusual powers, dedicated to destroying the patient by ruining her work, tampering with electronic circuits, and producing mischief in many ways. As I attempted to clarify the extent to which the patient recognized all this as reality or fantasy, Ms H immediately became suspicious of my attitude and intentions. She considered the possibility either that I might know X or that X had approached me in an effort to influence me. In any case, Ms H felt really threatened that I might become an enemy in alliance with X.

I considered the possibility that an image of a threatening, revengeful oedipal mother was being projected onto X and onto me in the transference, but it was impossible to link these paranoid developments in the here-and-now with significant aspects of the patient's past. In fact, over extended periods of the analysis, for weeks at a time, it was as if Ms H had no past, no personal history that I might work with in constructive or reconstructive ways, and as if everything was being played out in her relationships with X and myself. Indeed, there were times when I thought the patient might be psychotic. Any efforts to link these developments in the transference with the patient's past not only failed but ended up increasing the confusion in the hours, so that, in certain sessions, I felt as if I were being threatened by a crazy witch who was attempting to transform my efforts to understand what was going on into a destructive scrambling of my own thoughts. Bion's (1959) description of the patient's destructive attacks on anything felt to link one object with another, as an expression of the "psychotic" part of the personality, seems pertinent here. The analytic situation became totally chaotic, and now I experienced in my countertransference toward Ms H (I was being bewitched . . .) what she was telling me was occurring in her relationship with X; simultaneously, both she and, to some extent, I lost the capacity to sort out reality from fantasy.

I would like to stress the confusing effects on me of rapid alternations in the treatment between "crazy times," when "witch-hunting" seemed to go on, with the dominant question being who was the hunter and who was the hunted, and "oedipal times," when Ms H behaved like a typical neurotic patient: associating satisfactorily while exploring the positive oedipal transference and her relationships with other people in the present and in her past in light of these transference developments.

It was only after many months of clarification of these transference developments that I was able to interpret to Ms H that, regardless of the reality of X's behavior, Ms H had projected onto her an internal reality consisting of a mad "witch" woman who was trying to steal her thoughts, destroy her work and her future, and whose power was related to the patient's own intense admiration for and sexual attraction to her. That same "witch" woman was forcing her to undo her own creative work in the laboratory. It was only then that very early memories came to mind in which Ms H perceived her mother as both intensively protective and yet invasive—controlling the patient and reading her mind. It became apparent that Ms H had always felt penetrated by this image of mother. She felt that her body, her movements, her speech, her intentions, could no longer be trusted because they might really represent her mother's intentions.

Then the idealized figure of the aunt emerged as a split-off image of an ideal mother, loving without being invasive, tolerating distance without aggressively punishing her daughter. Ms H had lived with the perception in fantasy or reality that her mother could not tolerate her independence or autonomy during her childhood years. The fear of driving on highways or over bridges now became clarified as fear of being taken over by a mother who would punish her with death for attempting to escape from mother by racing through highways or over bridges. I was now able to analyze with Ms H how she was repeating her relationship with mother in her relationship with me, experiencing me as an invasive witch-mother who was assaulting her simultaneously in the sessions and at her workplace while, at other times, without being aware of it, identifying with this invasive mother in attempting to prevent me from contributing with my autonomous work to her understanding and from thinking independently. I suggested that the terrible confusion of whether her rival was indeed creating a "gaslight" situation at work or whether Ms H only fantasized such a development was part of this pattern. The analysis of Ms H's identification with a primitive, overwhelming witch-mother who had parasitically taken over her superego gradually led to the resolution of her self-defeating falsifications of her findings.

At that point, Ms H started to think more freely about what was going on at work. Both she and I discovered in the course of a few weeks that X was indeed actively attempting to undermine the patient's work, a fact confirmed by evidence from other coworkers.

It became apparent at the advanced stages of her analysis that the internal, unconscious submission to a mother from whom she could not differentiate herself represented the acting out of oedipal guilt, the split-off counterpart to her conscious oedipal fantasies and wishes in the transference. Ms H now became both more inhibited in the expression of her sexual fantasies toward me and consciously more fearful in her sexual involvement with men. The analysis evolved into an evaluation and working through of oedipal conflicts and ambivalence regarding both parents.

MRS. J

Mrs. J, a moderately successful painter in her early forties, consulted me after several failures in psychoanalytic psychotherapy because she had heard that I was interested in painting; in her fantasy, I therefore represented a "nonestablishment" analyst. This somewhat flimsy rationalization for her decision to start treatment with me soon turned into a source of great anxiety for her as she started to fear that I might become very envious of her ability to paint, and that this might endanger her treatment with me. Mrs. J suffered from moderate anxiety, conflicts in her current, third marriage, interpersonal difficulties with other women, lengthy periods of paralysis in her work, and mild self-mutilating trends. She bit and chewed the mucosa of her mouth and the skin surrounding her fingernails, and compulsively pulled out her pubic hair. She had formerly been a heavy drinker, but this symptom was under control by the time she started her treatment with me.

She was the only child of parents who, while boasting of their aristocratic background, had undergone serious financial difficulties, for reasons that were never made clear to the patient. Mother's resentment at father's incapacity to reverse their financial difficulties constituted a major theme of Mrs. J's childhood. I learned very little about her mother: she was described as strong yet nonintrusive, "always there" yet distant from the patient. Because Mrs. J's father had lived in Latin America in his youth, as had I, the patient developed elaborate fantasies about my personality, linking it to his.

Father emerged as friendly but frail and incompetent, and the patient explained in detail how she had searched for a more assertive and effective man in her own life but was always frustrated. She always ended up with men who were failures, a major source of her bitterness. Mrs. J's daughter from an earlier marriage was away at college, and Mrs. J missed her terribly. She thought her daughter's absence accentuated the difficulties with her present husband, a businessman who had not been able to sustain his own business and was now working for a former competitor. Mrs. J was teaching art in addition to painting and was able to contribute significantly to their joint income.

The initial impression Mrs. J conveyed was of a woman relatively free from symptoms in the sense that her self-mutilation, anxiety, mood swings, and interpersonal difficulties did not impress me as severe. After a more extended evaluation, however, I detected a sense of emptiness and confusion that caused me to revise my initial impression. She nonetheless had a capacity for introspection and motivation for treatment that seemed to favor undertaking psychoanalysis.

She was precise and clear in describing objective events or her past history and current life situation but became diffuse and even chaotic when portraying her family and closest friends. Important women in her life were fascinating yet threatening, close yet untrustworthy; men, in contrast—particularly her three husbands—were reliable but weak. Mrs. J was pleased with herself for having maintained a good relationship with her former husbands, but I did not get a clearly differentiated picture of one from the other from her narrative. Mrs. J had difficulty in conveying her view of herself: she enjoyed her art and teaching, but she also wondered whether there was something "fake" about her; she was troubled by her tendency to cling to relationships even when they seemed frustrating and produced conflict.

On the basis of all these elements, I diagnosed her as an infantile personality functioning in a borderline personality organization and initiated psychoanalytic treatment.

Again, what follows is a highly condensed summary of issues relevant for my purpose here. Her intense fears that I might envy her artistic talent, an early transference development, reflected the projection onto me of her envy of me and my professional work. She felt that I was an example of the successful man she admired and longed for and could never seem to have, a reminder of her bitter disappointment in her father and her husbands; she gradually became aware that it was hard for her to decide whether she wanted me as a man or wanted to be like me. Positive oedipal longings and penis envy, together with unconscious identifications with envied men, became a principal content of the early transference. In this connection, her unconscious selection of men whom she considered limited in order not to experience excessive envy and rivalry with them appeared as a first dynamic aspect of her marital difficulties. Later we found out that she was unconsciously contributing to keeping her husband in a subordinate position in his business.

A second theme that soon emerged reflected her relationships with other women. She was active in a women artists' group and worked closely with a few women having similar professional backgrounds and interests. She selected women to work with whom she considered very aggressive; she first admired and submitted to them and later developed intense rage reactions and terminated the relationship with violent arguments. This pattern had repeated itself often enough for the patient to be fully aware of it, of her fascination with these powerful women, and of her tendency to put herself into a position where they would exploit her. She would then develop an intense resentment of and, in her own view, an exaggeratedly violent reaction to that exploitation.

In fact, although Mrs. J could diagnose this pattern in retrospect, she was unable to diagnose it in the course of its development. My focus on why she could not recognize the pattern while it was in progress made her intensely anxious. Mrs. J now became fearfully aware that it was difficult for her to differentiate her own reactions from those of her women friends.

It now struck me that any effort to link her growing awareness of a pathological pattern of interpersonal relations in the present to her past proved fruitless. Quite similarly to what occurred with Ms H, all efforts at construction or reconstruction ended in confusion or the sense that I was partaking in a sterile intellectual exercise. In contrast to Ms H, however, Mrs. J was acutely aware of her confusion between her motivation and that of her friends, and of her fear that this confusion would prevent her from understanding herself and her difficulties and would also prevent me from understanding her. In fact, during such confused states, even her verbal communication in the hours became somewhat disorganized. In dramatic moments during some sessions, Mrs. J said with intense anxiety that her main problem was that she really was not a person separate from others but was so totally immersed in and influenced by relations with others that it was impossible to sort herself out; she could not see how I would be able to help her do this. Eventually, I told her that I thought she was afraid I could not tolerate her in her "unglued" state, a comment she experienced as very helpful. She now felt that she could "fall apart" in the sessions without fearing that I too would fall apart in my understanding. She no longer worried about provoking me to try to "put her together" in a forceful way that would limit her freedom and expose her to becoming an artificial product of my mind.

A long period followed in which the patient became chaotic in her comments in the sessions and in which certain themes emerged that never came up at other times. These included Mrs. J's sexual excitement with biting and chewing her mucosa and the skin of her fingers and the fantasy of sadistically attacking her body while controlling that attack and being able to erotically enjoy the pain it caused. At one point, Mrs. J herself was able to formulate the fantasy that it was as if she were engaged in a sexual perversion in which she was enacting the roles of sadist and masochist at the same time, with a sense of humiliating herself before me as well as being humiliated in a sexual delivery of herself that was eminently exciting.

Another issue that came up in fragmented ways during such periods of confusion was the thought that in many ways she was imitating her mother in her gestures and clothing, or that her mother was imitating her, as if there were telepathic communication between them. I should stress that it was extremely difficult for me to form a realistic picture of the mother during extended periods of Mrs. J's analysis, a problem similar to the one I experienced with Ms H. At times, Mrs. J used her mother's colloquialisms in ways that were slightly bizarre: she also used her mother's recipes for cooking with slight modifications that typically resulted in a ruined product. I was never clear about whether the disastrous result was caused by Mrs. J or by her mother's having deliberately modified the recipe.

It eventually became very clear that the patient's unconscious identification with an overpowering and dangerous mother could be undone only by means of an internal fragmentation, a generalized splitting operation, which reflected the fantasy that there was no danger in letting mother take over because there was no person there to be taken over—that mother would just get lost in the course of this attempt. And projecting Mrs. J's defensive sense of fragmentation onto mother brought about the fragmentation of mother's image and was an effective defense against fears of her. We now learned that Mrs. J's fearful concern over my getting lost when she felt fragmented in the hours was in fact an active effort to make sure that I would not threaten her in an invasive manner: my comment that she was afraid I would not be able to tolerate her sense of fragmentation was reassuring to her because it meant that I acknowledged her fragmentation and that I was not going to be able to overcome it. In other words, what I had experienced as my tolerating her state of regression without prematurely intervening interpretively she experienced as protection against me, as a dangerous primitive mother trying to mold her after me. In addition, my own sense of confusion, of fragmented thinking, in many sessions when the patient was in a regressed state could now be understood as the result of her projecting onto me her "endangered self" while unconsciously she enacted what she saw as her mother's invasively controlling behavior.

The clarification of all these issues in the transference brought about further clarification of her difficulties with women. The patient was able to assess and resolve more realistically the temptations to become involved in neurotic interactions with dominant women. At the same time, reconstructions of the early relationship with mother became possible, particularly their relationship during the rapprochement stage predating the major oedipal involvement with father.

It was only then that the infantile version of a powerful and desirable father emerged from behind the disillusion and disappointment with a weak and frustrating father, a later image in which realistic aspects of childhood experience and unconscious oedipal guilt feelings coalesced.

The fear of mother's envious attacks could then also be related to the patient's fantasy of becoming the powerful mother and, by using that powerful mother's controlling force, take over father "from inside" and become both of them, a powerful primitive father-mother. This fantasy, in turn, further clarified the unconscious need to choose men whom she experienced as disappointing but was able to control in subtle ways. This clarification led to changes in her relationship to her husband and to her capacity to support his efforts to improve his business situation.

TECHNICAL CONSIDERATIONS

Perhaps the most striking feature of the analyzable infantile personalities that I have treated or supervised is the sudden development of a
transference regression—brief or extended—that may not be immediately apparent because the patient continues to free associate and the
manifest behavior on the couch is not radically altered. Usually it is in
the countertransference that the analyst first observes the fundamental
change that has taken place.

The change consists in a sudden, dissociative shift into a type of free
association that enacts a primitive relationship in the transference while
disconnecting it defensively from its antecedents in the past and, at
times, even from external reality. It is as if a patient who ordinarily
functions on a neurotic level suddenly begins to function at a typical
borderline level, with a shift from total to part-object relations, from a
stable sense of identity (which facilitates the description of past and
present object relations) to a state of acute fragmentation, which distorts
or breaks up all communication about significant object relations other
than that enacted in the present with the analyst.

Then the analyst feels forced to shift his pace of work, to focus sharply
on the current transference relationship while having to accept that the
cues will come predominantly from his countertransference fantasies
and affects rather than from the manifest content of the patient's verbal
and nonverbal behavior. It is the suddenness of this shift that is so impressive and potentially disorganizing to the analyst.

At such points of regression, it is as if the transference channel (see
chap. 7) represented by the content of the patient's subjective experience
and the transference channel represented by the patient's nonverbal behavior in the transference fade out, leaving only the "analytic space," the
relatively constant yet silent background configuration of the relationship between patient and analyst that allows for the enactment of both
realistic and fantastic object relations. The latter has a direct impact on
the analyst's countertransferential disposition.

I have found that if the analyst now attempts to continue his ordinary
way of working with the content of a patient's free associations, increasing periods of confusion ensue. There is a real danger of artificially organizing the patient's communications in intellectual ways, which the
patient unconsciously interprets as an invasive takeover. It is, in fact, the
very absence of dramatic acting out, the absence of communication by
means of the nonverbal action channel, that tends to falsely reassure the
psychoanalyst that he may focus his attention on the content of the

patient's verbal communication. This assumption leads to premature efforts at interpretation, while the main issue being played out in the silent space between patient and analyst goes underground.

The clinical characteristics of these states of regression are subtle and yet dramatic in their effects on the analyst's countertransference. The patient may continue to free associate with affectively invested narratives of what is going on currently or he may talk about the past; there may be references to the analyst, without, however, the possibility of clarifying the deeper transference implications of these feelings. To the contrary, sometimes the patient may seem unusually "healthy" and "reasonable," and the central issue is the analyst's sense, over a period of days and weeks, that it is not possible to deepen the exploration of anything the patient says or that there is no depth at all to his material. Also, experience will teach the analyst that any efforts to penetrate to deeper levels, utilizing previously acquired knowledge about the patient's unconscious processes, will lead into a strange confusion, which will be detrimental to the analyst's efforts to understand what is going on. The issues that finally emerge are typically the patient's concern that he is being taken over, that his mind is being scrambled, that the analyst is being "lost" (as a consequence of projective identification); therefore the patient feels threatened that he will be abandoned.

Only gradually will the underlying primitive part-object relationship become clearer, in the context of rapid interchanges of the enactment of self and object representations. In the psychoanalytic psychotherapy of borderline patients, the analyst may be prepared to deal with only the unconscious implications of the dominant object relation in the here-and-now, postponing any effort to link the unconscious in the here-and-now with its genetic antecedents; the analyst is therefore, paradoxically, better prepared to deal with such severe regression. In contrast, in the analytic treatment of the infantile personality, these regressions are masked by the patient's apparently remaining within the frame of the analytic process that proved so productive and helpful earlier, thus temporarily—or permanently—confusing the analyst. Extensive acting out facilitates analytic exploration of primitive internalized object relations in a specific arena whether the action is with the analyst or others. In the circumstances I am describing—which are characteristic of patients who are being analyzed precisely because, among other reasons, acting out is not so great as to preclude analysis—the seeming continuity of the analytic process masks its underlying discontinuity.

Often, during the silent regressions typical of these patients, the analyst may feel that he is treating what is really not an analytic case, that the patient is talking emptily without any possibility of transforming the communication into useful material; the analyst may simply withdraw with a sense of helplessness. Underneath such helplessness the analyst may be unconsciously identifying with the patient's projected regressed self. I have had the opportunity to examine cases in which the analyst broke off the treatment because of extended periods of this kind. On the other hand, an analyst with a strong bias toward believing in a specific genetic origin for such states of regression may be tempted to interpret the verbal content in the light of such a genetic hypothesis, and the patient may respond with contents corresponding to such an interpretation while unconsciously acting out the fantasy that he is being taken over and that only further fragmentation will protect him.

In fact, the principal reason these frequent, sudden regressions in the transference of infantile patients occur may be the patients' conscious or unconscious awareness of the analyst's understanding of them and their feeling that any emotional understanding is equivalent to a dangerous invasion, takeover, or even sexual penetration, against which the enactment of transference regression becomes a ready-made defense.

My main point is that a helpful approach to such periods is precisely not to interpret specific verbal content at such times and to gradually prepare the interpretation of the dominant object relation enacted in the transference in an atemporal fashion—that is, without any effort to link this development to a specific period of the patient's past. Analyzing what is going on unconsciously in the here-and-now while tolerating the disconnection of this material from the patient's immediate external reality and from his unconscious past constitutes, in my experience, the best way to elicit meaningful information that will eventually make it possible to link the unconscious past with the unconscious present and other aspects of the patient's external reality.

The type of regression I have described requires, one might say, a different type of listening, or rather an awareness on the part of the analyst that the patient's channel of communication has radically shifted, from the verbal and nonverbal toward the most subtle and intangible channel of analytic space, the implicit but constant relationship between the analyst and the patient. Communication within that space reaches the analyst first through his countertransference. There is, of course, the danger that countertransference problems in a narrow sense—that is, derived from the analyst's transference dispositions—may bring about a period of failure to understand; the analyst will first have to tolerate such a period and then examine whether it stems from his own activated conflicts or from the sudden and radical shift in the nature of the communication from the patient. I should like to stress how long it took me to become aware of what was going on in each of the two cases reported; this was also true of the other patients of this type whom I have treated. These difficulties also present themselves in supervision, when the supervisee communicates lengthy periods of apparent stalemate in the analysis of his patient, or lengthy periods of not understanding, with the additional difficulty for the supervisor of opening up the exploration of countertransference problems without invading the supervisee's privacy. The supervisor's overall distance from the material in this instance, however, can be helpful.

One aspect of the reconstructive work of interpretation that emerges from experience with infantile patients is that reconstructions involving the regressive transferences can be attempted only belatedly, after analytic work has been completed with the unconscious meanings in the here-and-now carried out on an atemporal basis for an extended period of time. Such constructive work requires proceeding with issues of various kinds derived from the stages of what might be called neurotic transferences left unresolved, interrupted, hanging in midair. If the analyst can tolerate these discontinuities, these interrupted paths to the past, new patterns eventually evolve that impress him with logical, almost unavoidable connections between the two sets of information coming from periods of "borderline" regression and periods of more advanced or "neurotic" functioning. Only then has the possibility for connective genetic interpretations emerged for me in those cases.

The fact that in my two examples the dominant object relation enacted in the deep though apparently silent regression was with an unconscious aspect of the preoedipal mother points to a prevalent etiology of such regressive states, but should not be taken to mean that this is the interpretive line the analyst should expect or anticipate. There are cases, such as Mrs. J, in which a regression occurs to a condensed father-mother figure; the unreality of these regressions requires much more elaboration in the unconscious here-and-now before they can be traced back to the more realistic aspects of the parental images.

It is important to carry out analytic work along ordinary interpretive lines during such times when the patient seems to be functioning on a neurotic level. At these times, patients with infantile personality present a more direct expression of transference relationships that have a total in contrast to a part-object relation quality. The transference relationship can be connected more easily to other object relations in external reality and in the patient's past and therefore lends itself to constructive and reconstructive efforts. What is important is that the analyst tolerate the discontinuity in the analytic work during the "neurotic" times and during times of deep though subtle transference regression.

The severe transference regression I have been describing may be confused with the chronic resistances against transference regression so typical in narcissistic personalities. In fact, the analyst's protective withdrawal, his sense of impatience and boredom, which may signal the activation in the countertransference of regressive transferences in infantile personalities, may be confused with similar reactions to narcissistic transference resistances. The principal difference is that the patient's intense, clinging dependency on the analyst persists throughout the regression in infantile personalities, in contrast to the sense of distance and lack of emotional involvement with the analyst in the narcissistic transferences.

The nature of the patient's confusion that emerges when the analyst attempts to deepen the patient's understanding of the material presented during these severe regressions in the transference raises another question. Is one faced with loss or blurring of ego boundaries, so that it is no longer possible for the patient to ascertain whether thoughts are originating in his mind or the analyst's? And is a similar confusion contaminating the analyst's thinking as well? Or, as I believe, is this confusion the consequence of intense activation of projective identification in the patient—and, possibly, in the analyst as well—so that by rapid alternation between projective and introjective mechanisms there is an interchange of reciprocal roles between patient and analyst that tends to bring about a confusion of who is who, though without ever reaching a condition of actual merger between them? The situation is almost always of the second case, in clear contrast to authentic merger in the transference, which can be observed in the psychoanalytic approach to psychotic patients (chap. 12).

As I have pointed out in earlier work (1975), loss of reality testing in the transference consequent to the activation of projective identification must be differentiated from authentic merger experiences. The latter are typical of psychotic, particularly schizophrenic, patients in analytic modalities of treatment. Borderline patients in deeply regressive transferences maintain their capacity to differentiate themselves from the therapist, even when they temporarily seem to be "exchanging their personality" with him.

Bion (1957b) described "psychotic personalities" as the psychotic aspect of clinically nonpsychotic patients as well as the characteristics of schizophrenic patients in psychoanalytic treatment. These psychotic personalities or aspects of personality evince a predominance of extremely destructive impulses, hatred of reality expressed as aggressive destruction of the patient's capacity for awareness of reality, projective identification, and pathological splitting of projected material into minute fragments that constitute "bizarre objects."

Although I believe that Bion underestimated the differences between psychotic transferences proper and severe regression in borderline and other character pathology, his stress on the predominance of projective identification and other primitive defenses as a manifestation of aggressive attacks on the very apparatus of perception conforms with the characteristics of the transference regressions I have illustrated. But the severity of these features varies from case to case. The aggressive attacks on the perception of reality in particular may be quite limited. I think that Bion, in lumping together schizophrenia and character pathology, underestimated important differences in their respective transference regression and, even more important, in their technical management.

The analysis of the dominant object relation during severe transference regression proceeds very slowly. The unconscious fantasies throughout these periods may become clarified by means of the here-and-now, atemporal mode of interpretation I have already described. Typically, such regressive transference relationships appear with rapid role reversals between self and object—that is, rapid shifts from moments during which the patient identifies with his own self and projects his object representation onto the analyst to other moments during which the patient identifies with his object representation and projects his self representation onto the analyst. Both clinical cases described illustrate this rapid shift. In contrast, during "neurotic" transference periods such shifts are much slower and less frequent.

Ms H's alternation between identifying with the "witch" and projecting the witch image onto me illustrates this process. Mrs. J and I alternately enacted both sides of the invasive nature of the powerful overwhelming mother in relating to the defensively fragmented child. This rapid alternation of part-object relations is typical of borderline personality organization. In the course of analyzing such part-object relations in the transference, it is possible gradually to integrate mutually split-off part-object relations and thus to bring about an integration of the self and an integration of the representations of significant others and, with these developments, self constancy and object constancy. The consolidation of object constancy, in turn, tends to reinforce and further clarify the nature of both preoedipal and oedipal conflicts. Both cases also illustrate how the early analysis of oedipal material can be deepened later on, after working through the transference regression.

From a theoretical viewpoint, one might think there is nothing unusual about defensive regressions in the transference from oedipal to preoedipal periods of development. What is of interest, however, is that the regression in these cases is a structural one, reflected in the activation, in the transference, of the syndrome of identity diffusion. In these cases, as typically occurs in psychoanalytic psychotherapy of nonanalyzable borderline patients, the transference developments oscillate rather abruptly and sharply between advanced, or "neurotic," and regressed, or "borderline," transferences.

The dangers facing the analyst in treating patients who have such dramatic, radical shifts in their mode of communication are the following: first, by staying exclusively at the neurotic level of regression in the ordinary transference developments that these patients present in common with psychoanalytic cases, one may lose the connection with deeper, more primitive levels of development. As a consequence, treatment may end in a stalemate because the basic character structure is not changed, and these patients may surprise one again and again with bizarre, sometimes even violent acting out and with a lack of integration in their external life that seems to defy all the analytic work done. Under these conditions, the analyst may well conclude that this is a patient with basic ego weakness, without real insight, with very early deficits that cannot be repaired, and so on.

Second, if the analyst remains at the level of severe regression in the transference without being flexible enough to go back to analyze ordinary neurotic conflicts, there is a danger of losing contact with the healthy aspects of the patient's functioning and either maintaining the knowledge acquired about the patient's primitive functioning in a suspended state, unrelated to the healthier level of the patient's functioning, or "indoctrinating" the patient with interpretations at a primitive level that bypass the healthier levels of functioning and prevent the patient from fully integrating the primitive with the advanced, the more fantastic with the more realistic layers of his mind. Some endless analyses in which the patient seems almost artificially regressed by consistent primitivity of the analyst's level of discourse and interpretation and, by the same token, remains strangely unrealistic in dealing with ordinary day-to-day functioning may illustrate this danger of lack of a full integration of the patient's conflicts as part of the psychoanalytic technique. In some cases, chronic psychotic transference regression ensues and spills over into the patient's ordinary life.

I believe that the technical approach proposed herein may expand the field of indications for psychoanalytic treatment of severe personality disorders.

Part IV TECHNICAL APPROACHES TO SEVERE REGRESSION

Chapter 10 PROJECTION AND PROJECTIVE IDENTIFICATION: DEVELOPMENTAL AND CLINICAL ASPECTS

The term *projective identification*, **originally described by** Melanie Klein (1946, 1955) and elaborated on by Rosenfeld (1965) and Bion (1968), like other psychoanalytic concepts, has become blurred because it has been so variously defined by so many people. In my view, the problems with existing definitions are related, at least in part, to the different patient populations studied—for example, schizophrenic (Ogden 1979) versus borderline—and the failure to distinguish among defensive operations, the patient's general structural characteristics, and countertransferences.

I have found the phenomenon (as I defined it in 1975) extremely useful clinically, especially when it is considered vis-à-vis the mechanism of projection. Projective identification is a primitive defense mechanism. The subject projects an intolerable intrapsychic experience onto an object, maintains empathy (in the sense of emotional awareness) with what he projects, tries to control the object in a continuing effort to defend against the intolerable experience, and unconsciously, in actual interaction with the object, leads the object to experience what has been projected onto him.

Projection itself, a more mature form of defense, consists of first repressing the intolerable experience, then projecting it onto the object, and finally, separating or distancing oneself from the object to fortify the defensive effort.

Projection is typically seen in the defensive repertoire of patients with neurotic personality organization. In the treatment situation, the hysterical patient who expresses fears that her analyst might become sexually interested in her, has no awareness of her own sexual impulses or that she might be communicating such impulses by nonverbal means, so that her "fear" of the therapist's sexual interest in her occurs within an essentially nonerotic atmosphere, illustrates the mechanism of projection. Patients with borderline personality organization may use both projection and projective identification, but the latter clearly dominates the defensive repertoire and the transference situation. Patients with psychotic personality organization (characterized principally by loss of reality testing) typically use projective identification as a prevalent defense. Psychotic patients who do project—for example, homosexual impulses that they do not consciously experience in some persecutory delusions, or erotic feelings by patients who have no awareness of their own erotic strivings—are much less common than the early literature would imply. In short, although a patient may employ both projection and projective identification, projection is typical of a higher level of functioning, whereas projective identification is typical of borderline and psychotic personality organizations.

One important issue that confuses efforts to define projective identification is the extent to which it is a "psychotic" mechanism. Unless one thinks of *psychotic* as a synonym for *primitive*, an idea I consider untenable, projective identification is not necessarily psychotic. Only when internalized and external object relations occur under conditions of blurring of self and object representations and lack of differentiation between self and others may such object relations rightly be called psychotic.

Elsewhere (chap. 2) I describe how patients with psychotic object relations use projective identification in a desperate attempt to prevent themselves from lapsing into utter confusion regarding the differentiation of self and object. Under such circumstances, projective identification may permit a patient to localize aggression outside the self. In contrast, a person with borderline pathology uses projective identification to maintain splitting of all-good from all-bad ego states. Projective identification is thus not necessarily based upon lack of differentiation between self and object representations (although it may occur under such conditions), nor does it necessarily cause a loss of differentiation between self and object representations, although it weakens reality testing temporarily in borderline patients.

My concept of projective identification is supported by my clinical observations of the effects of interpreting this defense mechanism to a patient. The psychotic patient will be temporarily more confused and his reality testing will be diminished; the borderline patient will respond by an improvement in reality testing, even if only temporarily.

Projective identification, then, is a primitive defensive operation but is not necessarily linked to psychosis. It predominates in the psychoses, where it is accompanied by loss of reality testing and, from a structural viewpoint, by the loss of boundaries between self and object representations. In borderline personality organization, projective identification is accompanied by maintenance of reality testing, structurally underpinned by differentiation of self from object representations, and permits the utilization of particular therapeutic techniques to deal with it interpretively, with the result of strengthening reality testing and the patient's ego. Projective identification plays a relatively unimportant role in the neuroses (except when the patient undergoes severe temporary regression) and is for the most part replaced by projection.

DEVELOPMENTAL CONSIDERATIONS

I propose that a developmental line of defenses leads from projective identification, which is based on an ego structure centered upon splitting (primitive dissociation) as its essential defense, to projection, which is based on an ego structure centered upon repression as a basic defense. Generally, I believe, it is possible to trace a developmental line for other types of defensive operations. For example, we see a developmental line from primitive idealization, in which the splitting is between idealized and persecutory objects, to the idealization typical of the narcissistic personality (in which self-idealization, either ego-syntonic or projected, is the counterpart of devaluation), to the idealization typical of neurotic personality organization which reflects reaction formations against guilt, and finally, to normal idealization as part of the externalization of integrated aspects of the ego ideal. (Normal idealization, for example, plays an important role in falling in love.) Again, denial as defined by Jacobson (1957a), which is based on primitive dissociation of contradictory ego states, may be seen as the primitive form of negation, a more advanced mechanism based on repression and a typically neurotic defensive operation. In a different defense area, primitive introjection (when the subject lacks the capacity to differentiate self from object representations) may be seen as the precursor of introjections that occur in connection with identifications characteristic of advanced stages of ego and superego development. In short, whether splitting or repression is prevalent as a central means of defense determines whether projective identification or projection predominates.

If projective identification implies that the subject has the capacity to differentiate self from nonself, it can be assumed that the subject must have reached a certain level of development before projective identification is operational. I assume two conditions that must be fulfilled. Insofar as projective identification implies a fantasy—and in order to fantasize we have to assume the capacity for having one element stand for another and be manipulated in the direction of a desired goal—the capacity for symbolization must be present. And insofar as the wish is to expel onto another what is felt as undesirable, there must exist a capacity for awareness not only of the difference between the self and the other but also of how one feels—of one's subjective state. Only when we can recognize a particular subjective state as undesirable in comparison with other subjective states does it make sense to attempt to get rid of it by expulsion. These capacities probably exist by the time the infant is fifteen months old (Stern 1985).

For reasons which I elaborate on below (see also chap. 1), I assume that the core mental representations of self and object are established when the infant is stimulated by extreme pleasure or pain rather than when he is in a quiescent and merely alert state.

The effect of learning during peak-affect states differs from the effect of learning during alert quiescent states. In the latter, the infant has no wish to fuse with or separate itself from the other; hence the issue of boundaries is not present. But experiences during peak-affect states foster both fusion and differentiation. If the state is one of extreme pleasure, the infant wishes to fuse with the provider of that pleasure. If the affect state is one of extreme displeasure or pain, the infant's wish to expel the pain fosters differentiation. Projective identification is an essential defense mechanism to deal with intolerable psychic pain during negative peak-affect states, when self-awareness and symbolization are operational.

Projection, in contrast, requires the achievement of a further state of development in which a clear differentiation between representations of self and of object, and between self and external objects, is matched by a sense of continuity of self-experience under contradictory emotional circumstances. This implies the ability to tolerate ambivalence and to experience a sense of continuity—the "categorical self" of the philosophers. Self-awareness is now not only that of temporarily changing subjective experiences but of a subjective self as something stable against which each subjective state is evaluated.

Projection may be conceived as a "healthier," more adaptive outcome of projective identification, at least at early stages of integration of the self concept and consolidation of repressive barriers. Eventually, of course, projection has maladaptive consequences because it can result in the distortion of external reality.

TECHNICAL APPROACH

As I described earlier (chap. 7), the analyst has two channels of information, verbal and nonverbal, regarding the patient's subjective experiences. A third channel is constituted by the emotional ambience of the analytic situation, mostly communicated by the analyst's countertransference. And the analyst, under ordinary transference developments, experiences transitory concordant and complementary identifications with the patient (see chap. 6). Although all patients express significant information by nonverbal means, the deeper the patient's pathology, the more nonverbal behavior predominates. Projective identification usually comes into play in the nonverbal aspects of the patient's communication and is diagnosable through the activation in the analyst himself of powerful affective dispositions that reflect what the patient is projecting, and through his alertness to the interpersonal implications of the patient's behavior.

When verbal communication of subjective experience predominates, projective identification is less evident, less easily detected because its manifestations are subtle, but more easily handled interpretively if the analyst preserves his internal freedom for fantasy about the patient and does not suffer from undue countertransference reactions.

Patients with severe character pathology who unconsciously attempt to escape from an intolerable intrapsychic reality by projective identification onto the analyst make it easier for the analyst to detect this phenomenon and yet more difficult to interpret it, for the patient typically resists the analyst's efforts at interpretation because of the dread of what had to be projected in the first place.

The following clinical vignettes illustrate the activation of projection and projective identification and their technical management. These vignettes also show the different ways in which these mechanisms operate in neurotic, narcissistic, and borderline patients.

CLINICAL ILLUSTRATIONS

Mrs. K, in her early twenties, entered psychoanalysis suffering from a hysterical personality, consistent inhibition of orgasm in intercourse with her husband, and romantic attachments in fantasy to unavailable men. A few months after starting treatment, she expressed the fantasy that I was particularly sensual, in fact, "lecherous," and might be attempting to arouse her sexual feelings toward me so as to obtain sexual gratification from her. She said she had heard I came from a Latin American country and had written about erotic love relations. Furthermore, she thought I had a particularly seductive attitude toward the women working in the office area where I saw her. She believed all this justified her fears. She thought that I looked at her in peculiar ways as she came into my office and that I was probably trying to guess the shape of her body underneath her clothes as she lay on the couch.

She had initially been reluctant to speak about these fears, but my interpreting her fear of my rejecting her if she openly expressed her fantasies about me led to a gradual unfolding of this material. Actually her attitude was not seductive: on the contrary, there was something inhibited, rigid, almost asexual in her behavior and very little eroticism expressed in her nonverbal communications. My own emotional reactions and fantasies about her had a subdued quality and contained no conscious erotic element; I concluded that she was attributing to me her own repressed sexual fantasies and wishes. In other words, this typical example of a neurotic transference illustrates the operation of projection, with no activation of countertransference material (see chap. 7).

A year later, Mrs. K had changed significantly. Her fear of my sexual interest in her had led her to express disgust at the sexual interest older men have for younger women, to the discovery of resemblance to her father in such disgusting, lecherous older men, and then to the discovery that her romantic attachments in fantasy were toward men she perceived as unavailable and that she was afraid of sexual excitement with such previously unavailable but now potentially available men. Her recognition that sexual excitement was associated with forbidden sexual relations made her gradually aware of her defenses against sexual excitement in relation to me. Her repression and projection of sexual feelings in the transference decreased, and direct oedipal sexual fantasies about me emerged.

At one point, Mrs. K expressed quite candidly her fantasy of having a sexual affair with me, including taking a secret trip with me to Paris. I found myself having an erotic response to the patient, including a fantasy that I, in turn, would enjoy a sexual relation with her, especially as it would mean my breaking all conventional barriers. I would thus provide her with a gift: the fullest acknowledgment possible of her specialness and attractiveness. In other words, my response was complementary to her wish—that of a seductive oedipal father. Neither projection nor projective identification was operative here, however: the patient's sexual impulses were ego-syntonic, she made no effort to control me in order to protect herself against her sexual impulses, and in response I could maintain empathy with her central subjective experience. It should come as no surprise that a little later Mrs. K was angry at my failure to respond to her sexual feelings and felt I had teased and humiliated her; this led to our exploration of her anger with, as she experienced it, a teasingly seductive, rejecting father.

In this neurotic personality structure, the predominance of communication of an intrapsychic experience by verbal means led to the activation of a complementary identification in a transference relationship relatively free from more primitive defensive operations, particularly of projective identification. Repression and projection were dominant defenses, in addition to other typical neurotic defenses such as intellectualization, reaction formations, and negation.

Ms L, on the other hand, in her late twenties and unmarried, suffered from a narcissistic personality disorder with overt borderline functioning. She had periodic deep depressive episodes and impulses to commit suicide that had already led to several hospitalizations. Recently discharged from the hospital where I had seen her as an inpatient, she was continuing in psychoanalytic psychotherapy with me three sessions a week. Ms L was physically attractive, although the staff found her cold, haughty, and distant. She alternated between periods when she grandiosely and derogatorily dismissed all those who tried to help her and times when she experienced feelings of inferiority and deep despair.

She had a long history of chaotic relations with men. She became infatuated with men she admired and thought unavailable, but any man who was interested in her she treated with contempt. She considered herself a "free spirit" with no sexual inhibitions; she expressed her sexual wishes and demands unreservedly and maintained simultaneous relationships with several men.

Her dominating, controlling, intrusive mother, who came from a relatively humble background, had used her strikingly attractive daughter from early childhood on as a source of gratification for herself and (as the patient saw it) had no interest in Ms L's internal life other than what reflected on herself as her mother. The father was a successful businessman whom the patient described as stunningly attractive and sexually promiscuous. He died suddenly of illness during Ms L's adolescence. Because of his intense involvement with his business as well as his many affairs, he had been practically unavailable to his daughter.

Ms L had originally sought me out to treat her because I was the director of the hospital. But as soon as I became her psychotherapist, her initial feeling of triumph was replaced by doubts about whether she wanted to continue in treatment with me.

The following episode took place several weeks after her discharge from the hospital. She was to resume her graduate studies, but expressed strong doubts whether to continue in psychotherapy with me, in the "small town" we were located in; this, she said, would totally destroy her motivation and interests because the town was ugly, provincial, lacked stimulation, and had a horrible climate. San Francisco and New York were "the only two livable cities in this country," and she raised questions about my professional insecurity, reflected, as she saw it, by my remaining in such a small town.

She came to the session I am about to describe elegantly dressed. She told me about a former friend, now a prominent lawyer in San Francisco, who had invited her to live with him, an offer she said she was seriously considering. She went on to say how ridiculously unattractive in bed her current lover was; she thought she would drop him. He was nice but without subtlety or refinement, sexually inexperienced, and poorly dressed. She then said that her mother had asked, after seeing me for the first time, whether Ms L wouldn't benefit more from a therapist who was more energetic and who could be firm with her: I had impressed her mother as friendly but plain and insecure.

I asked her what her thoughts were about her mother's comments, and she said that her mother was a very disturbed person but at the same time very intelligent and perceptive. She then smiled apologetically and said that she did not want to hurt my feelings, but that I really dressed in a provincial way and lacked the quiet yet firm sense of self-assurance she liked in men. She also said that she thought I was friendly but lacked intellectual depth. She expressed concern about whether I would be able to tolerate her being frank with me. She sounded friendly enough, and it took me a few minutes to register the note of condescension infiltrating that friendliness.

Ms L talked about plans for meeting her friend in San Francisco. She considered the possibility that he might fly out to visit her here before that, and she had some ideas about how to make his brief stay in town an enjoyable experience in "cultural anthropology"—that is, the study of small-town culture.

As she talked, I experienced a sense of futility and dejection. Thoughts crossed my mind about the many therapists this patient had previously had and the general description they conveyed to me of her incapacity to commit herself to a therapeutic relationship. I thought that she was probably incapable of maintaining a therapeutic relationship with me and that this was the beginning of the end of her therapy. I felt like giving up and suddenly had the thought that I was having difficulty in thinking precisely and deeply, words the patient had just used. I also felt physically awkward and experienced empathy with the man Ms L had just dismissed with her derisory comments.

It was only in the final part of the session that I realized that I had become one more devalued man and that I stood for all the men whom Ms L had first idealized and then rapidly devaluated. I now remembered the anxiety she had expressed in the past over the possibility that I might not take her on as my patient, her desperate sense that I was the only therapist who could help her, and the intense suspicion she had expressed in the first few sessions that I was interested only in learning all about her difficulties and would then dismiss her, like a collector of rare "specimens." I decided there was an act of revenge in Ms L's devaluation of me, the counterpart of her earlier sense that I would assert my superiority and devalue her. And it then came to mind that I was also feeling much the way she had described herself as feeling when she felt inferior and in despair, when she felt stupid, uneducated, incapable of living up to the expectations of the brilliant men she had been involved with. And I recognized in her behavior toward me the attitude of quiet superiority and subtly disguised devaluation with which her mother, as the patient had described her, made fun of her because of the inappropriate nature of the men she selected for herself.

The session ended before I could sort out all these thoughts, and I believe I may have conveyed to the patient the impression of being both silent and slightly dejected.

The same themes continued in the next session, which included plans for meeting the desirable man from San Francisco, the final stages of the dismissal of the current lover, and more derogatory comments about the "small town." I now realized that during the last session she had even managed to activate in me whatever ambivalence I myself experienced about that town. Only now did I become aware that the town also stood for me in the transference, and the town and I also represented her own devalued self-image projected onto me, while she was identifying with the haughty superiority of her mother. I thought it likely that she was enacting one aspect of her grandiose self—the identification with her mother—while projecting onto me the devalued aspects of herself. At the same time she was submitting to mother's efforts to destroy her chances of getting involved with a man who might care for her. Now a memory came back to me, one that had been temporarily obliterated in the previous session, regarding fears she had expressed earlier that I would try to prevent her from leaving town because of my own needs to keep an interesting patient, and my earlier interpretation that this fear represented her view of my behaving like her mother, an interpretation she had accepted.

I now said that her image of me as intellectually slow, awkward, and unattractive, "stuck" in an ugly town, was the image of herself when she felt criticized and attacked by her mother, particularly when mother didn't agree with her selection of men, and that her attitude toward me had the quiet superiority, the seeming benignity and yet subtle devaluation that she herself experienced so painfully from her mother. I added that in activating the relationship with her mother with an inversion of roles she might also be very frightened that I would be totally destroyed and that she might have to escape from the town to avoid the painful disappointment and sense of loneliness that would come with this destruction of me as a valued therapist. Ms L replied that she could recognize herself as she had felt at other times in what I was describing, and that she had been dejected after our last session. She said she felt better now and asked if I could help her make the visit of the man from San Francisco a success so that he would not depreciate her because she lived in such an unattractive place. She was reverting to a dependent relationship with me practically without transition, while projecting the haughty, derogatory aspects of herself as identified with mother onto the man from San Francisco.

Ms L illustrates a typical activation of projective identification, including the projection of an intolerable aspect of herself, the behavioral induction of the corresponding internal attitude in me, the subtle control exerted over me by her derogatory dismissal and self-assertion that kept me temporarily imprisoned in this projected aspect of herself, and her capacity for empathizing with what had been projected onto me because, at other times, it so clearly corresponded to her self representation. My countertransference reaction illustrates a complementary identification and, beyond that, my temporarily getting "stuck" in it, a position Grinberg (1979) has designated as "projective counteridentification."

My third example, Mr. M, a businessman in his early forties, presented a paranoid personality with borderline personality organization. He had a history of psychotic episodes brought on by alcohol, which required brief hospitalizations. Both at work and socially he was alternately inhibited and subject to impulsive outbursts of rage. The latter had seriously interfered with his life in both spheres. He was extremely inhibited in sexual encounters with women, was frequently impotent, and was generally suspicious and distrustful of others.

Mr. M was the oldest of several brothers born to a pharmacist who had become prominent in the social life of the small town where they lived, a powerful, irate, extremely demanding, and sadistic man who punished his children severely for the merest trivial misbehaviors. The patient's mother was completely submissive to his father, and although she professed to love her children, he said she never went out of her way to protect them from father's rages. Shy and socially withdrawn, she left the care of her children to her older single sisters, several of whom lived in the household, acted as maids and "surveillance agents" for father, and treated his children with particular severity. The patient vividly recalled puritanical attitudes about sex. He felt that his younger siblings were able to escape from what he considered the dreadful atmosphere of his home while he, as the eldest son, could not escape the constant control of his father. Against his father's wishes, he went into a large farming-equipment business but, because of his personality difficulties, never managed to advance beyond middle-level managerial positions in spite of an excellent academic background, unusually high capacities in marketing analysis, and a better education than several colleagues who had been promoted above him.

In the transference, Mr. M oscillated between intense fears and suspicions about me perceived as a sadistic father and intense idealization of me linked to homosexual impulses. His transference illustrated typical splitting mechanisms. In the course of the first two years of treatment, I interpreted to him his emotionally opposite feelings about me as the enactment of aspects of his feelings about his father, first, an unconscious identification with his mother as she submitted passively to an idealized father who would provide love and protection, and second, rage against his sadistic father. He had gradually begun to tolerate his intense ambivalence toward his father and to talk quite openly about his murderous wishes toward him. The following episode took place in the third year of treatment.

Mr. M had met a woman who worked in the large complex of psychiatric institutions with which I was associated. For the first time, he had dared to become active in pursuing a relationship with a woman he found physically attractive and who was socially and intellectually his equal. In the past he had felt safe only with prostitutes or in asexual relationships with women. Any sign of involvement with a woman he valued caused him to quickly break away, become suspicious of her intentions toward him, and fear that he might be impotent. On several occasions, Mr. M had expressed the fantasy that I would be unhappy if he became involved with anyone who worked in an institution related to the one I worked in. He expressed the suspicion that I would warn such a person against him and interfere with the developing relationship. I interpreted this as an expression of oedipal fantasies, commenting to him that, in his mind, I was the owner of all the women in the institution and that his sexual approach to them was forbidden by me as father and, in his fantasy, would be severely punished. I also linked this fantasy to his fears of impotence with a woman who would seem fully satisfactory to him.

A few days after this interpretation Mr. M came in, livid with rage. He started by saying that he felt like punching me in the face. He sat down in a chair at the greatest distance from me and asked for a full explanation. When I asked, "An explanation of what?" he grew even angrier. After some moments of mounting tension, during which I became genuinely afraid that he might strike me, he finally explained that he had spent an evening with this woman, had asked her whether she knew me, and had learned that, indeed, she did. When he then pressed her for information about me, she grew reticent and asked him "ironically," as he saw it, whether he was a patient of mine. He then confronted her with what he considered a fact—namely, that she had known all along that he was a patient of mine. She then became even more distant and ended the evening by suggesting that they had better "cool" their relationship.

Mr. M accused me of having called her, telling her all about his problems, warning her against him, and causing the end of the relationship. My attempt to connect this with my earlier interpretations of his experience of me as owner of all the women of the institutional complex and jealous guardian of my exclusive rights over them further heightened his rage. He said I was dishonestly using my interpretations to deny the facts and to put the blame on him for the breakdown of the relationship. He now focused on my dishonesty; he could tolerate my prohibitions but not dishonesty. He demanded that I confess that I had forbidden her from entering into a relationship with him.

The patient's rage was so great that I was really in a dilemma: either I acknowledged his mad construction as true or I insisted that what he was saying was false, thereby risking being physically assaulted. Earlier doubts about whether the patient's paranoid traits permitted an analytic process added to my uneasiness.

Taking a deep breath, I told Mr. M that I did not feel free to talk as openly as I wanted to because I was not sure whether he could control his feelings and not act on them. Could he assure me that, however intense his rage, he would refrain from any action that might threaten me or my belongings? He seemed taken aback by this question and asked whether I was afraid of him. I said that I certainly was concerned lest he attack me physically and felt I could not work under these conditions. He would therefore have to reassure me that our work would continue in the form of verbal discourse rather than physical action or else I would not be able to continue working with him in this session.

To my vast relief, Mr. M then smiled and said I did not need to be afraid; he just wanted me to be honest. I said that if I answered him honestly he might get very angry at me; could he assure me that he would be able to control his rage? He said he could. I then said that I knew the woman, but I had not talked with her during the entire duration of his treatment and that his assertions were a fantasy that needed to be examined analytically. He promptly became enraged with me again, but now I no longer felt afraid of him.

After listening to a repetition of his reasons for believing that I was involved in the woman's rejection of him, I interrupted him to say that I believed he was absolutely convinced that I was responsible and added that he was now in the painful position of having to decide whether I was lying to him or whether we were in a mad situation in which one of us was aware of reality and the other not, and it could not be decided which of us was where. Mr. M grew visibly more relaxed and said he believed that I was telling him the truth. He added that for some strange reason the whole issue suddenly seemed less important to him. He felt good that I had been afraid and had confessed as much to him.

A rather long silence ensued, in the course of which I sorted out my own reactions. I had a sense of relief because the patient was no longer attacking me, a feeling of shame because I had shown him my fears of being physically assaulted, and a feeling of anger because of what I perceived as his sadistic unremorseful enjoyment of my fear; I was aware of my intolerance of his pleasure in his sadistic acting out, and I also was puzzled that the whole relationship with the woman had seemed suddenly less important.

I said that a fundamental aspect of the relationship with his father had just taken place—namely, the enactment of the relationship between his sadistic father and himself as a frightened, paralyzed child, in which I had taken on the role of the frightened, paralyzed child and he the role of his father in a rage and with a secret pleasure at intimidating his son. I added that my acknowledging my fear of him had reduced his own sense of humiliation and shame at being terrorized by his father; and the fact that it was safe to express rage at me without destroying me made it possible for him to tolerate his own identification with his enraged and sadistic father. Mr. M said that perhaps he had frightened the woman because of the inquisitorial way he had asked about me and that his own suspiciousness about her attitude toward him might have contributed to driving her away.

We see here projective identification being employed at an almost psychotic level. Initially the patient used projection in attributing to me a behavior that did not resonate at all with my internal experience. Then, in attempting to force me into a false confession, he regressed from projection to projective identification, activating the relationship with his father with reversed roles. In contrast to the previous case, the violent nature of the projective identification appeared to affect the patient's reality testing significantly, and my efforts to interpret projective identification directly were futile. My acceptance of the complementary identification in my countertransference as a realistic reaction to the transference was, I believe, a less regressive phenomenon in me than the more unrealistic counteridentification mentioned in connection with Ms L. At the same time, I had to initiate my efforts at interpretation by temporarily moving away from a position of technical neutrality, establishing a condition for continuing the session that implied a restriction of the patient's behavior. Only then could I deal with the projective identification itself by first establishing a clear boundary of reality or, more specifically, by spelling out the nature of the incompatible realities that now characterized the analytic situation. I think clarifying incompatible realities as a first step in facilitating the patient's tolerance of a "psychotic nucleus" in his intrapsychic experience is an extremely helpful way to deal with such severe regressions in the transference. Moreover, establishing the boundaries of reality also reestablishes the analyst's internal freedom to deal with his countertransference reactions. This technique must be distinguished from countertransference acting out, a difference that is sometimes rather hard to detect. Countertransference acting out, rather than reducing the enactment of the regressive transference, maintains and even feeds into the projective identification.

FURTHER CONSIDERATIONS ON TECHNIQUE

As part of my approach to interpretations of projection and projective identification I see the need for the analyst to diagnose in himself the characteristics of the self or object representation projected onto him. Only then can he interpret to the patient the nature of this projected representation, the motives for the patient's intolerance of that internal experience, and the nature of the relationship between that projected representation and the one being enacted by the patient in the transference. The persecutory nature of what is projected in projective identification typically induces fears in the patient of being criticized, attacked, blamed, or omnipotently controlled by the analyst. Systematic interpretation of this secondary consequence of the interpretation of projective identification may facilitate working through over a period of time.

The analyst's intrapsychic experience when projective identification is activated may disturb or help the analytic process. The analyst's firmly maintaining technical neutrality, avoiding communicating the countertransference to the patient, and refraining from setting up parameters of technique not originally planned for this particular treatment may all facilitate his internal freedom for fantasying during the sessions with the patient, and outside the sessions as well. I have found the latter helpful in gradually clarifying and working through countertransference reactions and developing alternative hypotheses and strategies to interpret the transference under such trying conditions. For the analyst to be preoccupied with deeply regressed patients between the treatment hours may be healthy, not necessarily neurotic. In fact, I believe that a significant part of the analyst's working through of his own countertransference reactions may have to occur outside the hours.

When borderline personalities with narcissistic and paranoid features undergo a temporary psychotic regression in the transference, it may be necessary for the analyst to stop interpreting and to clarify the immediate reality of the treatment situation, including asking the patient to sit up and discuss with him in detail everything that has led to his paranoid stance, a course suggested by Rosenfeld (1978). The analyst should absorb the patient's projective identification without interpreting it for the time being, acknowledging empathy with the patient's experience without accepting responsibility for it, thus demonstrating the capacity to tolerate the patient's aggression without crumbling under it or exhibiting counteraggression, an application of Winnicott's "holding" (1960) function. The analyst should consistently interpret projective identification in an atmosphere of objectivity that provides a cognitive "containing" function—Bion's (1968) approach. Finally, the analyst should set limits to acting out that may threaten the patient or the analyst's physical integrity (if such limits are objectively required), test the extent to which reality testing is still maintained in the interaction (with the assumption that interpretation of unconscious determinants cannot proceed before a common boundary with reality has been reestablished), and analyze mutually incompatible realities.

At times, the analyst's emotional dissociation from the situation, his temporary "giving up" on the analytic experience, may provide a distancing device that detoxifies the therapeutic relationship, but at the cost of potential disruption of the treatment or a temporary or permanent going "underground" of primitive transferences; this security valve, therefore, has its risks and dangers as well as its advantages.

These various techniques are largely compatible with each other, but there are differences in emphasis. My own approach utilizes Bion's (1968) "containing" and Winnicott's (1960) "holding" functions, Rosenfeld's (1971, 1975, 1978) understanding of the nature of deeply regressive transferences in narcissistic character pathology, and the techniques I have described to clarify the reality situation before further attempting interpretation of projective identification.

I believe, however, that Bion's avoidance of the analysis of countertransference issues with severely regressed patients and his assumption that the concept of countertransference should be maintained in its restricted definition, and therefore as an indication of pathology in the therapist, discourage the analyst's openness toward the total field of countertransference reactions. Particularly in the Brazilian lectures (1974, 1975), Bion conveys both an exquisite sensitivity to regressive transferences and a puzzling lack of concern for the patient's reality situation, which may be the counterpart of his deemphasis or countertransference. I believe that concern for the patient implies commitment to him, and commitment makes the analyst vulnerable to countertransference in a broad sense. My confronting the patient with incompatible views of reality is in contrast to Rosenfeld's (1978) recommendation of temporary abandonment of a confronting and interpretive stance with paranoid regressions.

Projective identification is a basic source of information about the patient and requires active utilization of the analyst's countertransference responses in order to elaborate its interpretation in the transference.

Chapter 11 PROJECTIVE IDENTIFICATION, COUNTERTRANSFERENCE, AND HOSPITAL TREATMENT

Projective identification can play a pivotal role when it occurs within a hospital milieu. The following description of two patients suffering from very different psychiatric illnesses, both undergoing long-term inpatient treatment, illustrates some features of hospital treatment that cut across different types of psychopathology.

LUCIA

Lucia, single and in her late twenties, was an attractive, intelligent, but emotionally unstable Latin American musician who had been educated in this country and whose wealthy parents financially supported her and her artistic career. She had a history of drug and alcohol abuse, several serious suicide attempts, and interpersonal difficulties at work and in intimate relations.

Lucia was the youngest of three children, but her parents treated her as their only and major concern. Father was seductive rather than loving with Lucia, and he was basically controlled by mother, clearly the dominant personality in the family. Mother was highly emotional, extroverted, and charming, but intrusive; in subtle ways she attempted to control Lucia's life while remaining indifferent or even hostile to her at a deeper level. For example, Lucia suffered from an allergy that prevented her from eating certain types of sweets; mother knew of her allergy but periodically sent her packages of those sweets.

Lucia's diagnosis on admission was (1) severe personality

disorder with predominantly narcissistic and borderline features, (2) mixed substance and alcohol abuse, and (3) minor depressive disorder with a relatively unpredictable suicidal potential linked to severe emotional crises. Because of her failure to respond to repeated efforts in outpatient psychotherapy, long-term inpatient treatment and simultaneous psychoanalytic psychotherapy were initiated.

From the beginning, Lucia's treatment had a VIP quality because of her parents' vast wealth and social connections and because the chairman of the hospital board as well as other board members were more than ordinarily interested in it. The director of the hospital, Dr. A, was always available to the parents when they came to visit—a most unusual circumstance. Dr. A, moreover, disagreed with the diagnosis; he thought it too "harsh" and believed that Lucia was merely infantile-hysterical. Dr. A told the psychiatrist assigned to Lucia that he was being too critical of this unusual family. Dissatisfied with what he considered this psychiatrist's excessively harsh, rigid, and unsophisticated approach, Dr. A asked me, a new unit chief in the hospital, to take on Lucia's hospital management. He told me he thought I would be able to handle the case better because I had graduated from a psychoanalytic training program, and the other unit chiefs, although ambivalent about psychoanalysis, respected hospital psychiatrists who had been psychoanalytically trained.

Lucia's psychotherapist, Dr. C (whom she was seeing four times a week while I saw her on average for fifteen to twenty minutes, five times a week), preferred to continue his treatment with her completely separate from the hospital management. He too had been trained psychoanalytically and was a close personal friend of Dr. A. In our brief encounters, Dr. C treated me pleasantly, but clearly as a very senior person condescending to a recent graduate.

Both Dr. C and Dr. A were also on the faculty of an institute for postgraduate psychodynamic psychotherapy, which I will call the Institute. The theoretical orientation of the Institute was somewhat different from my traditional psychoanalytic one, so I was clearly an outsider. The hospital faculty and staff, however, considered themselves better qualified than the Institute people to handle severely ill patients in long-term inpatient treatment, and so they viewed the Institute with a degree of ambivalence. They considered the (nonhospital-based) Institute psychotherapists too soft, even naive, in dealing with severely regressed patients; in their view, such patients required firmness and a clear treatment structure. I thus became, unwittingly at first, a representative of the philosophy of the Institute as opposed to that of the hospital staff, represented by the hospital psychiatrist I was replacing.

My relationship with Lucia started out with what might be described as a therapeutic honeymoon. She quickly informed herself of my own Latin American background and told me she considered that I represented the European-influenced Latin American culture that corresponded to her own background. She persuaded me to agree that the "rigidity" of her previous hospital psychiatrist in insisting she participate in hospital activities and work was unreasonable and counterproductive. She proposed that instead of her daily schedule of activities she take correspondence courses from a local university in order to answer to her educational requirements and facilitate her progress toward an advanced degree in music.

I agreed with this course of action, saw to the arrangements, and gave the matter little further thought. Although my relations with Lucia seemed to be developing satisfactorily, casual remarks by other unit chiefs and senior hospital staff suggested that these arrangements were being viewed with some skepticism, in the belief that both Dr. C and I were being manipulated by the patient.

Several weeks later the correspondence courses had not arrived, but Lucia had long since withdrawn from most of her scheduled activities. She had elaborate explanations for the missing courses. First they had been lost in the mail; then a replacement set was not delivered because of some error in the hospital mail office; the third set was being delayed at its source. I then went to the hospital mail office to try to trace the source of the trouble and was told that a large package had indeed just been delivered to my patient.

When I confronted Lucia with the discrepancy between her assertion that she had not received the package and the information from the hospital mail office, she became very upset, accused me of not believing her, of becoming like her previous hospital psychiatrist. She explained that the package she had just received (the contents of which she said she was willing to show me) was from her mother.

Late that evening I was called at home because Lucia was in an intense panic and insisted on seeing me. I returned to the hospital, where Lucia received me dressed in a transparent and highly revealing negligee. She was obviously trying to seduce me, and although I maintained my equanimity, I was aware of an erotic element in my affective reaction. She said she simply wanted to tell me how upset she had been by my questioning her earlier in the day, but she was most grateful for my responding to her call and felt better now that I had come. She stressed how important it was to her that our relationship be a good one.

That night I dreamed that I was in Lucia's room in the hospital, but it now looked more like a hotel room, and I was sitting on the bed with her in what was obviously evolving into a sexual encounter. Suddenly, with a seductive smile, Lucia put her index finger into my mouth, probing deeply, and I awoke in a state of intense anxiety. As I lay awake thinking about the dream, it suddenly occurred to me that what she had been doing to me in the dream was, in Spanish, *meterme el dedo en la boca* ("putting her finger into my mouth"). In Chile, where I was educated, this was a popular way of saying "making a fool of somebody." Wide awake now, I thought about the comedy of errors of the correspondence courses and decided that Lucia had probably been lying to me all along.

The following day, I confronted her with my belief that she had been lying to me, whereupon she confessed that she had received the package from the university and had thrown it away. She now became enraged and accused me of rigidly insisting that she take college courses she was not at all interested in. I reminded her that she had taken the initiative regarding these courses and that I had agreed with her. I expressed my regret about her inability to tell me she was unwilling to take these courses and to discuss with me possible alternatives. Lucia, apparently oblivious to what I was saying, continued to upbraid me for pursuing the idea of a study plan instead of showing concern for her interests and vocation.

It was standard hospital policy to inform a patient's psychotherapist of important developments regarding the patient, so, after telling Lucia I was going to inform Dr. C about this issue, I promptly did so. After listening to my report, he told me that he had been aware of the problem of the correspondence courses all along but thought that I was exaggerating its importance; after all, some manipulative behavior was to be expected from this patient. My efforts to stress the gravity, as I saw it, of Lucia's unwarranted deceptiveness led to his unbending enough to add that he understood this was an extremely difficult patient and that it was very important to understand the reasons for her need to behave in this way in light of the chaotic experiences she had suffered in her childhood. Our conversation ended without a meeting of minds. I thought Dr. C was underestimating the gravity of Lucia's superego pathology and her temporary displacement onto me of an aggressive deceptiveness in the transference; he thought I was overreacting in response to a narcissistic lesion and because of lack of experience with this kind of patient.

Later that day, I received a call from Dr. A's office, and an appointment was set up for me to see him the following week. The other unit chiefs soon let me know that the call resulted from a complaint about me that Lucia had lodged with him. I now had the strange experience of suddenly becoming the hero of the day in the eyes of the other unit chiefs and senior hospital staff because I had "stood up to" Lucia's manipulative behavior. Her deceptiveness had seemed clear to them all along. I also noticed, not without apprehension, that I was now perceived as part of the hospital front against the Institute.

Dr. A received me looking very stern. He told me that Lucia had complained about my rigid, obsessive, "policeman"-like attitude regarding her studies. He made it clear that he was disappointed in me. He said he had talked with Dr. C, who saw the situation exactly as he did. Both thought she should be treated more gently. I felt defeated and paralyzed, and was almost relieved when Dr. A told me that, in agreement with Dr. C, he planned to transfer Lucia to another hospital psychiatrist.

My immediate reaction was of anger and disappointment, but once that had passed I was concerned because I believed that Lucia's "triumph" in dismissing me indirectly through manipulation of Dr. C and Dr. A had profoundly self-destructive implications. In brooding over these events I had the strong support of Clara, the head nurse of my unit, who now told me that Lucia had always been perceived as seductive toward men in authority. I realized that she had certainly exercised her seductive powers with Dr. A, as well as with me. Clara also said she had thought my treatment of Lucia showed me to be quite naive; she thought the episode might turn out to be a good learning experience for me.

Shortly after Lucia was transferred to another psychiatrist she reverted to alcohol and drug abuse and finally left the hospital. Within a year, the hospital lost all communication with her and her family.

DISCUSSION

What I called the therapeutic honeymoon with Lucia might be described, in terms of my countertransference reaction, as my concordant identification (Racker 1957; also see chap. 6) with the patient's pathological grandiose self, her characterological narcissistic structure. My countertransference probably reflected my being drawn into the role of an admiring and potentially corruptible as well as seductive father.

But when I recognized Lucia's deceptiveness with regard to the college course, my internal reaction shifted sharply to a suspicious, persecutory stance—a complementary identification with the dissociated, sadistic superego precursors against which her narcissistic defenses had been erected, while she identified with her own dissociated, humiliated, and sadistically mistreated self. And it is probable that I became a primitive, sadistic mother representation, disrupting the sexualized relation with father in violent revenge.

One might speculate that had I not been so fearful of the activation of my sexual fantasies about her, and had I at the same time become aware of her narcissistic seductiveness, I might have tolerated my sexual fantasies and become alert to her seductive behavior and the control over my independent thinking that derived from it. As it was, I had been seduced by Dr. A's assignment into a sort of alliance with the patient's narcissistic defenses, which reduced the objectivity of my stance toward her.

Later on, in the sudden reversal of my relationship with her, I automatically identified with the "anti-Institute" sentience of the hospital staff, so that my complementary identification with Lucia's internal "persecutors" coincided with my identification with a rebellious ideology in the hospital.

The shift from concordant to complementary identification in my countertransference may also be related to the sudden activation of projective identification in the patient's defensive repertoire. Lucia dealt with me deceptively over a period of weeks. Her dishonesty may be considered a "psychopathic" defense against a feared "persecutory" attack from me that reflected the projection onto me of a sadistic, persecutory object representation, most probably a preoedipal mother image. Her description of me as a rigid, obsessive policeman was devoid of sexuality and implied a highly self-centered, callous, suspicious, primitive authority figure who disrupted the sexualized relationship with male authority (father).

That the patient could project onto me a persecutory, callous, and manipulative mother while still identifying herself with such a sadistic image (reflected by her self-protective, manipulative control of me) indicates the operation of projective identification rather than projection. What seems to me of particular interest here is the bridging function of my countertransference reaction: it was a response to both the patient's enactment, by means of projective identification, of a primitive internalized object relation and the hospital milieu's enactment, by means of a powerful though subtle role-induction and/or facilitation in me, of a submission to Dr. A and the Institute as a defense against the underlying rebellion against them. In other words, the patient's pathology of internal object relations and the hospital's latent social conflicts "clicked" in my internal reaction at the boundary between the patient and the hospital system.

Of equal interest, it seems to me, is the "withdrawal reaction" that occurred in me, in the patient's attitude toward me and the hospital, and in the hospital's attitude toward the patient. When I was dismissed I felt an emotional withdrawal from both Lucia and Dr. A. The subsequent cynical, almost gleeful withdrawal from Lucia by the hospital staff as her treatment gradually fell apart (the hospital psychiatrist who replaced me carried out his functions somewhat perfunctorily, and though many staff members were aware of the patient's acting out, their information no longer reached either Dr. C or Dr. A) was the third "withdrawal reaction" in the hospital system. All these developments may be subsumed under the category of a withdrawal to protect the self-esteem of "injured parties"—in other words, a defensive narcissistic withdrawal from an intense conflict around hostility. This general withdrawal of the hospital system from the patient, which became dramatic in the last few months before Lucia finally interrupted the treatment, may also be considered to represent a symbolic corruption of the total care that the hospital ideally should have continued to provide for her.

It is as if the patient had let me "die," and the hospital staff and I let her treatment "die" in return. The hospital staff also left me alone: once my "defeat" was obvious and I was dismissed from the case, no unit chief challenged Dr. A's decision in a clinical forum or ventured to reexamine the total therapeutic handling of the case. One could say that once I had served a function for the hospital ideology I was dropped from the scene and allowed to "die."

What is perhaps more striking than anything else was the replay of Lucia's family pathology within the hospital. The family's enormous wealth had created a situation that was effectively utilized by the patient's mother to support her daughter's control over the treatment against Lucia's better interests. This development was a continuation of the family history of a teasingly seductive but unavailable father who was controlled by the mother. Dr. A's "seduction" by the patient, an implicit repetition of the relationship with her father, was destroyed by the collapse of the treatment, an implicit consequence of the patient's and her mother's destructive effects on the hospital system. The family's control over their own world had found a dramatic counterpart in their daughter's self-destructive manipulativeness. Their effective control of the hospital's world similarly bred an atmosphere of corruption and revenge, and destroyed their daughter's treatment.

Ideally, I should have been able to explore Lucia's dominant pathology of internalized object relations as it was replayed in the hospital: her failure at work, her sexual seductiveness as a corruption of those who were there to help her, the symbolic destruction of a good relationship with an oedipal father because of the destructive effects of a sadistic, internalized image of the preoedipal mother, the projection of her sadistic superego precursors onto the environment, and her secondary defenses against persecution by means of dishonesty. The pathogenic features of her childhood environment, however, were replayed in her unconscious seduction of Dr. C, Dr. A, and me, and replayed as well in the large-group process activated in the hospital milieu.

RALPH

Ralph was single, in his early twenties, and with a history from early adolescence of a severe behavior disorder characterized by truancy, rebelliousness, school failure, and violent fights with other youngsters and teachers, all of which led to his having been expelled from several schools. In late adolescence he alternated occasional violent behavior with prolonged periods of social withdrawal. He was now considered "strange," was the butt of ridicule by peers, and showed occasionally bizarre behavior and a gradually deepening isolation from all social contacts. Ralph dropped out of high school shortly before graduation, spending days and weeks mostly in his room, practicing strange rituals, which he attempted to hide from his parents. He expressed a growing preoccupation with changes he thought were occurring in his face. Eventually he developed delusional ideas of bodily transformation and auditory hallucinations, was diagnosed as presenting a schizophrenic illness, and was hospitalized in several psychiatric hospitals for periods lasting from a few weeks to several months. He had responded to repeated treatment with high doses of neuroleptics and electroshock to the extent of being able to return to home and school. At such times, however, he presented frankly antisocial behavior; he was dishonest and aggressive, and exploited and cheated fellow students and teachers; he was occasionally violent and had to be expelled from school again. He then withdrew into his own room and presented symptoms of psychosis.

By the time he was admitted to our hospital, after at least eight years of a progressively worsening illness, he carried the diagnosis of a chronic undifferentiated schizophrenic illness. Because of the striking pattern of improvement with neuroleptic treatment and the subsequent development of pronounced antisocial behavior, followed by renewed regression into psychosis, he was considered to present one of the rare cases of "pseudopsychopathic schizophrenia."

Ralph's father was a foreign businessman who had developed new methods for large-scale recycling of industrial waste. Ecologically minded legislators and former associates in his country of origin were questioning his methods, and lengthy lawsuits had resulted in his having become embittered, feeling under siege, and having to spend an inordinate amount of time and energy on legal and political rather than business matters.

Ralph's mother never emerged as a real person in the course of all the interactions of the hospital staff with the family. She rarely if ever visited her son; it was father, accompanied by a personal legal counselor, who came to the hospital and made himself available for discussion of Ralph's treatment plans. In spite of occasional visits to this country to see Ralph, several older brothers and sisters also remained shadowy and distant figures during the treatment. The father candidly expressed his feeling of hopelessness regarding Ralph's treatment; he had selected this hospital as a last resort and implied that, though he did not have much time to invest in participating in the treatment effort, he would certainly be extremely grateful if Ralph could be helped.

This case, like Lucia's, was surrounded by a VIP climate. The aura of power emanating from the father's legal and political battles and the family's enormous wealth led to all sorts of rumors and speculations.

I was assigned this patient by Dr. B, the hospital director who replaced Dr. A (who had accepted a position elsewhere) about a year after Lucia left the hospital. Dr. B was much more closely in sympathy with the "hospital" philosophy than with the "Institute" philosophy; that is, he favored an empirical, no-nonsense approach to patients and was skeptical about applying psychoanalytic understanding to hospital treatment.

He told me he thought Ralph was a very difficult patient who would surely attempt to entangle me in arguments, and he trusted that I would be able to maintain a firm structure and avoid becoming involved in such contests. Dr. B seemed friendly and outgoing and had the reputation of wanting to avoid conflicts and of bending excessively to pressures from the chairman and members of the hospital board. Whereas Dr. A had been authoritative and even authoritarian in his dealings with faculty and staff, Dr. B tried to reach consensus whenever possible. In contrast to his predecessor, however, he did not support faculty or staff when influential people from outside exerted pressures on them. I understood that, as far as Ralph was concerned, I would have all the hospital support I needed unless the treatment ran into hot VIP waters.

I first met Ralph in his room staring in the mirror, scrutinizing his face because, as he explained to me, he was concerned about pimples. He said he was using various antiseptic facial creams to deal with irregularities on the skin of his face and neck. I could not detect any abnormality on his face. The room had a slightly rancid smell, which I never ceased associating with Ralph. It was filled with containers of facial cream and boxes of facial tissues, which he used to clean his fingers as well as for spreading the cream. Used and crumpled tissues were strewn over the bed, the chairs, and the floor.

Because it was questionable whether Ralph would be able to sufficiently differentiate a psychotherapist from an administrative hospital psychiatrist, I was assigned total hospital management of the case, including psychotherapy. Clara, the head nurse, told me her staff was in conflict about how to deal with Ralph. Should his room be cleaned up and a daily routine developed that would provide him with clear tasks, boundaries, and limits—in other words, an "ego psychological" approach? Or should he be permitted to regress further, with assiduous exploration of the psychological meanings of his bizarre behaviors as a way to establish contact with him and permit the eventual resolution of his psychotic regression by psychotherapeutic means—in other words, a "Chestnut Lodge" approach? The history of limited improvement with intense neuroleptic treatment and electroshock and the fact that Ralph resorted to antisocial behavior rather than to a more adaptive nonpsychotic state weighed heavily on my mind. I decided to postpone designing treatment strategy until I learned more about him.

I must say that my first emotional reaction to Ralph was one of disgust. It was impossible for me not to react to the rancid smell, the greasy doorknobs and chairs in his room, yet I was forced to see him in his room because he refused to leave it. In one of our early sessions, while I was sitting on a (greasy) chair and he on his bed, Ralph said: "I must seem pretty disgusting to you," and I was at a loss for words in view of the accuracy of his observation. And because I was responding as a disgusted authority figure, I did not see and could not acknowledge his obvious pleasure in playing with dirt, with a messy, sticky substance, with excrement. For the same reason, I was also unable to connect his pleasure in playing with dirt and waste with his conflict over whether to submit to, identify with, or rebel against his father, the "king" of transforming industrial waste into useful products and the man accused of polluting the environment with the products of his industry.

Ralph had a terrible fear of my entering his room without his having some time to "prepare" himself. He pleaded with me to knock until he opened his door (which could take several minutes), and he always looked extremely fearful and suspicious when I entered his room. I thought he was trying to clean up the room before I came in or to disguise or conceal the indications of some strange ritual, but all my attempts to discover why he wanted me to knock so lengthily only elicited a sheepish and odd-sounding laughter that I eventually read as ironic and derogatory.

While I was attempting to assess the situation, Ralph's behavior regressed further and further; any nursing staff efforts to mobilize him generated intense rage. He was a strong man and large, and female staff members were afraid to approach him. Indeed, the prolonged "knocking on the door" ritual led me to the fantasy that one of its functions was to portray me to the nursing staff as weak and fearful. The nurses did talk about Ralph's "granting audiences" to me and to selected staff members.

My efforts to help Ralph verbalize his fantasies and fears in connection with these issues led nowhere. He talked vaguely and evasively about his face and what he saw as the disturbing intrusiveness of the nurses. Eventually I devised a treatment plan with the nursing staff that would protect Ralph's privacy in his room for certain hours of the day but would also include a minimal program of activities (walking on the grounds, participating in a simple work group for regressed schizophrenic patients) for a regularly scheduled time. His room would be cleaned as all the other hospital rooms were, except that certain drawers would be reserved for whatever he wanted to keep in them, including his creams and tissues.

The plan worked, but with unforeseen results. A special mental health worker was assigned to Ralph for the morning period of activities and another one for the afternoon. Both mental health workers were instructed to carry out similar functions—that is, to help Ralph get appropriately dressed for outdoor walks and activities and to provide him with the opportunity to discuss whatever he wished regarding his daily life in the hospital. The morning worker was a black man, the afternoon worker was white. Clara, the unit head nurse, was black, and Clara's superior, the hospital director of nursing, was a white woman. Ralph developed an immediate affinity with the white mental health worker, who impressed him (and me, initially) as a friendly, outgoing, enthusiastic man. Ralph also developed an immediate and intense hatred for the black mental health worker, who impressed me initially as friendly, outgoing, and warm, but who gradually became tense and inhibited when confronted with Ralph's verbal and eventually physical assaults.

Both Clara and I thought this was a clear case of splitting that required psychotherapeutic exploration, but the patient's complaints about the black mental health worker soon reached the office of the director of nursing, who recommended changing him for another staff worker. Clara and I strongly resisted that recommendation: I thought it would reinforce Ralph's splitting operations and increase both his regressive omnipotence and his deeper fears of the destructive affects of his aggression. The situation was further complicated by a visit from Ralph's father and the development of friendly contacts among the patient, his father, and the white mental health worker, who, according to Ralph, had offered to provide total coverage for him and agreed that the black mental health worker was not really helpful. Ralph's father spoke to Dr. B, who talked with the director of nursing, who exerted strong pressure on Clara to remove the black mental health worker from the case.

Before long, the entire nursing staff seemed to be divided along racial lines. In addition, I had for some time been critical of what I considered the coldness and distance of the director of nursing (an opinion that coincided with that of most of the other unit chiefs). She, however, had social connections with members of the board, which apparently weighed powerfully in Dr. B's general support of her. Emotionally, I became a total ally of Clara and the black staff; and now the entire social system of the hospital, in ever-widening circles, appeared to be split: authorities on one side and rebels on the other.

In my discussions with Ralph, I attempted to help him verbalize his sense of being between two worlds, a "white" world of conformity, established authority, and protection against a "black" world of rebellion, danger, and violence. I also attempted to relate this to his own internal conflict between the need to submit to his powerful father by appealing to the "highest authorities" in the hospital to protect him against the rebels and the need to rebel against his father by refusing to leave his room and polluting the room with facial creams and tissues. While his father was recycling waste, he was producing material for waste. In short, I tried to convey to him that the division of his feelings between his two mental health workers represented an effort to deal with two aspects of himself. Ralph responded by becoming more suspicious and distrustful of me; he now clearly perceived me as an enemy, while his relationship with the white mental health worker seemed to grow closer each day.

I finally had a call from Dr. B, who discussed with me his concern lest the patient's family get upset and complain directly to the chairman of the hospital board. He suggested, in a very amicable way, that Ralph was probably a hopeless case anyhow, so why not give up on it? He felt that I was functioning under enormous pressure and that my energies and knowledge could be put to better use with other cases; he asked how I would feel about a transfer. After a long discussion I conceded, acknowledging my own limitations, and in fact I felt flexible and mature in so doing and appreciative for the friendly way he was discussing the case with me.

I left Dr. B's office in a relaxed frame of mind and started for home. Suddenly, while driving, I had an intense feeling of alarm and suspiciousness; it is probably not an exaggeration to say that I became paranoid. I had the fantasy that this friendly conversation was the first step in the process of getting me out of the hospital. I suspected Dr. B of having received instructions from higher up to get rid of me. I suddenly also remembered that that very morning Ralph had asked whether I had talked with Dr. B. I now thought that, without my knowing it, Ralph had already been told that he would be transferred to another hospital psychiatrist. I decided to drive back to the hospital at once and establish the "truth" by discussing the matter with Ralph.

Ralph denied remembering having asked me whether I had talked with Dr. B. I also had a sense that the white mental health worker, who was present, was looking at me triumphantly.

That same evening, I discussed the situation with Clara, who reassured me categorically that, from all she knew through the grapevine, there was no criticism of me in the hospital. She told me point blank that I was being paranoid in thinking I might be dismissed because of the conflict around this patient. She confirmed my view that Ralph had activated the potential for racial tensions in the hospital and agreed with my assessment of Dr. B as too willing to compromise and unable to take a stand. She felt that the director of nursing must have had a strong voice in this matter.

Ralph was transferred to another hospital psychiatrist. After six more months of his treatment in our hospital, the conclusion was reached that no real progress had been achieved, and the family decided to transfer him to yet another psychiatric institution. Follow-up information several years later, provided by indirect sources, revealed that Ralph had eventually been sent to a public hospital in his country of origin, where he died accidentally during a fire that broke out there.

Discussion

Here again a strong and disruptive countertransference emerged early in my initial reaction of disgust and in my delay in analyzing its implications. In my complementary identification with Ralph's dissociated and projected self-loathing ("I must seem pretty disgusting to you") I became inhibited by his suspicious expectation of such loathing from me and by his controlling behavior aimed to make me feel guilty for my reaction of disgust. Ralph's utilization of projective identification dominated the therapeutic relationship from the start. He identified with the depreciated, persecutory, and persecuted enemies of his father while fighting off his father's terrible authority, projected onto me in the ritual of delaying opening the door to his room. Simultaneously, with his tissues and creams he was also identifying with his father's control over industrial waste. The conflict between father's (white) authority and the dangerous (black) rebels against his father's empire was replayed in his splitting of the images of the two mental health workers and the subsequent triggering of a similar conflict in the larger arena of the hospital's social system.

Again, my complementary identification in the countertransference, a consequence of the patient's projective identification, led me to identify with his "enemies" and to my alliance with (black) Clara and her supporters as against the (white) director of nursing and her supporters, which finally led to my dismissal from the treatment by the alliance of Dr. B, the director of nursing, and the patient's father.

It is of interest that, even within the extremely regressive scenario played out in this case, an oedipal constellation was activated in my allying myself with Clara against the director of nursing, the cold, distant, emotionally unavailable, yet dangerous mother figure who only much later resonated in my mind as a symbolic replica of the patient's own mysterious, distant, unavailable mother.

I believe that these events also illustrate the corruption of the hospital social system in eventually yielding to the patient's demands to get rid of his black mental health worker, in the shift of therapists, and in the efforts of the hospital director to keep things "cool," given an obvious "special patient."

In addition, these events illustrate the repetitive, dramatic reversal of the roles of victim and persecutor so typical of primitive transferences. Ralph's paranoid reaction to me for "irrupting" into his room, the defensive ritual of insisting that I knock on the door, his pathetic efforts to hide tissues and creams, were like the last-ditch protection of a fecal world threatened with destruction by the "clean and powerful." My own intense "paranoid" reaction on driving home after the interview with Dr. B illustrates my identification with the patient as a victim, my fear that my own world as a unit chief was being destroyed, my sense of being attacked and defeated.

Here again, then, the patient's projective identification activated a powerful countertransference reaction in me, a complementary identification reinforced by latent conflicts in the hospital, triggered by the patient's deeply regressive behavior. In my functions on the boundary between the patient and the social system of the hospital I unconsciously contributed to "switching on" the correspondence between intrapsychic and social pathology.

I think now that I should have quickly clarified the meanings of the patient's "disgusting" world of "industrial waste," his unconscious identification with victim and victimizer, and interpreted his efforts to split the staff as a way of externalizing the internally intolerable tension between these two sides of himself. If I had been able to identify with the patient's own pleasure in smearing the world of his powerful father, and if I had not felt so guilty over my identification with a persecutory, "disgusted" authority, I might have utilized the understanding of this primitive object relation in the transference of victim and persecutor and attempted to reduce rather than play into the split between Clara and the director of nursing. It might then have been easier to interpret gradually the patient's enjoyment of "fecal rebellion," his fear of being destroyed by father, the revengeful turning of the hospital into a fecal mess, and the identification with his father in controlling the hospital treatment.

REGRESSIVE GROUP PROCESSES IN THE HOSPITAL

The patient's behavior within the therapeutic milieu tends to induce interpersonal disturbances within the hospital staff that unconsciously reproduce, in the patient's social surround, his intrapsychic world of object relations (Main 1957). As Stanton and Schwartz (1954) masterfully described, such patient-induced disturbances in the social system of the hospital activate potential social conflicts that predate the patient's entry into that system and contribute to a circular process in which intrapsychic and social pathology reinforce each other. We have just seen the widespread effects of projective identification. Projective identification is central to the patient's induction of complementary identifications in the hospital therapist's countertransference and in triggering the interpersonal conflicts of the staff interacting with the patient and even of the entire hospital social system, with the final consequence that the therapist's countertransference is further reinforced and its acting out potential dangerously strengthened.

The second theoretical frame utilized here is a psychoanalytic open-systems-theory approach to the large-group processes activated in social organizations (see Kernberg 1976). The patient's hospital psychiatrist stands at the boundary between the patient and the hospital social system and thus is in the position of carrying out a leadership function for the patient within the hospital and for the hospital with the patient. This leadership function has, of course, a task-oriented aspect derived from the therapist's technical, professional, and administrative authority, but it also contains a primitive "shadow," a silent but powerful aspect—that of the leader of a potential regressive large group represented by the hospital milieu (Turquet 1975). A further aspect is even more subtle and ever present: playing a "leadership" role in the patient's internal scenario of pathological object relations activated and enacted in the hospital.

As the leader of these reciprocal large-group formations, the interface of which is located precisely in his emotional experience, the hospital therapist is prone to being sucked into roles that are complementary to roles enacted by the patient's self-experience and by the potential large-group processes of the hospital milieu. The patient's family pathology, projected onto his relations with the therapist and hospital staff, and the hospital staff's latent conflicts around professional, social, and ideological commitments produce a specific emotional turbulence around each patient. As the target for the patient's projective identification, the hospital therapist may be regressively tempted to enact the patient's dominant self and object representations and simultaneously become the potential leader of a regressive large group in the hospital (Kernberg 1984). The clarity or ambiguity of the hospital's administrative structure and delegation of authority, the therapist's skills and knowledge, his personality, his specific countertransferences to the patient, his relationships to professional and task groups, and their corresponding ideologies in the hospital—all contribute to a configuration that typically, and uncannily, combines to amplify the patient's intrapsychic pathology in the social system and to enact dominant conflicts in the hospital social system.

Elsewhere (1980, 1983) I have dealt with large-group processes and their diagnostic and therapeutic use in hospital treatment. Here I would like to stress the correspondence between patients' regressive ego states and regressive large-group processes in terms of the induction in all the participants of "narcissistic" and/or "paranoid" reactions. We have seen the narcissistic withdrawal syndrome of everybody involved in Lucia's treatment. We have seen the paranoid developments in Ralph's social surround. Large-group processes tend to result in a group that is self-satisfied and leans to a narcissistic leadership, or they might produce a dynamic "mob" moved by aggressive impulses toward external enemies, led by a paranoid leader (Kernberg 1983).

Perhaps most disturbing and dramatic is the corruption of moral values that typically takes place as part of the regressive processes I am describing. Freud (1921) originally described how the members of a mob project the ego ideal onto the idealized leader. The effect is to eliminate moral constraints as well as the superego-mediated functions of self-criticism and responsibility of each of the members. In large groups—that is, in groups of 30 to 150 people who can still communicate with each other (and thus are not yet a mob) but who do not have (at least momentarily) a functional leadership—the projection of superego functions onto the leader cannot, of course, develop (Turquet 1975; Kernberg 1980, pp. 219–220; Anzieu 1985).What obtains instead is a projection of primitive superego functions onto the group itself. Instead of projecting the mature superego functions of each individual member onto the group at large, the large-group members tend to project a minimal, highly conventional morality onto the group. The rigidity and lack of discriminating characteristics of this conventional morality create a generalized fear of "how others may react," while the individual members of these groups are strangely "liberated" from their ordinary, mature superego functions and tend to attempt to "get away with what they can." The combination of a diffuse conventionality and a reduced individual sense of responsibility creates the preconditions for a general corruption of the adherence to moral values within this group setting. This is the background against which the self-indulgent group ideology fostered by a narcissistic leader and the rationalization of aggression facilitated by a paranoid leader reinforce the moral corruptibility of regressive large groups.

Zinoviev (1984) described the characteristics of groups whose egalitarian ideology fosters the projection of moral authority onto the group at large and finally, to protect their egalitarianism, onto external "persecutory" authority figures. He described the prevalence, under such conditions, of careerism, selfishness, and neglect of functional tasks, the enjoyment of others' failures, a tendency to gang up against those who get ahead, a search for propitiatory victims, and a search for an authoritarian leader to mediate the threatening conflicts within the group. Such groups also show a negative attitude toward individuality, the differentiation of individuals, and courage. This description, derived from the study of the egalitarian structure of group processes in factories, schools, and other social organizations in the Soviet Union, dramatically replicates the studies of the psychology of large-group processes carried out in experimental settings by Rice (1965), Turquet (1975), and Anzieu (1984). My point is that, given the great potential for activation of superego corruption in the large group under regressive conditions, a dramatic and dangerous potential exists for the replication in the hospital's social system of patients' specific superego pathology as well.

Projective identification, then, is a powerful primitive defensive operation that may induce intense countertransference reactions in the therapist in the form of complementary identification and, simultaneously, regressive group processes in the hospital setting by directly triggering latent conflicts in the hospital's social system. The therapist's leadership functions for the large group thus activated create the condition of mutual reinforcement of the patient's pathology, the group's pathology, and the therapist's countertransference, leading under the worst circumstances to an uncanny replication within the social system of the patient's social, familial, and intrapsychic pathology. When this pathology includes significant superego deterioration, a potential corruption of the social system of the hospital may replicate and amplify the corresponding aspects of the patient's intrapsychic pathology.

Chapter 12 IDENTIFICATION AND ITS VICISSITUDES AS OBSERVED IN PSYCHOSIS

My principal aim in this chapter is to illustrate, by describing the treatment of a schizophrenic patient, the vicissitudes of psychotic identification as observed in the transference and to trace the development of a sense of identity. In this context, I shall expand on the development and functions of the mechanism of projective identification explored in previous chapters and on the nature of very regressed self-object-affect units.

Edith Jacobson's ideas (1964, 1971b) and my own previous development of these ideas (1976) constitute the theoretical frame within which I propose the following terminology.

I use *internalization* as an umbrella concept to refer to the building up of intrapsychic structures that result from both actual and fantasied interactions with significant objects under the impact of drive derivatives represented by specific affect states. The basic unit of internalization, as I see it, is dyadic, consisting of a self and an object representation in the context of a specific affect representing libidinal and/or aggressive drives. I conceive of *introjection, identification,* and *identity formation* as developmentally progressive levels of internalization.

Introjection, the most primitive of these, occurs during the symbiotic stage of development (Mahler and Furer 1968; Mahler et al. 1975), when self and object representations are not yet differentiated from each other; *identification* takes place when self and object representations have been differentiated from each other—that is, in the stage of separation-individuation. *Identity formation* refers to the more general

intrapsychic process of integration of libidinally and aggressively invested self representations into a cohesive self, in parallel to the simultaneous integration of libidinally and aggressively invested object representations into broader representations of significant objects. Ego identity is
the result of this process. It includes both a longitudinal temporal and a
cross-sectional integration of the self.

Identifications are normally partial or selective: they imply modification of the self concept under the influence of the object. At the same
time, an increase in differentiation between self and object is implied in
the discrimination among aspects of the object that are and are not incorporated. Identifications thus have progressive or growth-promoting functions.

Identification that normally takes place during development can be
contrasted with *psychotic identification,* a pathological process that
may take place at any time in the context of the development of a psychotic process. Psychotic identifications reflect a defensive regression to
aspects of the symbiotic stage of development. They are characterized by
the internalization of an object relation that is defensively re-fused, including the re-fusion of all-good self and object representations under the
dominance of real or fantasied gratification as a defense against the dread
of annihilation resulting from the parallel re-fusion of all-bad self and
object representations that reflect internalized object relations dominated by aggression.

It is important to distinguish what takes place during normal symbiosis
from the psychotic process. Normally during symbiosis, all-good fused
self-object representations result from gratifying relations with the object. Normal introjections build up fused or undifferentiated self-object
representations separately under libidinally invested and aggressively
invested relations with the object. In contrast, defensive destruction of or
escape from object relations and defensive blurring of the boundary between self and nonself with a consequent loss of reality testing are
characteristic of psychosis but not of normal symbiosis. In normal symbiosis, the infant-caregiver relationship is consolidated; in psychosis, the
re-fused self-object representation has a fantastic quality and implies a
withdrawal from object relations in reality. In essence, psychotic identification is a defense against the dread of annihilation.

In my view, psychotic identifications include two mechanisms: *psychotic introjections,* characterized by a defensive re-fusion of all-good
self and object representations that threatens the destruction of the self
as a consequence of defensive blurring between these self and object
representations (Jacobson 1964), and *projective identifications,* repre-

senting efforts to escape from an intolerable world of aggression within which self and object can no longer be differentiated. I have already suggested (chap. 10) that projective identification may constitute the means whereby a distressed infant tries to differentiate itself from the object under conditions of negative peak affects. Normal introjection, in contrast, facilitates the infant's cognitive differentiation of self from object. Extreme pleasure states establish an all-good undifferentiated self-object representation within which self and object components will then be gradually differentiated as heightened attention is drawn to these experiences; extreme unpleasure states motivate efforts to escape from and eliminate this unpleasure by placing its source "out there," creating an all-bad fused self-object representation in the process. Here again, self and object are thus gradually differentiated.

The effort during normal symbiosis to eliminate an all-bad relationship implies an effort at differentiation but also the creation of a potentially dangerous external reality, which, because it is dangerous, needs to be controlled to avoid "persecution." A potential distortion of external reality occurs here, so that primitive projective mechanisms bear some resemblance to the regressive projective processes in psychosis. In contrast, more adaptive projective mechanisms, encountered in neurotic structures, do not aim at controlling the object of projection.

Therefore, as I said in chapter 10, I designate the earliest or most primitive form of projection *projective identification* and reserve the term *projection* for more adaptive, later forms of this defense. I am using the term *projective identification* instead of *psychotic projection* because the former is more current even if the latter is perhaps more accurately descriptive. The normal early projective mechanism and those observed in both psychotic and borderline psychopathology are practically identical, justifying one term—projective identification—for both normal and pathological early projection; and the term *projection* is most frequently described with characteristics that correspond to later, more adaptive forms of the mechanism observed in neurotic disorders. In contrast, normal introjection and psychotic introjection are clinically different from each other; psychotic introjection is in fact observable only in psychosis. Therefore, I refer to introjection as the normal process and psychotic introjection as its psychotic counterpart.

As mentioned in chapter 10, I believe that projective identification is not necessarily a psychotic mechanism, unless the term *psychotic* is used as a synonym for *primitive,* an idea I reject. When projective identification occurs in patients presenting a psychotic structure, it represents a last-ditch effort to differentiate self from object, to establish a boundary between the self and the object by means of omnipotent control of the latter. Projective identification is the patient's way of trying to avoid a complete loss of self, which would result in psychosis. Without recourse to projective identification the patient would lapse into a confusional state in which he or she would no longer know whether aggression came from the inside or the outside.

In patients with borderline personality organization, whose boundaries between self and object representations and between self and external objects are well differentiated, projective identification serves different functions. Here it is the primitive dissociation or splitting of all-good from all-bad ego states that the patient attempts to maintain. In patients with borderline personality organization, projective identification weakens the ability to differentiate self from external objects by producing an "interchange of character" with the object, so that something internally intolerable now appears to be coming from the outside. That exchange between internal and external experience tends to diminish reality testing in the area of the exchange, but the patient maintains a boundary of sorts between the projected aspects and his or her self-experience.

In psychosis, psychotic identifications, including psychotic introjections and projective identification, predominate. These processes lead to delusional distortions or re-creation of external objects and pathological efforts to control them within an overall context of loss of reality testing derived from the loss of ego boundaries that results from self-object blurring. Psychotic identifications, as I said earlier, signify regression to an abnormal symbiotic phase. They bring about an obliteration of the self under the influence of psychotic introjection, and destruction of the object world under the influence of projective identification (Jacobson 1964). The ultimate cause of the activation of psychotic identifications is the upsurge of inordinate aggression, which triggers a defensive re-fusion of all-good self and object representations and activates projective identification to deal with the threatening infiltration of aggression into all internalized object relations.

As an important consequence of all these developments, there is a profound sense of loss or dispersal of identity in psychosis, a phenomenon usually obscured when the psychotic transferences are active (true merger experiences in the transference), which reflects the patient's inability to differentiate self from object representations. It is only when psychotic transferences are being resolved that the problem of loss of a sense of identity in the psychotic patient and a struggle for its recovery becomes apparent. The case description that follows illustrates some of these aspects of identification processes in psychosis, including the emergence of struggles around a sense of personal identity when the psychotic transference is being resolved.

The patient I am about to describe fulfilled what Michael Stone (1983) considers positive criteria for intensive psychotherapy with psychotic patients—namely, a capacity for relatedness, a character structure free of all but the slightest measure of antisocial features, psychological mindedness, and average to better-than-average intelligence. In addition, the fact that my initial contacts with the patient took place before her psychotic break may have been a beneficial factor in her treatment.

THE CASE OF MS N

Ms N, an attractive young woman in her early twenties, was referred by an internist she had consulted for a variety of somatic complaints for which no organic basis could be found and because she had complained of a growing sense of confusion and lack of purpose in her life. Her history disclosed no major psychopathology—her parents were caring and accepting, the mother on the controlling side (occasionally very domineering), the father more passive. Ms N had been a good student, bright, sociable, if a bit willful. After graduating from college she had performed effectively in a position that called for considerable responsibility and for working with other people. It was shortly after the marriage of one of her three younger brothers that the first signs of trouble appeared.

About two years before our initial interview, Ms N, for reasons she did not make clear to me, left her job and undertook psychotherapy with a Dr. R, who, Ms N emphasized, "rescued" her from what had become a boring and unsatisfactory profession by encouraging her to shift to painting and the decorative arts and to increase her body awareness by a special type of relaxation exercises.

Ms N referred to a number of relations with men, an area of her life she portrayed so confusingly that it was impossible for me to gain any understanding of it. She said, in response to my questions, that she had always felt very erotic, yet sexually unresponsive to men. She was interested in men but did not feel committed to them. She said she had had intense erotic feelings for Dr. R but had never been able to discuss these or any of her sexual difficulties with him. She said these feelings were why she had stopped the treatment with him and, against his advice, had decided to enter a workshop on "bodily awareness" in a distant city.

This four-month workshop, which ended a few months before her first consultation with me, created in Ms N an increasing sense of confusion. She felt that the woman in charge of the workshop was trying to break down her free will and her mind, to "grind me down to self-oblivion" so that she could "reconstruct myself again." She implied somewhat confusedly that the workshop leader, in attempting an unimaginably awful invasion of her mind, was repeating what she described as her mother's dominant, controlling, infantilizing behavior. She had never been able to tell "who was crazy," herself or her mother. The picture I had of the patient's father and her three brothers was extremely vague, but the picture of her mother as controlling was clear enough.

In ensuing interviews, she impressed me as losing contact with reality. She had used up all her money, the savings of four years, after she left her job, and she now had trouble differentiating the loss of money from the loss of her capacity to think about what was going on in her life. She felt she had difficulties in communicating her feelings to others but was unable to clarify what the problems in communication were.

She showed some anxiety and, at times, anger when talking about the manipulative behavior of others, particularly her mother. When I shared my observations about her confusing way of talking, she became more disorganized, thus demonstrating a definite lack of the capacity to understand ordinary social criteria of reality and a loss of reality testing in our interaction.

Further exploration of her sexual life led to vague comments about her being sexually excited with women as well as with men, occasionally with her mother, but an affirmation of her basically heterosexual nature. Ms N denied having hallucinations or delusions but said she had a heightened sensitivity to the environment: she could anticipate when her telephone would ring, and she was aware of people's sex, age, and occupation even if they approached her from behind. She could not explain this capacity, which puzzled and both frightened and excited her. She felt that it implied a change in her body and mental functioning that she could not account for. This change in her mental functioning was, at the same time, a major source of anxiety.

Throughout the diagnostic interviews Ms N became increasingly restless and suspicious. She saw me as a "traditional psychiatrist," not like the free, open, and "nonestablishment" Dr. R. She was afraid that I would force her into verbal communication when, in fact, she felt she needed to increase her body communication; only through the arts and workshops lay the road to psychological liberation. Before I had a chance to start treatment, Ms N decided to stop her sessions, although I had formulated to myself the diagnosis of a schizophrenic illness and stressed to her the need for further evaluation and treatment.

A few weeks later, her worried parents asked me to see her because her condition had worsened alarmingly. When I saw her again her anxiety level was high and her speech pressured. She described what seemed to me delusional thinking and hallucinatory experiences. She felt that her physical energy was blocked and at the same time expanding from her body through her neck into her head and external environment, so that she had an increased sensitivity to all stimuli to an extent she found very confusing. Her detailed description of the flow of energy in her body had a clearly delusional quality, and she presented auditory hallucinations on several occasions. She showed no marked mood fluctuations; her sensory and cognitive disturbances clearly predominated over any affective ones.

Ms N accepted my recommendation that she be hospitalized. Once the diagnostic conclusion of schizophrenic illness, undifferentiated type, had been reconfirmed, the staff decided to treat the patient with a combination of neuroleptic medication (Thiothixene, up to 40 milligrams daily), hospital milieu therapy, and psychoanalytic psychotherapy, which I would carry out. A staff psychiatrist, Dr. S, would continue to control her medication when the patient was able to move into the day hospital and would also take care of practical decisions affecting her daily life, her relations with her parents, and any other decision making that might be indicated in support of her psychotherapeutic treatment. After about six weeks, the patient was discharged to the day hospital and into a halfway house, where she stayed for about six months before moving to an outpatient status. She continued in her psychotherapy with me and weekly controls with Dr. S.

Because of the development of extrapyramidal symptoms, Thiothixene was first reduced and then changed to Thioridazine at a daily dose of 300 milligrams, which was gradually reduced over the next six months to 150 milligrams and in the following five months to 50 milligrams daily. The effect of neuroleptic medication was dramatic. In six weeks, Ms N's anxiety and agitation decreased enormously. During the final week of her hospital stay, she was no longer agitated, only moderately anxious, and though she still experienced energy flows and blockings, these thoughts had a less compelling quality, and there was a marked reduction of her experience of sensorial overstimulation and physical symptoms. Ms N responded to initial reductions of Thioridazine with increased agitation and anxiety, but later reductions did not increase anxiety or restlessness. To the contrary, the patient was pleased because she no longer had a feeling of muscular rigidity or mental "dullness," which she attributed to the medication.

The First Year of Psychoanalytic Psychotherapy

During the first month of treatment, Ms N was hospitalized in an acute treatment unit. The content of our sessions was filled with her references to the energy flow from her body through her spine into her head and out into space, "blockings" of these energy transfers, and various somatic symptoms she attributed to these blockings. I considered these statements to represent her sense of loss of boundaries between her self and external reality. There was an atmosphere of intense erotization of these references to energy floating throughout her body, expressed in a seductive attitude and with exhibitionistic display of her body, while she simultaneously manifested intense anxiety and agitation. Any questions I raised about what was so frightening about these experiences immediately shifted Ms N's attention to the female nursing staff, whom she accused of being sadistic and controlling. She bitterly complained that I had betrayed her trust in me by hospitalizing her in this prison run by women torturers.

My initial efforts to clarify her fears that her body energy might dissipate and get out of control intensified her agitation. She implied that by trying to induce her to tolerate her energy flow and energy loss I was attempting a sexual seduction that would deliver her into the hands of the nursing staff as a punishment for illicit sexual relations with me. She denied having sexual feelings for me and clearly implied that any questions about her sexual feelings reflected a sexually seductive assault by me. I thought that I represented a sexually seductive father, attempting to disguise his wish to rape his daughter by accusing her of sexual advances toward him to an enraged and punishing mother (represented by the nurses). But when I tried to share this idea with Ms N, her agitation, denial, and terror increased. I was trying to drive her crazy and deliver her to the nurses by talking about sex. I think this episode illustrates the temporarily disorganizing effects of an interpretive approach to the activation of projective identification.

At the same time, any efforts to question whether her concerns about energy transfer in her body might be imaginary also led to increased anxiety, agitation, and rage. In other words, the patient could not tolerate my pointing to any differences between her views and mine—that is, any threat to the re-fusion of her "good" images of herself and me in her remaining area of trust and reliance on me. And so I decided to sit back and listen, adopting the stance of a neutral and benign observer. Now Ms N occasionally produced a warm smile and expressed her appreciation of my presence. Such fragmentary moments, however, were quickly followed by a resumption of pressured speech and the description of energy flows. Ms N also presented auditory hallucinations, macropsia, and micropsia.

Both the intensity of her erotic behavior and her rage and suspicion decreased, and she became verbally more coherent.

Ms N, having now entered the day hospital and moved into a halfway house, was able to come to my office for her sessions, much of which she spent vigorously complaining about the mistreatment she had suffered from the nurses and Dr. S, her hospital physician. These complaints gradually crystallized in a description of the hospital as a sadistic institution for control and repression. She said she was deeply disappointed in me for having delivered her into the hands of that mindless team of nurses and doctors.

I thought she was now expressing her fears and rage toward a combined sadistic father-mother image in more reality-couched terms and referring more directly to realistic aspects of her parents as she had perceived them. At the same time, she was attempting to preserve her relationship with me by portraying me as the relatively innocent, misguided victim of the parental ideology that was replicated by my medical background and training. When I attempted to express these thoughts to her, telling her that she was trying to maintain a good relationship with me by dissociating me from the rest of the staff of the hospital, thus avoiding a frightening perception of me as possessing the features of both her parents, Ms N became more anxious but did not seem to become more confused. For the first time, she seemed able to tolerate an interpretive approach without immediate regression into confused thinking. In fact, there were moments when she smiled as if acknowledging that my not dissociating myself from the rest of the hospital team implied an act of honesty on my part.

Ms N now started to talk about her previous therapist, Dr. R, describing how he had stimulated her to move into the world of art and to express herself physically, how free and open he was regarding sexual matters, encouraging her to have affairs with men without being so bound by traditional moral constraints. When I tried to connect what she was saying with her fear that I would seduce her and deliver her to the nursing staff, and when I reminded her that she had previously said she had never discussed sexual problems with Dr. R, Ms N grew agitated and disorganized and angrily accused me of trying to smear Dr. R. She indicated, in short, that she had to deny this aspect of her relationship with Dr. R and had to maintain the split between her paranoid reaction to me and her idealization of him in order to avoid a psychotic sense of confusion. She was afraid of losing control of her dangerous sexual impulses toward both of us as father images.

A curiously confusing and confused series of sessions evolved over a period of two months. The patient focused endlessly on how she was dealing with her daily life and denied any aspect of her internal life of fantasy. She accused me of trying to "rehabilitate," "reeducate," "resocialize" her. At the same time she was actually making what seemed to me to be intelligent use of the efforts on the part of the day hospital and her hospital psychiatrist to help her adapt to the life of the local community.

I tried to clarify that, though I was in agreement with these immediate arrangements, this did not imply that I had any long-range master plan for her and what she wanted to do with her life. But Ms N angrily accused me of being dishonest. Why, she asked suspiciously, could I not acknowledge openly that these were my own ideals?

I eventually concluded that the real issue was tangential to this manifest theme: the patient's concern was that she had no way of protecting herself against *any* plan about her life suggested by Dr. S, the day hospital staff, or myself, because we controlled her thinking completely. It became evident that Ms N could not separate her own thinking from mine. Thus she felt that if I appeared to be arguing with her in the session, my anger would contaminate her mind with anger, we would both be engaged in battle, and she would no longer be able to differentiate herself from me. The patient was now able to verbalize her sense that any sexual feelings toward me would immediately activate similar feelings in me and lead to a destructive orgy.

Ms N's fear of confusing herself with me first became apparent to me when, provoked by her into a minor argument about the philosophy of her daily life, I found myself in such confusion about who was saying what that I was unable to clarify even to myself, after the session, what we had been talking about. One might say that, in response to her psychotic identification with me and the related blurring of the boundaries between her self representation and her representation of me, a concordant identification with her in my countertransference induced in me a corresponding temporary loss of differentiation between her and myself. Any effort to maintain empathy with the subjective experiences she was conveying led me immediately into a sense of confusion and to paralysis of my own thinking.

I now discovered that Ms N felt compelled to follow to the letter whatever "instructions for healthy living" Dr. S (in reality) or I (in her fantasy) might give her. Such instructions confused her and made her feel as if she had no identity of her own. She experienced herself as an automaton, a behavior machine controlled by Dr. S's and my will; she was projecting her decision-making process onto us and at the same time experiencing us and herself as a single psychic unit. I believe these developments illustrate the mechanism of psychotic introjection, which, together with projective identification, characterizes psychotic identifications.

Once I became aware that the patient's central fear in the sessions was of her mind being invaded by my thoughts and wishes, I was able to spell out these fears. Ms N immediately confirmed that that was exactly what she was afraid of. She also made it clear that she found it reassuring when I pointed to differences between how she perceived me in the sessions and how I perceived myself. The issue was not to convince each other but to acknowledge our differences in perceiving reality. Further exploration of these issues led to moments when indeed Ms N repeated something I had previously said as if she herself had said it and also attributed to me statements that she had made. The confusion between herself and me as a consequence of pervasive introjective and projective processes was dramatically evident in the hours; her major task seemed to have become to disentangle her thinking from that of Dr. S and myself.

At the same time, there was a marked diminution in the erotic atmosphere in the sessions and a sudden suppression of all sexual behavior and fantasies. Ms N now came dressed in an inappropriate, childlike fashion, giving an impression of asexuality, in stark contrast to her previous presentation. She also seemed to have adopted a sense of indifference toward herself, as if she were merely going through the motions of "adjusting" to external life. Only at occasional moments did she suddenly fix me with an intense gaze that I experienced as sexually seductive, but in a fashion so dissociated from the rest of our interactions that it was gone before I had a chance to think about it clearly.

After about six months Ms N left the day hospital and the halfway house and moved into an apartment, and her life in the outer world assumed aspects of normality. She found herself a position suitable to her capacities, but in her hours with me a marked change occurred. I can best describe what took place as a process of emptying out. She spoke monotonously, without conviction or depth, about the superficial relations she was establishing at work and in her social life. All intensely aggressive, sexual, or dependent feelings seemed to have become unavailable. She not only looked sleepy but sometimes seemed almost to fall asleep during the sessions. Yet, from the information provided by Dr. S, and from what Ms N said about herself, she seemed perfectly awake in her daily interactions with others.

And I, too, found myself sleepy in the hours, to a degree I had never before experienced. What I think was taking place was a reactive withdrawal on my part. Because these sessions were punctured by brief moments when Ms N looked at me intensely in an eroticized fashion, I commented that she was withdrawing from any contact with me to avoid the emergence of sexual feelings that would create the danger of sexual response from me and a frightening emergence of her fears of being sexually attacked by a father figure. I thought my own sleepiness was partly a defense against intense oedipal feelings in the countertransference and, by concordant identification, a reflection of the patient's defensive withdrawal from sexual impulses crystallized in a stereotyped oedipal form.

She immediately talked about her fear that, had she experienced and expressed sexual feelings toward Dr. R, her former psychotherapist, he would have responded sexually and created the experience in her of having sex with her father. This surprisingly direct response to my interpretations, however, was immediately submerged in what might be called a sea of sleepy meaninglessness and left no traces in the sessions of the following days and weeks. I therefore focused on the emptiness itself. When Ms N once asked me if I was falling asleep, I told her I had to struggle to keep awake, and I wondered if this could be related to her own experience of having to struggle against falling asleep in the hour. She readily acknowledged her struggle to keep awake and said it was easier to fall asleep than to face the sense of complete emptiness in our encounter. I agreed with her that the hours felt empty, and I wondered whether it came from her trying to tell me that she felt totally lost and abandoned in a confusing landscape of infinite and veiled spaces. In fact, as I spoke, I had a very concrete image of an endless surface of ice and a pervasive fogginess. Ms N accepted that image as corresponding to her own experience, and both of us abruptly became wide awake as we spoke.

This incident initiated a period of exploring her sense of living from one emotional reaction to another without any sense of continuity, any sense that she was really a person living these experiences. I believe her sense of having no wishes, no initiative, illustrates the loss of a sense of self, of ego identity. She could look at herself and describe what she was experiencing at any particular moment, but she felt that there was no central person in her putting all of this together. I acknowledged my understanding of what she was saying and added that it was as if, inside of her, there was nobody taking care of her, concerned for her, so that she was living, as it were, in an artificial state of calm that was hiding the fact that the natural caretaker had abandoned the field of her inner life. And she could not even feel anxious about that. Ms N said she felt I understood. Both of us were henceforth able to tolerate that experience without having to escape into sleepy withdrawal.

I think this stage of her treatment illustrates what might be considered the loss of identity in psychosis, a condition usually masked by the dominance of primitive part object relations in the transference. The empty space of identity diffusion is populated, so to speak, with psychotic fusion experiences. In other words, psychotic identifications mask the painful absence of an integrated self experience. Ms N could now articulate very fully her sense that she was no longer worried about herself, that she did not know what she wanted, that she had no wishes, no initiative, and that she was not even able to worry about the absence of these functions which she remembered having experienced in the past. When I said that it was as if she had been left alone by herself and by me, during these times when I seemed to become sleepy, Ms N said she was no longer worried over the similarity between her experience and mine, which I took to mean that she was less afraid of confusion between herself and me. I acknowledged that and said this also meant that she was beginning to be able to tolerate her own internal confusion. At the same time, I added, in experiencing herself as safely different from me, she was also feeling very much alone.

Following that session the patient brought in a newspaper article about "the laying on of hands," adding something about the influences of radiations that originated in the body. I suggested that she was testing to see whether I could accept her own past experiences of energy flowing from her body, thus indicating that I could tolerate her "crazy" experiences. Ms N laughingly acknowledged that it would please her if I also became confused about what was scientific reality and what was "crazy."

A repetitive sequence of events now followed, which eventually became predictable. Sessions in which Ms N felt I understood her sense of isolation and drifting were followed by sessions in which she would dare to talk briefly about her fears of discussing sexual matters, fears that would rapidly escalate into fantasies about seducing me sexually and the conviction that I would respond to such seductiveness with a sexual attack. This set of experiences was followed by intense anxiety and a sense of confusion on Ms N's part about the extent to which these were her fantasies or mine. These sessions in turn were followed by "empty" sessions in which she again appeared aloof and distant, emotionally unavailable, and I sensed the lack of any meaningful material emerging. The cycle repeated itself over three months, with the patient becoming increasingly aware of the cyclical nature of the process.

She then returned to an earlier theme, accusing me of being too square and conventional, disapproving of her wishes and fantasies of a free and promiscuous sexual life, and so forth. A replay of her earliest relationship to me seemed to be taking place at a more reality-oriented, less disorganized level. But now I could interpret these wishes to escape and her image of me as a defense against her frightening fantasies of sexual involvement with me as her father. Such interpretations were no longer followed by gross disorganization in the hours.

I understood Ms N's accusations as serving to establish a boundary between us, a "mental skin," so to speak. They were also a residue of her confusion of herself with me, a working through of her psychotic identifications.

Discussion

In the course of psychoanalytic treatment, when the analyst communicates to the patient his observations not only about the patient's behavior but also regarding the patient's self-awareness, the boundaries of that self-awareness expand, incorporating the perceptions communicated by the analyst. The patient's self representations also become more sophisticated, absorbing into the self concept the self-reflecting aspects that were the analyst's focus of attention and were incorporated by the patient in identification with him.

I suggest that the self always includes two layers, or rather, what might be visualized as a central sphere of self representations and a surrounding sphere of self-reflectiveness derived from identification with the observing and concerned mother in the original dyadic relationship when self and object representations are differentiated from each other. One might also describe this dual nature of the self as a grouping of functions of self representations, one group centering on self differentiation, the other on retaining the observing functions of the parental images internalized into the self.

What is missing in psychosis as a consequence of lack of differentiation between self and object representations is not only reality testing but also the capacity for self-awareness normally derived from the early identification with the differentiated object. My patient illustrated this state of affairs dramatically when, in spite of the fading away of her primitive, affectively charged internalized object relations in the transference, her lack of differentiation of self and object representations was so clearly shown by her confusion between her own and my thinking. At the same time, she had a sense of being completely alone and abandoned, with no concern for herself or any central awareness of herself as a person.

Ordinarily, the intense activation of primitive object relations in psychotic transferences totally occupies the field of analytic exploration, with the lack of an integrated concept of the self remaining in the background. But when there is a relative lull in the activation of intense primitive affect states, as occurred with Ms N when she was under intense medication during the early stage of treatment, the underlying structural characteristics of the failure to differentiate self and object and the painful loss of a sense of identity represented by the absence of the "surrounding sphere" of self-reflectiveness may become dramatically apparent.

I would now add that the patient's struggle with her painful sense of confusion and of being controlled by sadistic parental authorities, and her seduction fantasies regarding the paternal image, left her with two alternatives. She could either increase her sense of confusion by a total fragmentation of all intrapsychic experiences or, by withdrawing from the emotional situation into a total psychological isolation, be condemned to face her sense of loss of an integrated view of herself, of what might be called the "self-holding" function of ego identity: the normal identification with a parental or maternal attitude toward one's own self, which is part of the double-layered self structure I have described.

Patients with borderline personality organization also lack an integrated concept of the self, the syndrome of identity diffusion. With them, however, this syndrome serves the defensive function of avoiding the destruction by aggressively invested internalized object relations of libidinally invested ones. The self-reflective function of ego identity is also missing in borderline patients, not because they do not have the capacity for self-reflection but because of the defensive splitting of contradictory aspects of self-reflectiveness as well as contradictory aspects of self representations in a narrow sense. In each of the mutually dissociated ego states of borderline patients there exists a capacity for some self-reflectiveness. The interpretation of their splitting mechanisms permits borderline patients to integrate self-reflectiveness as the first phase of an integration of the self concept.

The borderline patient, as a result of interpretation, may become aware of the contradictory aspects of his experience, behavior, or thinking and painfully face his conflicts around ambivalence. The psychotic patient, in contrast, does not have the capacity for self-reflection. The confusion between self and object representations masks the lack of a self-reflective function. If and when the patient begins to tolerate the notion of differentiation between himself and the therapist, the sense of aloneness and the absence of a sense of concern for himself may emerge. This loneliness differs from the loneliness that reflects the depressive experience of abandonment or a guilt-determined sense of loss of the relation with good internal and external objects. Depressive loneliness emerges only with further integration of part-object into total object relations, a later phase in the psychoanalytic therapy of psychotic patients characterized by integration of all-good and all-bad internalized object relations.

The first psychotherapeutic task with severely regressed psychotic patients, particularly schizophrenic patients who have lost the capacity for ordinary verbal communication, require protective treatment in a hospital setting, and have only the most tenuous grip on reality, is to establish significant contact. In Searles's (1961) terms, the therapist facilitates the transformation of "out-of-contact" states into primitive transferences at whatever level of regression, within which primitive defensive operations—particularly projective identification, psychotic introjection, omnipotent control, extreme forms of splitting or fragmentation, and denial—are predominant. These primitive transferences at a symbiotic level involve a full display of the patient's psychotic identifications.

The patient's capacity to gradually experience intense all-aggressive, all-sexualized, or all-ecstatic emotional states may signal development of the capacity for symbiotic transferences within which self and object representations cannot be differentiated but which are differentiated from each other in terms of their dominant affect. Splitting now permits the dissociation of mutually opposite affect states and their corresponding undifferentiated object relations. Under these conditions, the capacity for self-reflectiveness is still absent, the "surrounding sphere" of the self-structure is totally unavailable, and the "central sphere" of fragmented self representations is not yet differentiated from the corresponding object representations. Here, in short, problems of identity are still irrelevant.

At a second stage of treatment of psychotic patients, or with psychotic patients who come into treatment with intense primitive transferences under the influence of mutually dissociated aggressive and primitively idealized object relations, the principal task is to gradually increase the patient's tolerance of fusion and confusion and then to contribute to differentiating his self experience from that of the analyst. In other words, the patient gradually has to become aware that, in contrast to his confusion of the experience of what comes from him and what comes from the therapist, he and the therapist have different experiences, so that they may live in incompatible realities. The patient has to learn to tolerate exploring this incompatibility without having to resolve it. This tolerance leads to the acceptance of separateness from the therapist and facilitates the development of self-reflectiveness.

Later on, defensive withdrawal protects the patient from dangerous fusion experiences but also, at the same time, from full awareness of the absence of an integrated sense of being a person in his own right. Now the interpretive work may proceed simultaneously to increase the patient's tolerance of fusion experiences, analyze the nature of these fusion experiences, and, at moments of beginning consolidation, analyze the patient's fear and avoidance of the sense of disintegrated aloneness. This is the stage of the treatment that prevailed with Ms N.

In advanced stages of the treatment of psychotic patients, once the capacity for reality testing has been restored, a beginning internalization of the concern and the observing function of the therapist consolidates nuclei of self-reflectiveness and thus creates the possibility of eventually interpreting the functions of defensive splitting of self-awareness against the tolerance of ambivalence. This technical approach is related to Winnicott's (1960) conception of "holding" in the transference, although Winnicott did not differentiate the psychopathology of psychosis from that of borderline conditions.

Now the analyst carries out a holding function, not only in the sense of resisting the patient's aggression without being destroyed, of assuring the patient of his continuing existence and availability, and of being available as a potential good object on whom the patient can depend. He also becomes an agent whose interpretations link the islands of self-reflectiveness in the patient's mind and permit the consolidation, through identification with the analyst in this function, of the patient's self-awareness simultaneously with integration of the dissociated self representations under contradictory affective experiences. This phase frequently causes the patient to experience intense depressive loneliness.

The integration of all self representations longitudinally (throughout time) and cross-sectionally into a central, comprehensive concept of the self is matched by a parallel integration of a surrounding sphere of self-reflectiveness that provides a background of ongoing self-evaluation. This surrounding sphere of self-reflectiveness merges temporarily with the central self in conscious action in concrete areas; it submerges itself, one might say, under conditions of nonself-reflective consciousness, but remains as a potential "split in the ego" in a descriptive sense. In other words, self-evaluation may become a preconscious structure of the ego, which carries out a supraordinate ego function, the self-observing function of the ego (Freud 1933; Sterba 1934).

Unconscious roots in the repressed id as well as in the repressed aspects of the superego codetermine the functions of the double sphere of the self at all times. Self-observation may be taken for granted in the neurotic personality organization; self-reflectiveness, thus considered, is a precondition for, but not equivalent to, emotional introspection or insight. Neurotic defenses (such as rationalization, intellectualization, and negation) may reduce emotional introspection even in patients with solid ego identity and excellent reality testing. Self-observation is always a crucial focus of the interpretive work with borderline personality organization, where defensive dissociation of the self represents a major ongoing resistance. The absence of self-reflectiveness and of the corresponding internalization of a self-concerned agency derived from the originally symbiotic, dyadic relationship may become a basic concern in some stage of the psychoanalytic psychotherapy of psychotic patients, as illustrated in the case reported here.

Chapter 13 VICISSITUDES OF AND PLEASURE IN HATRED

In this chapter I explore the clinical manifestations of pleasure in experiencing and expressing primitive hatred, with particular emphasis on the secondary defenses against hatred in the transference.

In my experience, primitive hatred may be differentiated from the affect of rage in the transference by its relatively stable, enduring, and characterologically anchored qualities (chap. 2). Regardless of its origin and the concrete unconscious fantasies it encompasses, the most impressive characteristic of such hatred, as Bion (1970) has pointed out, is the patient's intolerance of reality.

A strange process occurs in the patient dominated by primitive hatred: a common defense against awareness of such hatred is the destruction, by means of acting out, projective identification, and even, at times, a fragmentation of cognitive processes, of the patient's capacity to be aware of it: the patient's mind can no longer "contain" the awareness of a dominant emotion. Thus the defense is at the same time an expression of the impulse against which it is directed. Intolerance of reality becomes hatred of psychic reality directed against the self and against the hated object.

Hatred against the self shows directly in self-destructive impulses, such as self-mutilating or suicidal behavior, or in masochistic perversions. Intolerance of psychic reality also brings about a self-directed attack on the patient's cognitive functions, so that the patient is no longer able to use ordinary means of reasoning or to listen to such reasoning from the therapist. Under the sway of intense hatred, the patient may present the combination of focused curiosity, arrogance, and the pseudostupidity described by Bion (1957). In essence, the patient attempts to destroy the means of communication between himself and the therapist to erase awareness of his own hatred. In addition, intolerance of the object is reflected in the patient's intense fear and hatred of the analyst, who is perceived as a persecutor. This leads to paranoid developments in the transference, which may go so far as to result in transference psychosis, with what amounts to a desperate display on the part of the patient of projective identification. By means of this defense, the patient attempts to locate his aggression in the therapist by provocative behaviors that reinforce the projection, omnipotent control, and intolerance for any interpretations from the analyst.

The intolerance of the therapist as a good object, evidenced in periods when paranoid mechanisms are not in effect and the therapist is perceived as a potentially good object, is reflected in the patient's inordinate greed, the voracity with which he solicits the therapist's attention, time, and interpretive comments, and a concomitant, unconscious destruction of what is received: whatever the therapist contributes the patient experiences as inadequate; the greed continues.

A major question is, why is the patient unable to tolerate awareness of the intensity of his rage? Why does he have to deny the pervasive, constant, overwhelming quality of his hatred? I believe this intolerance is the expression of the deepest fears of losing the love object, originally the good mother threatened by the destructiveness of the patient's hatred. But the patient is immediately, as the result of his intolerance of his hatred, threatened by the fantasy of his own destruction as a consequence of pathological projective mechanisms that transform the frustrating and hated object (the bad mother) into a powerful, dangerous enemy who might well annihilate the patient. The fantasied threat of annihilation, of bodily and mental destruction, is the immediate source of attempts to fight off both the influence of the object and the awareness of the self under the impact of hatred.

The therapist's own hatred in the countertransference, a product of the patient's projective identification and omnipotent control or, more concretely, the natural consequence of the patient's consistently provocative behavior, his active destruction of meaning and of everything he receives in the therapeutic relationship, may generate in the therapist a wish to cut through the madness that invades the sessions, to free himself from endless entanglement in trivial bones of contention that seem to drown all opportunities for the patient's learning in the hours, and to escape from this destructive relationship.

To what extent is the patient's intolerance of reality of self and other and the concomitant destruction of the communicative process a defense against, rather than a direct expression of, primitive hatred? I believe that what is typically being defended against under such conditions is the patient's direct experience of hatred as an affect, the derivative affect states of gleeful, sadistic enjoyment of the destruction of the object, and the enjoyment of disgust, contempt, cruelty, and humiliation expressed toward the object. If and when the patient can tolerate the conscious experience of sadistic pleasure in the transference, a first step in the containment of hatred has been achieved. At this point, the patient is characteristically less afraid of the destructive effects of his aggression; his need to project aggression diminishes, and therefore his perception of the therapist as a bad object diminishes. The patient may now begin to be dimly aware that the object of his love and of his hatred is one.

Hatred exists in a dialectic relation with love. Hatred implies an intense involvement with an object of past or potential love, an object that at some time was deeply needed. Hatred is, first of all, hatred of the frustrating object, but at the same time it is also hatred of the loved and needed object from whom love was expected and from whom frustration is unavoidable. In its origins, hatred is the consequence of the incapacity to eliminate frustration through rage, and it goes beyond rage in a lasting need to eliminate the object.

But hatred also has a differentiating aspect; if love is associated with attempts at fusion or merger, hatred attempts to differentiate the self from the object. Insofar as hatred cannot be tolerated and is projected outside the self, it contributes to differentiating self from object and counteracts the urge to merge. Hatred may thus contribute to differentiation, the experience and testing of personal strength, self-affirmation, and autonomy; hatred may evolve into serving the sublimatory functions of aggression as healthy self-affirmation. It is only at the most primitive level of rage itself—the original source of hatred—that maximum intensity of rage (a peak affect) is experienced as fusion with the object.

Primitive hatred at a sustained intense level, however, creates a circular reaction that not only perpetuates but pathologically increases hatred itself. By projective mechanisms, particularly projective identification, rage at the frustrating object brings about distortion of the object, and the frustration is now interpreted as a willful attack. This sense of being attacked by a formerly needed and loved object is the most primitive experience of love betrayed and produces potent resonances throughout the entire sequence of preoedipal and oedipal stages of development.

The experience of love betrayed further increases hatred, with even greater amplification of hatred through projective identification; now the object is perceived as cruel and sadistic. The internalization of this distorted object relation perpetuates the experience of an enraged, humiliated, debased self and a cruel, sadistic, contemptuous object; the corresponding derivative ego and superego identifications bring about a general distortion of internalized object relations. The identification with the aggressive, triumphant object in this dyadic relation in turn triggers cruelty and contempt in the expression of hatred toward the object when the intolerable, debased concept of the self can be projected onto it, and, in identifying with the object, aggression toward the self as well.

Now the state described a few moments ago has been reached: hatred is destroying external and internal object relations; the defensive process of destroying the perceiving self to eliminate both pain and dangerous hatred is a major force in the patient's defensive organization. Projective identification may be replaced by an exacerbation of splitting mechanisms, leading to fragmentation of affective experience and of cognitive processes as well, a development Bion (1959) described. A lesser intensity of splitting may preserve a divided world of idealized and persecutory objects, and of an idealized and a bad self, with alternating behavior patterns clinically reflected in chaotic object relations, in destructive and self-destructive acting out, alternating with defensively idealized relations with objects.

A CASE VIGNETTE

To illustrate some of the vicissitudes of primitive aggression and pleasurable hatred in the transference in the course of a psychoanalytic psychotherapy, I introduce Mr. X, a foreign-born but American-educated man in his early thirties with a history of serious suicide attempts over an eight-year period. He would overdose on multiple drugs, some of them prescribed for antidepressive and anxiolytic purposes, some obtained by illegal means. These suicide attempts frequently ended up with the patient in a coma for two or three days; they had disrupted several psychotherapeutic efforts in the past. The psychotherapist who referred him to me ended his treatment after three years because of Mr. X's tendency to telephone him at all hours of the day or night, and particularly over weekends. During the sessions, Mr. X was mostly silent, proclaiming an inability to speak, but he felt free to talk to this therapist on the telephone outside treatment sessions, with desperate demands for attention.

The patient was diagnosed as presenting a borderline personality organization with a predominantly narcissistic personality and infantile and antisocial traits. During the diagnostic interviews, he oscillated between

an amiable, childlike, almost ingratiating manner and occasionally suspicious, pouting, distrustful behavior. He was highly intelligent, with a
particular interest in music, but had failed in college because of irregular-
ity in his patterns of work. His suicide attempts clearly developed at
times when his family, women friends, therapists, or teachers would not
accede to his pleas for special treatment. In spite of good surface relations
with others, he had gradually isolated himself because of his school failure, a drifting life-style, and the discouraging effects on everybody around
him of his suicide attempts accompanied by guilt-evoking maneuvers.

In the treatment, I first set up a formal structure aimed at blocking any
secondary gain of his suicide attempts; I made it very clear that I would
see him regularly twice a week, but that if he was suicidal, he would have
to go to a psychiatric emergency room or, if he had already swallowed
drugs, to a medical emergency room. I would be available to him once he
had been cleared psychiatrically and was ready to resume outpatient
treatment. I also made it clear to him and to his family that, in my view,
he presented an unavoidable risk of suicide. Because of this risk, I had
decided to involve the family in the treatment planning. The only alternative to the proposed treatment arrangements was long-term hospitalization, but, I told them, I doubted that long-term hospitalization would
be of help in his case, given the possibility of secondary gain derived from
a passive, even parasitic existence within such a setting. I also offered to
discuss with him fully his suicidal tendencies in the hours if and when he
was able to do this rather than act on his impulses. I made it clear to the
patient that if he called me before losing consciousness in the middle of a
suicide attempt, I would do all I could to save his life but would then end
my treatment with him and refer him to somebody else: this situation
would indicate that the treatment as planned was unfeasible.

The patient finally accepted these arrangements, but not before several
sessions of expressing his rage in reaction to the conditions I had given.
His parents, in contrast, accepted the proposed arrangements with remarkable ease. Once the treatment had started, the patient's silences in
the hours were so prolonged that he spoke barely a few sentences in the
first twenty sessions. I interpreted his silence as an expression of his fear
to directly vent his rage because I was not willing to agree to various
arrangements he had suggested regarding our sessions and, of course,
because of my conditions regarding his suicide attempts. The patient
finally began to talk, but, significantly, only at times when he was enraged with me. He had early asserted that he was unable to talk freely in
the hours. Now I could point out to him that he was able to talk freely if it
was under the sign of hatred, but not at moments of relaxed and open

communication in the course of which both of us might be able to learn more about his difficulties.

The patient then developed a new pattern of behavior. He would ironically mimic my statements in the hours, enter into arguments around relatively trivial matters, and then refuse to leave at the end of the sessions, claiming that he had important issues to discuss with me. Shortly thereafter I noticed that the patient would waste endless time on small issues and bring up what seemed to be pressing life problems only in the last few minutes, and then refuse to leave my office on time.

Mr. X also began to call me at all hours. I made it clear that I would be available to him at any time in case of an emergency, but if we did not agree that it was indeed an emergency, I would tell him that the call was unwarranted; and if an unwarranted call was followed by another one, I would not answer any telephone calls from him for a week. I further said that should this pattern then recur, I would not be available to him for telephone calls for a month; should it recur further, I would take no telephone calls for a year; he would thereby run the risk of the possibility of dying because he would not be able to reach me in case of a real life-threatening emergency.

This additional structuring effectively eliminated the telephone calls, and, after approximately one year of treatment, the patient was able to leave the sessions more or less on time and not telephone between the hours. Above all, from the beginning of treatment he made no further suicide attempts. They were replaced, however, by intense rage attacks in the sessions.

So far, I have been stressing the savage nature of the patient's acting out of aggression and the need to structure the treatment in order to control it. The provision of structure in this case tended to locate the patient's aggression and the defenses against it in the sessions. My overall treatment strategy focused on the analysis of the severely self-destructive impulses as they became concentrated in the sessions.

My first interpretations dealt with the patient's incapacity to talk to me in the sessions except when he was enraged. I interpreted this as the effect of an internal enemy agency that was interfering with his efforts to be helped by me, forbidding him to enter into any relationship with me except a destructive one. Because of his "righteous indignation" at every aspect of my relationship with him in which he thought that I was being dishonest, manipulative, or indifferent (he expressed these accusations very frequently), I interpreted the agency in his mind that was opposing a good relationship between us as pseudomoralistic. I said that this agency was pretending to be morally righteous when, in fact, it was a completely corrupt agency that would distort reality in order to justify angry outbursts and undermine his desperate needs to communicate with me regarding problems of real importance in his life. These problems included his difficulties in his studies of music and in relationships with women.

My descriptions of this internal enemy agency became more and more precise as the patient's patterns revealed additional information regarding the "enemy." It was, I pointed out to him, as if the internal enemy interfering with his capacity to communicate with me also made him feel strong and powerful, morally superior to me, as if it were instructing him to be enraged with me until I was willing to apologize for my shortcomings. It was like a primitive, sadistic, caricaturized version of a schoolmaster or a harsh, tyrannical parent who enjoyed the control and humiliation of a rebellious child. I suggested that the patient was enacting the role of that tyrannical parent and placing me in the role of the misbehaving, rebellious child, roles that he rapidly reversed at the end of the sessions: at that time, acting as if I were unfairly throwing him out, the patient experienced himself as a helpless, tyrannized, impotently rebellious child, while I became the harsh, cruel, sadistic tyrant parent.

Repeated interpretations of this object relation in the transference led the patient to discuss, in the brief moments available to talk calmly about issues other than his rage with me, his stepmother, whom he described, not surprisingly, exactly as I had described the internal enemy agent with which he tended to identify in long segments of the sessions.

It was thus that I learned that in the patient's early childhood his stepmother had brutally punished him for any minor rebelliousness, had beaten him so severely that he was ashamed of undressing for the beach. I learned that the stepmother, when annoyed, refused to speak to the patient for several weeks, expecting not only apologies but the right kind of apologies. The patient's father, a rather shy professor of foreign languages, frequently urged him to apologize to his stepmother even if, she was wrong, "for the sake of peace in the house."

I now began to interpret that this internal enemy was indeed his stepmother as the patient perceived her, and that, for reasons still unclear, the patient felt obliged to repeat his relationship with her, with constant role reversals, in his relationship with me. Interestingly enough, these disclosures brought about brief moments of introspective thoughtfulness and more information about his past, followed by savage attacks on me. I concluded that he was presenting a primitive type of negative therapeutic reaction in that he needed to destroy what he was receiving from me precisely when he felt that I had helped him. In other words, his most intense resentment of me came after moments in which he experienced me as a good object.

At the same time, he started to talk more freely about conflicts in his external life, and I discovered in him an intense sense of entitlement and greediness. For example, his aunt had promised him a desk for his birthday, the patient asked for authorization to buy it himself, and, with that authorization, he bought an extremely expensive desk, many hundreds of dollars more expensive than his aunt had authorized. When his aunt called this to his attention, the patient went into the most violent rage he had experienced for many months.

He also resumed his music studies and constantly attempted to obtain particular privileges for himself—dispensation from the work that had to be done by all the other students. He reacted with rage and despair when his attempts failed. He also complained more and more strongly about his total incapacity for studying or rehearsing precisely at crucial moments before final tests. These were times when he had to absorb a significant amount of technical material, and as it soon turned out, he bitterly resented having to make this effort; he wanted to master everything at once without effort. To make an effort to absorb what others had acquired and knew well was an insult.

In the second year of his treatment, new elements appeared. Mr. X seemed to be very curious about what I was thinking, listened with great interest to everything I said, but followed it with immediate dismissal or a simple "I don't see that at all," which meant that the subject was now closed. Efforts to draw his attention to this automatic discarding of everything coming from me and the strange contradiction between this behavior and his intense curiosity about everything I had to say led him again into immediate intense rage. He haughtily rejected my comments as "sheer stupidity" or ironically repeated what I had said, with sufficient distortion to justify his opinion of my contributions as worthless. Attempting to pinpoint the source of his rage, I finally discovered that it was the self-confidence with which I spoke, my calmly interpreting his silences when, as far as he was concerned, nothing was going on during those silences. On several occasions he made fun of what I had to say, suggesting that I was merely spinning new theories for future publication.

Mr. X reminded me of Bion's (1957) description of the combination of curiosity, arrogance, and pseudostupidity characteristic of patients who cannot tolerate acknowledging their intense greed and envy. In fact, his attempts to learn everything that was on my mind were extremely greedy, and he manifested intense envy and resentment of my contributions, dismissing them categorically, except for any statement in which I fully "agreed" with his assertions of justified indignation.

My efforts to point to this greediness or to analyze his defenses against envy of me proved useless at this point; in fact they provoked intense rage attacks without the possibility of further exploration. In contrast, my persistent interpretation of the repetition in the transference of his internal relationship with his stepmother slowly took effect. The patient first tried to deny that what was going on between us had anything to do with his relation to his stepmother, but his denial was relatively feeble and ineffective.

At one point, the patient said that my personality really was like his stepmother's. I invited him to explore with me my personality as he perceived it, as a new edition of his stepmother in the treatment. He responded with intense anxiety, obviously disturbed by my willingness to carry his stepmother's personality, as if afraid that he would no longer be able to differentiate his stepmother from me. At the same time, his own assertion that I was different from his stepmother forced him to consider the possibility that his rageful attacks on me might not be justified. He was thus confronted with the inappropriateness of his rage at me. I pointed out this dilemma to him, particularly his fear of acknowledging the pleasurable aspects of his destructive behavior in the sessions, knowing that he could count on my availability, my lack of vengefulness, and with the frail hope that I might help him extricate himself from the control of the image of his stepmother operating from within him.

The patient now began to experience more direct enjoyment of his destructive behavior toward me. He started to call me "F" in the sessions; my middle initial, he asserted, should stand for "fucker," an intended insult he used in connection with arrogant and depreciative comments related to my incompetence, as, for example, "You really are an asshole, F." This way of addressing me obviously gave him pleasure. The patient also would sit at places other than the chair on which he was expected to sit, in a playfully aggressive way that could easily shift into rage when he thought I was going to interfere. Several times he opened the session by sitting in my chair, forcing me to sit elsewhere, and giving a mocking imitation of me in action.

It would be easy to conclude that I am describing the playful behavior of a child teasingly trying to assure himself of his parents' tolerance, availability, understanding, and patience. But this behavior occurred particularly when he was faced with urgent problems in his external life. He manifested unmistakable pleasure in his efforts to exercise control and eliminate envy, in that nothing could be expected from me anyhow; this pleasure was in sharp contrast to his sense at the end of the sessions of humiliation, of being expelled, and his greedy wish for more time that was no longer available.

I began to point out to him the relation between his enjoyable attacks on

me, which I called violent destruction of his own time and, by implication, of what he might receive from me, on the one hand, and the inordinate voracity in his demands for more time to replace what had been
wasted, on the other. But if I attempted to point to this destruction of
time in the middle of hours when he seemed to enjoy making fun of me,
he immediately became enraged. Retrospectively, I realized that I was
prematurely interpreting the defensive aspects of his pleasurable mocking of me: after all, I had been trying to help him become conscious of his
sadistic pleasure, and now, when he dared to enact it, I was interpreting
its function in destroying time in the sessions. When I passively went
along with his behavior, describing what he was doing but without pointing to its destructive implications, the patient adopted a childlike, derogatory, but tolerant attitude toward me; at the end of the hour, however,
his bitter disappointment at feeling thrown out seemed unavoidable.
During the sessions, he manifested an amiability that struck me as artificial but tended to induce in me temporarily a pseudofriendly attitude
toward him as well.

I now attempted to interpret this pseudofriendly relationship with me
as representing a tolerant bystander who, however, was not moving a
finger to get him out of his predicament. As I explored, over a period of
time, the implications of this object relation enactment in the transference, it gradually emerged that this was an enactment of the relationship
with his father. He was in fact provoking me to act spinelessly to avoid
conflicts, as his father had done in the past. This again led to the patient's
rageful denial that what was going on in the session had anything to do
with his past. On the basis of past experience, however, I remained convinced that this was exactly what was going on, and that his rageful
devaluation of my interpretation reflected the envious destruction of
what he was receiving from me. Yet I felt that his increased tolerance of
his open enjoyment of destructive behavior in the hours reflected an
unmasking of aggression that had previously presented itself under the
guise of righteous indignation. At the same time, I thought, he was still
under the sway of major, unacknowledged primitive aggression acted out
as envious destruction of what he was receiving from me.

I should add that I met with the parents once every year, together with
the patient, to renegotiate our basic contract. In our meeting after two
and a half years of treatment, the parents told me that the patient had
changed significantly, that his intense rage attacks and chronic difficulties with various family members had markedly abated, and that they
were pleased that he was working as a musician, was able to pay for part of
his treatment, and, above all, was no longer attempting suicide.

I have offered this vignette to illustrate the expression of primitive aggression in the transference, first in violent forms of acting out, later in direct attacks on the therapist and everything coming from him in the hours, and, most important, on the very process of communication, particularly on the patient's own thought processes. In structural terms, this relationship involved the relation between an aggressively infiltrated grandiose self and the depreciated and devalued aspect of the patient's normal self.

In the course of the treatment, the initial dissociation between violent aggression and self-aggression, on the one hand, and surface friendliness, on the other, was gradually overcome. There was a recovery of aggressive affects in the sessions including the cognitive, affective, psychomotor, and communicative aspects of aggressive affect reflected in hatred, with a gradual emergence of its previously dissociated pleasurable quality. My work consisted mainly in interpreting his defenses against aggression and the functions of its direct expression in the context of gradual deepening primitive object relations in the transference. The joyful destructiveness of aggressive affects is most difficult to tolerate and integrate and must gradually be worked through in order to bring about the ascendance of the ambivalent relationships of later stages of development.

Chapter **14** PSYCHOPATHIC, PARANOID, AND DEPRESSIVE TRANSFERENCES

The superego pathology so frequently found in borderline patients becomes an important issue in the treatment strategy with these patients, particularly in dealing with the transferences that evolve as a result and expression of this superego pathology.

PSYCHOPATHIC TRANSFERENCES

Of high priority in the treatment of borderline patients is evidence of the patient's conscious, deliberate deceptiveness in communicating with the therapist, so that he will be misled in assessing the patient's emotional state and reality. This deceptiveness may assume the form of suppressing information, outright lying, or engaging in manipulative behavior aimed at disorienting the therapist or exploiting him in some way.

It is striking how difficult it is for therapists to acknowledge to themselves and to their patients that the patients are treating them deceptively. Typically, a patient who manifests deceptive behaviors also projects such tendencies onto the therapist. In fact, the patient's conviction that his therapist is dishonest is the most salient aspect of the transference in many of these cases; further, the more dishonest the patient, the more dishonest he believes his therapist to be. In some cases, verbal communication is vitiated to such an extent that it becomes a mockery of ordinary psychotherapeutic communication.

I have coined the term *psychopathic transference* to refer to periods in the treatment when deceptiveness and its projection prevail. In my view, it is essential to explore such transferences in great detail and to resolve them interpretively before proceeding with other material. For the psychoanalyst accustomed to patients in ordinary psychoanalytic treatment or psychoanalytic psychotherapy, this may seem in defiance of the open-endedness of the therapeutic process. In practice, however, these psychopathic transferences tend to infiltrate and corrupt the entire psychotherapeutic process and are a major reason for stalemates and failure. Treating a patient psychotherapeutically requires straightforward and full communication between patient and therapist, and it is for this technical reason, to open the field of communication—and not for any "moralistic" one—that the therapist has to address the problem of resolving these psychopathic transferences.

The relationship between the patient's antisocial behavior and the dominance of psychopathic transference is complex. No strict correlation exists between antisocial behavior and psychopathic transferences. In fact, a small group of patients who present antisocial behavior out of an unconscious sense of guilt may not present a borderline personality organization at all but a neurotic personality organization; they do not present psychopathic transferences and are perfectly suitable candidates for standard psychoanalytic treatment.

A central aspect of the therapeutic approach to psychopathic transferences is to confront the patient tactfully but directly with his deceptiveness. This confrontation may bring about an immediate angry attack from the patient, who may accuse the therapist of aggression or dishonesty. By means of projective identification and omnipotent control, the patient may try unconsciously to provoke the therapist to deceptive or dishonest behavior, or at least to inconsistencies in his behavior that the patient may then interpret as dishonesty.

In many cases, patients have intrapsychic conflicts between a desire for honesty and a corruption of this desire in another part of themselves, usually reflecting unconscious identification with a parental image perceived as profoundly inconsistent or dishonest. In patients with narcissistic personality disorder, the enactment of a sadistically infiltrated, pathologically grandiose self that operates against the healthy, dependent part of the patient's self constitutes a frequent dynamic underlying psychopathic transferences.

In some patients, a stubborn and silent protracted tendency to lying may defy the therapist's efforts to explore the reasons for this deceptiveness. Others may insist, over an extended period of time, that there are issues they will not discuss with the therapist. This honesty in communicating their unwillingness to participate in the treatment may permit the analysis over an extended period of time of the reasons for their fearfulness and distrust.

In somewhat different yet related cases, the communication seems to be open, except that the patient treats everybody else with total ruthlessness and lack of consideration, expects the psychotherapist to treat him the same way, and acts as if an honest mutual commitment between two people could not exist. Here, the patient's assumption is that any closeness or commitment is deceptive and that the therapist, by pretending to be interested—beyond any financial, scientific, or prestigious benefits he may gain from the patient—is really being dishonest. This may be an unconscious dynamic or a consciously experienced fear.

What these cases have in common is pervasive corruption of ordinary human intimacy, dependency, emotional commitment, and love. Typically, following the exploration of the origins of these psychopathic transferences and their effects on the therapeutic relationship, they tend to shift, after a time, into a different transference disposition. The patient gradually begins to understand that complete openness may be necessary for psychotherapeutic work to proceed but that this exposes him to the danger of rejection, criticism, and attack, as he sees it, from the therapist. The patient's projecting his own deceptiveness onto the therapist gradually or suddenly transforms a psychopathic transference into a paranoid one. The patient who treats all other people as "objects" typically fears that the abandonment of that protective distance from the therapist will endanger his security. The therapist, he believes, must hate him for this attitude, or else treat him as an "object" who is now defenseless.

Clinical Examples

Mr. T, a nineteen-year-old high school dropout, was brought to treatment by his father, a businessman, who had threatened the patient with withdrawal of all support if he did not enter treatment. Mr. T had shown violent, rebellious behavior from early adolescence on, had been expelled from various schools because of his aggressive, confrontational behavior toward teachers and peers alike, had been abusing alcohol, marijuana, and various other drugs in recent years, and had become involved with the law because of drug dealing at his local high school. He was sexually promiscuous but also tended to establish childlike, dependent relationships with some girls, who were able to manipulate this otherwise self-assertive individual in a surprisingly effective way.

The patient's older brother and sister were successful married professionals and maintained only distant contact with their parents. They agreed that the parents were extremely dominating and yet indifferent to their children, and they criticized their father's overwhelming efforts to control the patient as well as the basically uninvolved attitude of their mother. In joint interviews with the parents and the patient, father's sense that he must be absolutely in control and mother's wishes not to be bothered were evident. The parents concurred only in their desire to prevent their youngest child from having further problems with the law and help him become an independent and responsible citizen.

In the course of his psychiatric evaluation, Mr. T evinced a narcissistic personality functioning on an overt borderline level; ego-syntonic aggression expressed in his domineering, violent, confrontational actions; antisocial behavior represented by lying and manipulativeness at school and at home; a paranoid stance in relationships with all "outsiders"—that is, those who were not part of a small group of peers jointly involved in drug dealing; and what amounted to a parasitic dependency on wealthy parents. He showed, in short, the characteristics typical of the syndrome of malignant narcissism.

In his three-sessions-per-week psychoanalytic psychotherapy with me—a treatment he accepted under pressure from his parents and as a condition for their continuing financial support—he presented himself at first with a bonhomie that impressed me as false, a tendency to fill the sessions with trivial information about his daily life, and a total blackout regarding his relationships with his male and female friends. I had made it clear to the parents as well as to the patient that I was willing to try this psychotherapy but that, given Mr. T's lack of motivation and the nature of his difficulties, I was not certain I would be able to help him at this time; if I concluded that the treatment was not viable, I would so inform all of them and be available to counsel them regarding alternative treatment.

After several weeks of desultory psychotherapy sessions, I shared with the patient my impression that he was consciously suppressing the most important aspects of his daily life. Mr. T, in indignant denial, accused me of having a "policeman's" attitude similar to his father's. I explored with him his fantasy that I saw my task as extracting the truth from him and delivering him to his father's wrath. The patient challengingly said that if I learned about criminal behavior he was involved in, I would probably share what I had learned with his parents or even the authorities. I told him that if I concluded that he was potentially damaging to himself or others I would indeed take measures to protect him or others, but only if and when it appeared, in discussions in the sessions, that he was not able to control such behaviors himself. In any case, I added, I would certainly inform him about my thoughts and any action I might plan to take.

This led Mr. T to announce triumphantly that he had unmasked me as an ally of his father. Now ensued a series of discussions in which I attempted to clarify several issues. I stressed that my purpose was to help him understand the nature of his difficulties and, I hoped, to achieve more effective ways of pursuing his life goals: Mr. T had said that he wanted to go to college and that he was interested in more satisfactory relationships with girls. At the same time, I added, he would always be free to accept or reject what I said, even to the extent that, although his parents had apparently forced him into treatment, it was in his hands to end it. I also said that he automatically tended to attribute to me many of his father's judgments and attitudes, accusations that had no basis in reality.

The patient interrupted me loudly and angrily, with the implication that, in attempting to differentiate my relationship with him from his father's, I was lying. I asked him whether he really believed that I was lying and he flatly said yes. I told him I believed him and that we should examine why I would have to lie to him, a subject he was not at first willing to explore further.

When Mr. T once challenged me to admit that I was lying to him, I told him that as far as I could tell I was not lying, but that he had only my word to go on and evidently could not trust that. I reminded him of my conviction that he was not talking about the most important aspects of his life and was being deceptive by omission, and said that we were both convinced that the other person was lying. I added that I could understand that he might be lying, because of his profound suspiciousness and distrust of me, but why should I be lying to him? What was in it for me?

The patient smiled as if he had won a battle, implying that we were both crooks; it seemed to me that he no longer felt threatened by what he viewed as my "district attorney's" attitude. In a much more relaxed fashion, he told me that everybody lied and that the closer people were to somebody who had power over them, the more they lied. Even his father lied unashamedly to businessmen more powerful than he was or to the patient's mother, to hide his sexual activities. I, father's hired hand, was there to carry out father's designs on the patient.

During the next several weeks the focus was on my motivation for being Mr. T's psychiatrist, his view of me as a totally corrupt agent of his father, and the consequent impossibility for him to obtain any real benefit from our sessions. He repeatedly figured out how much of his own time, in addition to his father's money, was wasted on this imposed treatment. I shared with him my sense that he was being more honest now in expressing both his suspicion and his devaluation of me, and I noted how stressed and on guard he must feel all the time having to deal with either controlled underlings—as he saw me—or more powerful crooks than himself—as he would see others. I also wondered how, if everybody was a crook, there could be any satisfaction in a relationship with a woman other than a purely sexual one; I added that I was not surprised that, as I knew from the information he had provided during his evaluation, he was not able to sustain any relationship with a girlfriend. I also said that, if there is no honest science or profession, and college is simply a ticket to power, his reluctance to dedicate himself to studying was only natural.

A short time later Mr. T arrived at a session clearly in a state of intoxication. He was giggling, euphoric, and somnolent, telling me how great he was feeling and that it was much easier to tolerate what he called "this bullshit" while being "high." I said he seemed less afraid to acknowledge to me his use of drugs and the loss of control over his daily life in connection with drug abuse, and I wondered whether he had come by car. He assured me that he was not driving in such a condition, and he thought my question was stupid. Then, as he seemed to be falling asleep, I suggested that we end the session for that day because no further work could be done.

In the following session I explored with him his growing openness by means of action, implying that he was less afraid of me, but, at the same time, his assumption that I was rather foolish to tolerate this behavior. In effect, the patient confirmed that he was much less afraid of me and that he thought I was rather stupid and not really dangerous. I suggested that, while his fear might diminish under these circumstances, the pointlessness of the sessions must also increase in his mind. If I was not even dangerous—that is, if I had no power—and was stupid to boot, there was nothing to be expected from me. If he really needed help, hope might be evaporating. Mr. T then explained to me that one can't trust the powerful and that the weak can't help, but that one has to talk to somebody! Without giving me time to recover from that sudden acknowledgment of a human need, he went on to tell me about how he felt mistreated by his current girl, who was dropping him for one of his closest friends.

For the first time, he supplied some information about his chaotic world of what amounted to an informal gang of youngsters from his own socioeconomic level dedicated to a drifting, purposeless daily existence. I was able to point out to him how naively he had ignored this girl's behavior, which should have alerted him to what amounted to her exploitation of him. I expressed my surprise that with so many girls surrounding him he should have become infatuated with one who was so clearly manipulative.

Two changes now took place simultaneously. On the one hand, he began to talk openly to me about his daily life, problems with his studies and with his parents; on the other, he became very demanding. He was enraged if I kept him waiting for a session and for giving him what he considered insufficient time (that is, he refused to leave at the stipulated time) and demanded for rather flimsy reasons that I change his hours.

I told him it seemed to me that he was testing my honesty, reliability, and strength all in one and treating me no longer as an "innocent fool" but rather as a powerful potential exploiter. In effect, the patient agreed that I was "playing the innocent," that I had gotten all that information from him, and that I was all for myself and not interested in him. He now felt that I was ruthlessly attempting to dominate him, that I disliked and even hated him, and that I was trampling on his sensitivity about time. If he needed me, I would exploit him.

The transference had shifted from a psychopathic into a paranoid frame.

A twenty-seven-year-old woman had been referred by her internist for the treatment of chronic anxiety and hypochondriacal concerns. Unbeknown to the internist, she worked as a call girl with a select upper- and upper-middle-class clientele constituted mostly of businessmen.

During her early childhood, Ms Q's father, a chronic alcoholic, after many extramarital affairs abandoned Ms Q's mother altogether. He had maintained only occasional contact with Ms Q through the years, and neither he nor she had seemed interested in any further contact for the last decade. The patient had always experienced difficulties with her mother in her childhood. Mother worked hard to maintain her four children and increasingly relied on the patient, the oldest, to help her, which the patient bitterly resented. Conflicts with mother finally led to Ms Q's leaving home after graduation from high school. She moved across the country to New York, where, after various jobs that included modeling for sex-oriented magazines, she finally established herself independently as a prostitute.

She lived in what she described as a rather elegant apartment and spent most of her free time alone, very suspicious of being exploited or betrayed by other women. She had become pregnant shortly after arriving in town, decided to have the baby, and brought her daughter up until she felt that rearing a child would interfere with her work. Ms Q had sent her daughter away at age five to relatives in another city, to whom she regularly sent remittances for the child's upkeep. She also frequently visited the child, who was now nine years old. Her love for her daughter seemed sincere and consistent; the girl seemed to be the only person in her life she cared for and felt responsible for. She had years ago broken off all contact with her mother and her sisters and brother; the only other relationships that seemed of some significance to her were with a few of her clients. Two of them had proposed establishing a stable and exclusive relationship with her, which she had refused.

Clinically, she impressed me as presenting a combination of narcissistic and infantile characteristics. She was strikingly attractive, discreetly and elegantly dressed. She was proud of having acquired, over the years, tastes and manners that permitted her to accompany men to parties and official functions without embarrassing them or herself. At the same time, she impressed me as cold and aloof; there was something almost asexual in her demeanor. Although her way of supporting herself raised in my mind the question of antisocial tendencies, she seemed remarkably straightforward and honest with me, as far as I could tell, regarding all information about her life and activities.

She insisted on a businesslike, nonexploitative relationship with her clients. She seemed proud of the fact that all interactions were guided by money and that everybody got exactly what they paid for. She gave a history of promiscuous sexual behavior from early adolescence on, in the context of bitter fights with her mother, who was helplessly attempting to control her. No other information indicated that she was dishonest or deceptive. She was afraid of becoming addicted to anxiolytic medication and wanted to have psychological treatment because she had been told that her symptoms most probably had a psychological origin.

Although her motivation for treatment seemed adequate, she showed a remarkable lack of emotional introspection and a concreteness in her observations about herself and the people who had been important in her life, which at first defied my efforts to gain further understanding about her current unconscious conflicts. Her surface friendliness masked an underlying aloofness that, at first, made the sessions with her difficult for me to tolerate. I decided to see her in psychoanalytic psychotherapy for two sessions per week and to deal with my ethical dilemma (being paid from income derived from her activities as a prostitute) later on. After several months of psychotherapy, because of her marked narcissistic personality structure and the absence of contraindications for psychoanalytic treatment, I decided to shift the treatment to psychoanalysis proper, four sessions a week.

After several months, the dominant theme in the sessions was the patient's efforts to satisfy two of her clients who were, as she saw it, making inordinate demands of her. I gained the impression that her very openness and concreteness together with her marked aloofness, in addition to her sexual availability, attracted these men to her.

My early efforts to interpret Ms Q's "parading" her men before me as an assertion of her independence and a protection from becoming emotionally involved with me led nowhere. I was unable to detect any development in the transference, except her consistent emotional unavailability. At one point, however, I was struck by her saying that she had recently told one of her clients that she really loved him and that he was the only man in her life, and, only a few days later, had told exactly the same thing to another man.

This was the first time I was aware of having observed her lying, and I expressed my surprise. She responded that she had not been lying at all, that she meant what she said in both instances. She was completely honest, she said, and if these men extrapolated from her statement that her feeling would last forever, that was their problem.

She said this in such a natural way, obviously not attempting to be provocative, that I found it hard to respond without sounding moralistic. I asked her whether she did not believe that, in relationships between men and women, some more stable feelings might evolve, so that a statement such as "You are the man of my life" would be assumed to have the meaning of a commitment. Ms Q smiled in a derogatory way and said that this was certainly true in the movies but not in real life. She added that she believed that all relationships were nothing but commercial transactions, and that was fine with her.

Over the next few weeks, pointing out the contradiction between that statement and her commitment to her daughter, I attempted to point out the defensive nature of her denial of emotional relationships. Ms Q then talked about men's sexual promiscuity, their incapacity to maintain any relationship—which led her directly from her relationship with her current customers to memories of her father. She insisted, in this context, that she was not angry at or resentful of her father, that she had no feelings for him whatsoever, and that she enjoyed the company of both of the men who were trying to extend their relationship with her. These two men, she went on, were married, of course, and were simply trying to enrich their lives by having a paid mistress in another city. But, she said, fortunately she was not one of these stupid women who really need sex and protection mixed into one, and she was able to keep her head clear and avoid falling into emotional traps.

It was then that I introduced the subject of her coldness and aloofness in our sessions. She treated me, I said, as if this were another commercial arrangement: she was paying me in the hope that I would fulfill her need to get rid of her symptoms while watching herself lest she get trapped in an emotional relationship, which, for some reason, she saw as dangerous. Ms Q said that of course this was a commercial transaction; she commented that she appreciated my objective, businesslike attitude and added that she had no doubt that, under other circumstances, she would have no difficulty in seducing me sexually.

I asked her what she meant, and she said that for all my talk about emotional commitment, she could get me to go to bed with her; she knew that I was married, but she was convinced that I was no different from any other man. She added that she knew, or rather assumed, that I would not go to bed with her while she was my patient because I would not want to threaten my professional standing by so doing. However, if she were to try to pick me up at a certain elegant hotel in town, she was totally certain she would be successful.

I then suggested that we explore the implication of such a fantasied success: what would it say about me if, not knowing her otherwise, I were tempted to go to bed with her in the course of such an encounter? She first refused to explore this matter further, declaring it to be a ridiculous "mind game." She went on to say that it gave her a sense of power to know that she could seduce any man she wanted, including me. But she also disliked the idea that I could be seduced. As she developed her fantasies of what all this implied about me, she became angry and upset for the first time in her treatment.

She was angry because I would be unfaithful to my wife, and, by implication, I would have destroyed her confidence in my being "different." She corrected herself, saying that this was absurd because, given the premise of the situation, I would be just an unknown to her, but she was upset anyhow. I said that she impressed me at this point as being both moralistic (to go to bed with any woman other than my wife would make me a worthless, dishonest person) and afraid to confess to herself and to me that she had developed an ideal image of me as a man who would not have sex as part of a commercial transaction but only as a commitment to a love relationship. I added that her usual indifference and aloofness protected her against both the moralistic attitude about sex and a secret hope of the integration of sex and love, and that she was trying to depict me in her mind as a male robot, to avoid her hatred of me as an immoral man and her love for me as an ideal man for whom sex was not only a commercial transaction.

In the following weeks several developments took place simultaneously or in rapid alternation. The patient felt annoyed at my having called her moralistic and said that, to the contrary, she always suspected *me* of being moralistic, critical of her because she was a call girl. Eventually, it became clear that my alleged moralistic attitude reflected the projection, in the transference, of her guilt-raising, "puritanical" mother. She also said that of course I defended men's feeling that they had the right to have sex with many women because that was very convenient, but that I would certainly not tolerate my wife's going to bed with other men. She also was angry with me because she felt I was manipulating and controlling her. She wondered whether I explored all these issues because I wanted to involve her with me emotionally as a "sick form of sexual seduction," and she contrasted me with the straightforwardness of the two men she was involved with.

Ms Q illustrates the transformation of a narcissistic aloofness and uninvolvement in the transference into a transitorily psychopathic transference ("everybody is trying to get the most out of everybody else, and feelings don't count"). In analyzing the psychopathic transference, paranoid transferences emerged in the context of her hatred of the promiscuous, betraying father and her unconscious identification with and projection of a resentful, moralistic, prohibitive mother.

At a later stage in Ms Q's treatment, mourning processes emerged over the loss of a potentially good relationship with a man in her late adolescence together with intense feelings of gratitude toward me mixed with resentment of my relationship with my wife and envy of her, developments I shall not explore further here.

In this case the patient assumed that any closeness or commitment is deceptive and that the therapist, in pretending to be interested, is really dishonest. It can be argued that this is an ordinary narcissistic transference rather than psychopathic. But the pervasiveness and diffuseness of the conviction that all human transactions are "commercial" and that no commitments exist throughout time made this a psychopathic transference. It is true, however, that, in contrast to Mr. T, Ms Q was never deceptive in her interactions with me.

In general, patients with severe narcissistic character pathology may manifest another type of transference in addition to the psychopathic, a type I call *perverse*. This type of transference is characterized by the patient's gleefully transforming love into hatred, trust into corruption, and whatever he perceives in the therapist as good or potentially helpful into something bad and damaging. The perverse transference contains both libidinal and aggressive elements in which love has been corrupted by hatred. In contrast, in the psychopathic transference, dishonesty and deceptiveness are an essential defense against the upsurge of a paranoid transference, with less intrinsic pleasure linked to the destructiveness in the transference.

Both psychopathic and perverse transferences tend to shift into paranoid transferences in the course of their analytic resolution. While narcissistic transferences in general also may shift into paranoid transferences, the transference developments of many narcissistic patients without antisocial elements, ego-syntonic aggression, or paranoid personality features may evolve directly into depressive transferences during the resolution of narcissistic resistances (depressive transferences will be described further on).

In terms of technique, even with patients whose psychopathic transferences do not dominate, it is helpful for the analyst to be alert when the patient appears to be suppressing important information or hesitant to discuss an issue that has emerged in the session. There are times when the analyst may have a vague sense that the patient is not fully sharing what is on his mind. I am not referring here to the ordinary inhibitions in the flow of free association, or to extended silences, or to the analyst's assumption that there is a specific secret or area of his experience that the patient is reluctant to bring up. I am referring to the analyst's continuing sense that important issues in the patient's mind or life, issues that are centrally related to the treatment situation, are consciously being withheld.

When faced with such situations, I have found it helpful, often simply on the basis of long-term developments in my own countertransference reactions, to share with the patient my sense that he is not being fully candid with me. I may say something like: "I am struggling with the feeling that you are not completely candid with me, that important issues are being withheld here in the hours. I cannot pin it down more precisely, and I cannot even tell whether this is, indeed, your problem, or some problem in my experience of you. What are your thoughts about this?"

In reaction to such exploratory comments, some patients search within themselves for what they might be withholding without full awareness, whereas others confirm that they have indeed been withholding information and share some of the reasons. In general, patients without psychopathic transferences will experience concern and even alarm at the "distrust" the therapist is expressing, whereas patients with truly psychopathic transferences may simply dismiss the therapist's concern, tell him that it is his problem, and proceed as usual or as if nothing had happened.

In short, the patient's reaction to the therapist's exploratory comments about the possibility of deceptiveness in the transference usually opens up roads to further exploration of this issue. In the typical case of a patient who, like Mr. T, challengingly confirms his deceptiveness, the therapist may then explore with the patient what his conviction that he cannot be honest in their interaction means and how it destroys the possibility of authentic understanding and help from the treatment. The exploration of an internal world in which deceptiveness and distrust are the rule and to be honest is perceived as being condemned to being destroyed reminds one of George Orwell's *1984*. It is this internal world that needs to be explored, its self-destructive features in the transference clarified and interpreted, and the implications for the patient's life in general confronted.

PARANOID TRANSFERENCES

There are many patients with borderline personality organization whose predominantly negative transferences contain strong paranoid elements from the beginning of treatment. Although very paranoid borderline patients may appear to be more difficult treatment challenges than more smoothly functioning patients with psychopathic transferences, it is actually much easier to explore the projective identifications that reflect primitive internalized persecutory object relations in the paranoid transferences. Obviously, patients with paranoid psychoses (not transference psychoses but psychotic structures predating the treatment) also present severe—and often psychoanalytically not approachable—delusional paranoid developments in the transference. Where such paranoid transferences are the outcome of previously worked-through psychopathic transferences, the paranoid elements may be particularly powerful and expressed as serious distortions in the therapeutic relationship, even to the extent of the development of a transference psychosis.

Here the technique that I described in earlier work (1984) on dealing with paranoid regression in the transference may be helpful. If the patient seriously distorts the reality of the therapist's behavior, the therapist tells the patient that, in his view, their realities are completely different and incompatible. Confronting the patient with these incompatible realities reproduces the situation that occurs when a "mad" person and a "normal" person try to communicate without an outside witness or arbitrator to clarify what is real. The only alternative to the existence of truly incompatible realities at that point would be that the therapist is lying to the patient; and if the patient were so convinced, that would need to be explored further.

Interpreting to the patient what the therapist thinks lies behind the idea that he is dishonest may lead directly to other aspects of psychopathic transferences and their antecedent object relationships in the patient's early life. In some instances, the therapist must examine the patient's paranoid regression in terms of the activation of a "psychotic nucleus" (an area in the transference in which reality testing is consistently lost and an isolated but stable delusion regarding the therapist dominates the treatment situation) in the transference, sorting out once more the extent to which unresolved psychopathic transferences (the patient's assumption that the therapist is lying) need to be reexplored later on.

In my experience, in the case of a delusion in the transference, the therapist's communicating his tolerance of incompatible realities and examining fully the implications of the patient-therapist relationship under such conditions may gradually lead to the interpretive resolution of the psychotic nucleus and of the paranoid transference itself. Predominantly paranoid transferences are typically characterized by profound primitive aggression in the form of "purified" aggressive internalized part-object relations split off from the patient's idealized self and object representations.

Clinical Examples

Mr. R, a businessman in his late forties, consulted because he was selectively impotent with women from his own socioeconomic and cultural environment, although he was potent with prostitutes and women from lower socioeconomic backgrounds; he had fears of being a homosexual and problems in his relationships at work. Mr. R also was drinking excessively, mostly in connection with the anxiety related to his sexual performance with women. He was the son of an extremely sadistic father who regularly beat his children, and a hypochondriacal, chronically complaining and submissive mother whom the patient perceived as ineffectually attempting to protect the children from father. The patient himself, the second of five siblings, experienced himself as the preferred target of both father's aggression and his older brother's teasing and rejecting behavior. His diagnostic assessment revealed a severely paranoid personality, borderline personality organization, and strong, suppressed homosexual urges. The treatment was psychoanalytic psychotherapy, three sessions per week.

At one point in the treatment, Mr. R commented several times in a vague sort of way that I seemed unfriendly and when greeting him at the start of the sessions conveyed the feeling that I was annoyed at having to see him. In contrast to these vague complaints, one day he told me, with intense anger and resentment, that I had spat on the sidewalk when I saw him walking on the other side of the street.

I asked him whether he was really convinced that, upon seeing him, I had spat; he told me, enraged, that he knew it and that I should not pretend it was not true. When I asked why I would behave in such a way toward him, Mr. R angrily responded that he was not interested in my motivations, just in my behavior, which was totally unfair and cruel. My previous efforts to interpret his sense that I felt displeasure, disapproval, and even disgust with him as the activation, in the transference, of his relationship with his sadistic father had led nowhere. He had only angrily replied that I now felt free to mistreat him in the same way his father had, just as everybody in his office felt free to mistreat him as well. This time, he became extremely enraged when I expressed—in my tone and gesture more than in my words—my total surprise at the assumption that I had spat upon seeing him. He told me that he had difficulty controlling his urge to beat me up, and, indeed, I was afraid that he might even now become physically assaultive.

I told him that his impression was totally wrong, that I had not seen him and had no memory of any gesture that might be interpreted as spitting on the street. I added that, in the light of what I was saying, he would have to decide whether I was lying to him or telling him the truth, but I could only insist that this was my absolute, total conviction.

Mr. R seemed confused by my categorical statement; he seemed relieved by my strong emphasis and by my attitude toward him, which he could not fail to see as concerned and honestly trying to communicate with him. At the same time, he tried to explain away the contradiction between his observation and my statement by telling me that I was probably not aware of my behavior on the street and that, without being fully aware of it, I had seen him there.

I insisted on the essential incompatibility of his view of reality and mine. I told him that his accusation culminated a period of weeks of vague comments about my behavior and that, in the light of his statement about my behavior in the street, I saw all of it as an indication that one of us must be crazy. Either I was totally oblivious of my behavior toward him, or he was systematically misinterpreting my behavior in terms of his convictions. I also told him that his wishes to beat me up and make a violent scene expressed not only his rage at my behavior but also an effort to create in the reality of our interaction a fight that would confirm his view of reality and reassure him against awareness of the total incompatibility between what he and I were seeing as real.

His attributing to me the aggression that he did not dare to acknowledge in himself—while attempting to control my behavior and to induce in me the aggressive reaction he was afraid of—and, at the same time, his attempting to control me as an expression of fear of his own, now conscious, aggression reflect typical projective identification. But rather than interpret this mechanism, I stressed the incompatibility of our perceptions of reality per se, thus highlighting the existence of a psychotic nucleus, which I described to him as madness clearly present in the session, without locating it in either him or me.

Mr R's reaction was dramatic. He suddenly burst into tears, asked me to forgive him, and stated that he felt an intense upsurge of love for me and was afraid of its homosexual implications. I told him I realized that in expressing this feeling he was acknowledging that his perception of reality had been unreal, that he was appreciative of my remaining at his side rather than being drawn into a fight, and that, in this context, he now saw me as the opposite of his real father, as the ideal, warm, and giving father he had longed for. Mr. R acknowledged these feelings and talked more freely than before about his longings for a good relationship with a powerful man.

I returned, however, to his experience of my having spat when I saw him. I was concerned that a splitting operation had occurred, with a sudden shift in the transference reflecting a dissociation of the psychotic experience rather than its resolution. Mr. R was very reluctant to continue discussion of that perception of me as depreciating him. Over the next few sessions, he felt that my efforts to return to that perception meant a rejection of him and his wishes to be accepted and loved by me. Eventually, after elaborating this fear, he became able to explore his fantasies about the meanings of what he assumed to be my depreciation of him. It turned out that, in contrast to my earlier interpretation that it was the transference to his father that permeated his suspiciousness of me, my "crazy," derogatory behavior reminded him of the hypocrisy of his mother, who pretended to love her children while avoiding any confrontation with father in defense of them. The overall transference was to a combined image of a primitive, extremely sadistic parental image and superego precursor.

I should emphasize the extreme delicacy and potentially risky aspect of dealing with conditions of severe paranoid regression. The technical approach I describe has important limitations: it would certainly be contraindicated in patients with general loss of reality testing—that is, with active psychotic illness. I cannot emphasize enough the importance of an accurate differential diagnosis between paranoid personality and paranoid psychosis before deciding on psychoanalytic psychotherapy with a significantly paranoid patient. I also have found this technical approach useless in attempting to treat psychotherapeutically antisocial personality disorders. The syndrome of malignant narcissism, in my view, is at the boundary of what still may be approached with a psychoanalytic psychotherapy.

Speaking generally, it is important to evaluate the severity of the patient's characterologically integrated aggression, his impulse control, the extent to which some superego features such as ordinary morality are still present, all of which determine the risk of dangerous acting out of aggressive behavior as part of a paranoid regression. On the positive side, the successful diagnosis and analytic resolution of a psychotic nucleus in the transference and of severe paranoid regression in general may have dramatic therapeutic consequences in terms of the improvement of severe character pathology.

I have also applied the technique of the interpretation of "incompatible realities" in the treatment of patients with strong masochistic personality features and related sadomasochistic transferences, as illustrated in the following case. Ms S, a painter in her late thirties, consulted because of chronic depression and difficulties in her relationships with men and with close women friends, who ended their friendship with her after a period of time for reasons that remained obscure to the patient. So far, she had not been able to establish a long-lasting, satisfactory relationship with a man. She was the only child of parents who had been in constant marital conflict. Mother was addicted to a variety of drugs throughout her life and suffered from severe depressions and emotional crises, when she screamed, scolded her passive and meek husband, and tyrannized her daughter. The patient described the chaos in her early life, her dread of mother, and brief spells of warm relations with her father, separated by long intervals in which he did not seem available to her, mostly because of his extended absences. He was engaged in work abroad and also, presumably, avoided his family and home.

The diagnostic evaluation of Ms S revealed a person with a solid ego identity and neurotic personality organization, but severe character pathology with a predominance of sadomasochistic and paranoid features. I recommended psychoanalysis, and Ms S entered treatment with me, four sessions per week. In the second year, sadomasochistic features began to dominate the transference relationship. Particularly at times when the patient felt understood and emotionally close to me, she developed an intense fear in the sessions without being able to clarify its source; she then suddenly experienced me as being impatient, domineering, and controlling.

Sometimes, the atmosphere of the session would change in the course of a few minutes from a relaxed, trusting communication of emotional experiences to an intense suspiciousness and anger, and when I expressed surprise at this change, even further anger at my denial, as she saw it, of my impatient, harsh attitude. The issues under consideration might vary, but the sequence was always the same. Efforts to clarify what in my attitude or statements had impressed the patient as nonunderstanding, critical, or impatient led only to endless ruminations about the particular significance of a word or a sentence I had used and efforts on her part to obtain reassurances from me that I still thought well of her, liked her, and was not critical. All efforts to deal analytically with these demands, with her sudden need for reassurance, seemed ineffective.

My working hypothesis at that time was that Ms S was afraid of deepening her positive feelings toward me because they might have sexual implications and that her guilt feelings over positive oedipal fantasies were determining the activation of sadomasochistic features in the transference. Efforts to explore the material along these lines, however, were unsuccessful. Ms S denied any sexual feelings toward me and accused me of attempting to brainwash her with my theories. As these sequences— sessions of quiet exploration of her feelings, followed by intense recriminations for my mistreatment of her—went on, her angry reaction to the assumed slights from me increased in intensity.

Ms S now began to imitate me, caricaturing my voice and statements, while accusing me of making fun of her. She also began to feel more depressed. She berated herself as worthless and despicable and berated me for being sadistic, unfeeling, rigid, and indifferent.

I finally said that all my efforts to clarify why she felt mistreated by me seemed to fail and that we had to face the fact that she was experiencing herself under the simultaneous impact of three threats. First, she felt that I was attacking her mercilessly; second, she was attacking herself mercilessly, declaring herself worthless and feeling ever more depressed; third, in response to what she perceived as my attacks on her, she was also attacking me violently, caricaturing me and making fun of my statements, and accusing me of being a completely worthless and untrustworthy analyst. She thus was also losing me as a potentially helpful therapist.

I said she felt that she herself was under this tripartite attack, the common feature of which was a relentlessly hostile, sadistically teasing, and depreciatory person, sometimes located inside of her and attacking me, at other times located in me and attacking her, and all the time located also in herself in the form of self-attacks. I said that this reminded me of how she had described her relationship with her mother in the past, and that, in her relationship with me, she was enacting the relationship with mother with frequent interchange of roles: she felt that I was treating her as mother had treated her, or she was treating me as mother had treated her, and, most of the time, she was treating herself as if mother inside of her were attacking her.

Ms S angrily dismissed my interpretations as attempts to whitewash my own behavior. Over a period of several months, all my efforts to interpret this pattern failed. Eventually, I decided to confront the patient with my conviction that none of the aggressive behaviors she ascribed to me corresponded to reality. I told her I was convinced that her views were totally irrational and beyond reality, so much so that I would no longer explore all the instances she was giving as demonstrating my bad behavior. At the same time, I underlined, I did believe that she was convinced I was mistreating her, so that we were faced with a situation of incompatible realities in our sessions.

Ms S expressed her astonishment at the narrowness and rigidity of my approach. I was not behaving at all sympathetically and understandingly, as she had been led to believe psychoanalysts would. I agreed that her perception of me was so at variance with that of an understanding therapist that it would be reasonable for her to ask herself whether the problem was hers or whether she had landed in the office of a closed-minded, rigid, and incompetent psychiatrist.

Ms S immediately accused me of trying to get rid of her by attempting to convince her she should end the treatment. I said I was merely exploring the logic of the situation, not asking her to end the treatment, but noting an inconsistency in her willingness to continue a therapeutic relationship she described as only making her suffer and feel worse. Ms S was so genuinely alarmed that I might terminate her treatment that she was able to recognize the contradiction. I interpreted this contradiction as her enactment with me of the relationship with a bad mother: I was a terrible mother, but, in her fantasy, the alternative was to be left completely alone.

Ms S began to explore this possibility in a thoughtful way, but only a few sessions later was again accusing me of harsh, domineering, impatient, callous behavior. I immediately let her know that we were again in the realm of incompatible realities, and this time my comment led her to explore further the frightening and chaotic relationship with her mother. In other words, my confronting her with incompatible realities facilitated her becoming aware of the distortions in her views of me in the transference regression; she could then resume analytic work.

One could argue that in flatly dissociating myself from her transference distortion I was carrying out a kind of "transference deterrence," the reverse of the need to facilitate the deepening of the transference in order to interpret it; in other words, I was carrying out a supportive maneuver to reduce the transference regression. It might also be argued that in bringing my judgment sharply and categorically into opposition to the patient's judgment, I was denying the possibility of my participation in the transference-countertransference bind and exercising an arbitrary display of power.

I would counter that I had attempted to interpret the unconscious determinants of the transference over the many months during which this transference regression had evolved and that I had attempted to analyze the reality issues that might have triggered or even justified the patient's reactions in the transference. And, of course, there is always some element of the reality in the therapist's attitude around which transference regression crystallizes. Here, however, such careful exploration had not permitted resolving the transference regression analytically or separating reality from fantasy. Insofar as I was not attempting to convince the patient that I was right and she was wrong but, to the contrary, was stressing that right and wrong were less important than the existence of incompatible realities, I was not simply attempting to reduce the transference regression; rather, I was highlighting the structural aspects of the regressive transference. Under ordinary circumstances, when the patient is still able to separate transference fantasies from the reality of the situation, the technical approach I have described would not be necessary or indicated.

In stating how I perceived reality, following Ms S's insistence that I was trying to get rid of her, I asked her whether she really believed that should I want to end the treatment with her I would not say so directly. Ms S, after some thought, responded that she did believe I would not be afraid to let her know if I did not want to continue seeing her. The directness of my statement helped her to see that I would not be afraid to tell her the truth. This exchange marked the beginning of Ms S's capacity to acknowledge the contradictory aspects of her behavior in the sessions and her unconscious efforts to maintain the persecutory and idealized representations of me completely separate.

The analyst's discussing the truth—including the truth about aggression—has a reassuring function for the patient, the assurance that in the analytic situation everything can be discussed without danger. The long-range outcome of this phase of Ms S's analysis was her gradual working through of the condensed oedipal-preoedipal mother transference. The past almost psychotic relationship between her mother and herself had been blocking the way (via primitive superego identifications) to exploration of more advanced oedipal conflicts.

From a technical viewpoint, it is important that when the therapist stresses incompatible realities in the treatment situation, he do so not in the form of arguing with the patient, in a countertransference acting out resulting from severe sadomasochistic transferences, but from a position of technical neutrality—that is, with concerned objectivity. It goes without saying that if countertransference acting out has taken place in response to such regressive transferences, the therapist should acknowledge his behavior, without further burdening the patient with the deeper sources of his countertransference.

DEPRESSIVE TRANSFERENCES

Depressive transferences are those indicating the patient's capacity for acknowledging previously unrecognized, unacceptable aspects of himself, particularly unacknowledged aspects of aggression. Jacobson's (1964) description of layers of superego development provides a theoretical basis for understanding the relationships of psychopathic, paranoid, and depressive mechanisms. Assuming the successive development of, first, aggressive, persecutory superego precursors; a second layer of idealized superego precursors; and still later, more realistic superego introjects derived from the oedipal period—and the gradual integration of these layers—permits a summary of the pathological developments of superego functioning.

Where excessive early aggression predominates, whether because of genetic, constitutional, or environmental factors related to the early infant-caregiver relationship or to inordinate family pathology in the first five years of life, the aggressive layer of superego development is so dominant that, by projection, it populates the early world of experience with persecutory figures. This persecutory world interferes with the setting up of the idealized superego precursors. Instead, a predominantly paranoid world of object relationships is built up and eventually reflected in paranoid transferences. The almost total absence of compensatory idealized relationships may lead to the almost total destruction of internalized object relations; either investing the self with power or, as a secondary development, the psychopathic manipulation of relationships, the "paranoid urge to betray" described by Jacobson (1971b), are the only ways to survive. Psychopathic developments and the corresponding transferences, then, are a secondary elaboration as a defense against an underlying paranoid world.

If, in contrast, sufficient opportunities for idealized relationships remain to allow setting up both idealized and persecutory object relationships, then self-idealization and the narcissistic denial of dependency needs may be an alternative development to paranoid fears. These conditions lead to the dominance of narcissistic defenses as a protection against underlying paranoid tendencies and, when the pathological grandiose self is infiltrated with aggression, to the development of perversity. In ordinary borderline patients, splitting mechanisms facilitate the alternate activation, side by side, of idealizing and paranoid transferences.

If, however, the idealizing superego precursors and the persecutory superego precursors can be integrated and mutually toned down, more realistic superego introjections from the oedipal period may be internalized as well, leading to the normal integration of the oedipal superego with full development of the capacity for realistic self-evaluation and self-criticism. Melanie Klein (1940, 1946) first formulated the dynamics of the intimate connection between what she called paranoid-schizoid and depressive mechanisms; although her proposed developmental timetable and her failure to give sufficient consideration to the structuralization of the advanced superego are limitations in her approach, the overall mechanisms and relationships between paranoid and depressive transferences she described are relevant here.

The decrease of projective mechanisms and paranoid transferences implies that the patient is gradually recognizing the intrapsychic sources of his own aggression and the development, for the first time, of authentic experiences of guilt, remorse, concern for the therapist, and anxiety over the possibility of repairing their relationship. The patient becomes aware that his attacks were directed not at the bad, sadistic, tyrannical, or dishonest therapist but at the good therapist who was trying to help him. This development marks the beginning of depressive transferences, characteristic of advanced stages of the psychodynamic psychotherapy of borderline patients as well as of any stage of the psychoanalytic treatment of patients with neurotic personality organization, indicating that a significant degree of integration is taking place. Patients now begin to be able to reflect on the meanings of their behavior and to integrate the previously split-off images of the idealized and the persecutory therapist, in the context of also developing an integrated view of their parental images in terms of the idealized and persecutory aspects of their representations.

The most important problem at this advanced stage of the treatment may be the therapist's unawareness of the beginning of change in the patient. An early manifestation of a depressive potential may be the patient's more considerate behavior toward others in sublimatory functioning outside the treatment situation. One reason such an improvement may go undetected is the development of negative therapeutic reactions out of an unconscious sense of guilt. This is a higher-level negative therapeutic reaction than that which obtains in narcissistic personalities, whose negative therapeutic reactions usually reflect unconscious envy of the therapist.

The most dramatic indicators of the dominance of depressive transferences in the advanced stages of the treatment of borderline patients are the growing evidence of the patients' capacity to empathize with feeling states of the therapist—at times to the extent of developing an uncanny capacity to interpret the therapist's behavior; their concern for "maintaining alive" what is being learned in the psychotherapy; their capacity for independent work on the issues developed in the treatment outside the treatment hours; and their expressions of dependency on and love for the therapist rather than a superficial "as if" show of cooperativeness in the search for additional gratifications.

What I have described is necessarily schematic and oversimplified. Given the periods of chaotic condensation of transferences from many sources and levels of development in the treatment of borderline patients, depressive, paranoid, and psychopathic features may coexist or intermingle in the same transference reaction. Of greatest importance is that the therapist be oriented to the order of priority in exploring such chaotic transferences: I have found it extremely helpful to take up and resolve psychopathic transferences before focusing on the paranoid aspects of the material and then to resolve persistent paranoid elements before examining in depth the depressive developments.

Part V THE PSYCHODYNAMICS OF PERVERSION

Chapter 15 THE RELATION OF BORDERLINE PERSONALITY ORGANIZATION TO THE PERVERSIONS

Several roads have led me to a consideration of perversions. First, the psychoanalytic or psychotherapeutic treatment of patients with borderline personality organization has regularly revealed certain dynamic features that provided understanding of their apparently chaotic sexual fantasies and behaviors, and these same features were also to be found in the unconscious conflicts of perversions. The second road has stemmed from my studies of pathological love relations, and the third road, from my proposals regarding the syndrome of malignant narcissism.

Laplanche and Pontalis (1973, p. 306) give what seems to me an elegant and brief psychoanalytic definition of perversion:

> Deviation from the "normal" sexual act when this is defined as coitus with a person of the opposite sex directed towards the achievement of orgasm by means of genital penetration.
>
> Perversion is said to be present: where the orgasm is reached with other sexual objects (homosexuality, paedophilia, bestiality, etc.) or through other regions of the body (anal coitus, etc.); where the orgasm is subordinated absolutely to certain extrinsic conditions, which may even be sufficient in themselves to bring about sexual pleasure (fetishism, transvestism, voyeurism, exhibitionism, sadomasochism).
>
> In a more comprehensive sense, "perversion" connotes the whole of the psychosexual behaviour that accompanies such a typical means of obtaining sexual pleasure.

In contrast to the current tendency in the United States to call sexual deviation or perversion "paraphilia" (as in DSM-III and DSM-III-R), I prefer the psychoanalytic terminology of "perversion" in order to broaden the exploration of this field in light of the recent contributions from British, French, and Canadian authors.

In what follows, I shall adhere to the definition offered by Laplanche and Pontalis, with two major modifications. I exclude homosexuality for reasons that will emerge in the course of this discussion, and I restrict the definition to fixed, repetitive, obligatory behaviors required to obtain sexual gratification.

In earlier work (1975) I described how, in borderline patients, the small child's pathologically intense pregenital and particularly oral aggression tends to be projected onto the parental figures, causing a paranoid distortion of the early parental images, especially the mother. Because the child projects predominantly oral-sadistic but also anal-sadistic impulses, the mother is experienced as potentially dangerous; hatred of the mother later extends to hatred of both parents because the child experiences them in fantasy as a unit. A contamination of the image of father by aggression primarily projected onto the mother and then displaced onto him and failure to differentiate between the parents under the influence of splitting operations produce in both boys and girls a dangerous father-mother image, with the result that they later conceive of all sexual relationships as dangerous and infiltrated with aggression. In an effort to escape from oral rage and fears, a premature development of genital strivings takes place, but the effort often miscarries because of the intensity of pregenital aggression, which contaminates genital strivings as well.

What is typically found in these borderline patients includes the following. First, there is an excess of aggression in oedipal conflicts so that the image of the oedipal rival acquires terrifying, overwhelmingly dangerous and destructive characteristics; castration anxiety and penis envy in grossly exaggerated form; and prohibitions against sexual relations having a savage, primitive quality, manifested in severe masochistic tendencies.

Second, the idealizations of the heterosexual love object in the positive oedipal relation and of the homosexual love object in the negative oedipal relation are also exaggerated and have marked defensive functions against primitive rage. Thus one observes both unrealistic idealization of and longing for such love objects and the possibility of rapid breakdown of the idealization, with a reversal from positive to negative (or negative to positive) object relation in a rapid and total shift. As a consequence, the idealizations appear frail as well as exaggerated, with the additional complication, in narcissistic character pathology, of easy devaluation of idealized objects and total withdrawal.

Third, the unrealistic nature of both the threatening oedipal rival and the idealized desired one reveals, on careful genetic analysis, the existence of condensed father-mother images of an unreal kind, reflecting the condensation of partial aspects of the relations with both parents. Each particular relation with a parental object turns out to reflect a more complex developmental history than is usually the case with neurotic patients, in whom transference developments are more closely related to realistic fixations of past events.

Fourth, the genital strivings of patients with predominant preoedipal conflicts serve important pregenital functions. The penis, for example, may acquire symbolic functions of the feeding, withholding, or punishing mother, and the vagina may acquire the function of the hungry, feeding, or aggressive mouth. Although many neurotic patients and patients with milder types of character pathology also present these characteristics, their existence in combination with excessive aggressivization of all the pregenital libidinal functions is typical of patients with borderline personality organization.

Fifth, these patients typically show what might be called a premature oedipalization of their preoedipal conflicts and relations, a defensive progression in their instinctual development, which is reflected clinically in early oedipalization of the transference. The displacement of oral-aggressive conflicts from mother onto father increases castration anxiety and oedipal rivalry in boys and penis envy and related character distortions in girls. The girl's inordinate pregenital aggression toward the mother reinforces masochistic tendencies in her relationships with men, superego prohibitions against genitality in general, and the negative oedipal relation to the mother as a defensive idealization and reaction formation against the aggression. The projection of primitive conflicts around aggression onto the sexual relations between the parents leads to distorting and frightening fantasies of the primal scene, which may become extended into hatred of all love offered by others. More generally, the defensive displacement of impulses and conflicts from one parent to the other fosters the development of confusing, fantastic combinations of bisexual parental images condensed under the influence of a particular projected impulse.

It has become apparent to me that my observations regarding borderline patients correspond to the dynamics of the perversions as formulated in recent psychoanalytic contributions referred to below. For example, the reinforcement of the negative Oedipus complex in boys under the influence of intense preoedipal fears of mother combined with the displacement of preoedipal conflicts around aggression from mother onto father (with the consequent intensification of castration anxiety) may lead to a type of homosexuality in men that is largely preoedipally determined. The unconscious wish is to submit sexually to father in order to obtain from him the oral gratifications denied by the dangerous, frustrating mother. In these cases of predominantly orally determined male homosexuality, both father and mother (and heterosexuality) are perceived as dangerous, and homosexuality is used as a substitute way of gratifying oral needs.

My observations on the dynamics of borderline patients also relate harmoniously to Chasseguet-Smirgel's (1970) and McDougall's (1970) focus on preoedipal conflicts with mother as codeterminants of perversion, and to Stoller's (1976, 1985), emphasis on the central role of aggression in erotic excitement. Stoller stresses the preoedipal roots of this aggression. My observations also dovetail with Meltzer's (1977) idea of the defensive confusion of sexual zones in perversion, the aggressive infiltration of all object relations in these cases, and the perverse nature of the transformation of dependent relationships into aggressively destructive ones. From a different frame of reference, Person and Ovesey's studies (Ovesey and Person, 1973, 1976; Person and Ovesey 1974a, 1974b, 1974c, 1978, 1984; Ovesey 1983) of the common dynamic features of male transsexualism, transvestism, and homosexual cross-dressing in men also reveal conflicts of separation-individuation, disturbances in identity formation, and structurally borderline characteristics.

André Lussier's study on fetishism, *Les deviations du desir* (1982), uses fetishism as a paradigm for the general study of perversion. It lists the following characteristics of male fetishistic patients: (1) the need to exert absolute, even sadistic, control over a woman and utilization of the fetish as a symbolic reassurance of this control and of independence from the frustrating woman; (2) use of the fetish as a symbol of the safe possession of mother's breasts, thus protecting against separation anxiety and depression as an expression of fears over oral frustration; (3) fear of complete helplessness and abandonment related to fear of the destructive effects of the aggression induced under such conditions, aggression projected onto mother and defended against by possession of the fetish; (4) intolerance of anxiety or tension from any source, and the functions of the fetish as a source of supreme enjoyment and a denial of severe anxiety; (5) an extremely sadistic and masochistic conception of the primal scene, with confusion about whether father or mother is aggressor or victim and uncertainty about whether it is preferable to identify defensively with the aggressor of this ambiguous sexual scene or to submit masochistically to destruction by such an ambiguous, terrifying figure; the fetish, Lussier states, facilitates the defensive identification with both parents in the primal scene and provides reassurance against both castration and the dangerous phallic mother who condenses preoedipal and primal-scene aggression; and (6) fear of the homosexuality linked to submission to the sadistic father and to the castrating phallic mother in this primal scene; again, the fetish reassures against the unconscious fantasy of a feminine phallus as well as against castration.

Lussier points to the combination of oedipal and preoedipal conflicts, to ego splitting in relation to preoedipal conflicts, and to the unusual intensity of all the components of oedipal conflicts in the patients he studied.

PERVERSION AND THE RELATIONSHIP OF THE COUPLE

The second road to my interest in perversions has stemmed from the opposite end of the spectrum of psychopathology, namely, the important function of polymorphous perverse fantasies and activities in mature love relations.

In earlier work (1974a, 1974b, 1980a, 1980b, chap. 14 above) I concluded that for a man and woman to develop a healthy, stable love relation both partners must, first, have the capacity for broadening and deepening the experience of sexual intercourse and orgasm with sexual eroticism derived from the integration of aggression and bisexuality (sublimatory homosexual identifications). Second, they must have the capacity for an object relation in depth, which includes transforming preoedipal strivings and conflicts in the form of tenderness, concern, and gratitude, and the capacity for genital identification with the partner, coupled with sublimatory identification with (and yet leaving behind) the parental figure of the same sex. Third, they must have the capacity for depersonification, abstraction, and individualization—that is, maturation—in the superego so that infantile morality has been transformed into adult ethical values and a sense of responsibility and moral commitment, which reinforces the couple's emotional commitment to each other.

In exploring jointly the couple's sexual behavior, object relations, and superego functions, I concluded that sexual gratification derives its intensity from a freedom for experimentation that includes the expression of unconscious fantasies reflecting both oedipal and preoedipal object relations. This means bringing sadistic and masochistic, exhibitionistic and voyeuristic elements into the sexual relation and the enactment of complex fantasies. Such developments require time. The enactment of homosexual fantasies as well as of aggressive derivatives of preoedipal relations is included here: in the couple's capacity to transitorily free sexual activity from a rigid relation to a total object relation so that the participants can treat each other as "sexual objects." What is required for this is a capacity for sexual play, contained by an implicit frame of an emotional relation that transcends that play.

This conception links intense sexual excitement with the fantasy world of perversion and pornography. Sexual freedom of the couple in love expresses, at one point, polymorphous perverse fantasy that temporarily frees both participants from their specific object relation—although their total sexual involvement is still contained by that object relation. This last characteristic naturally makes sexual play an erotic art in contrast to the restricted, mechanical quality of pornography. I also use the term *pornography* to focus on one more dimension of sexual freedom—namely, its opposition to socially sanctioned sexual behavior, usually directed against the aggressive and generally pregenital components of sexuality. The aspects of sexuality that are conventionally accepted as part of a couple's love life are typically shorn of the intensity and excitement derived from pregenital features. There is a surprising similarity in the role of aggression in perversion and in normal love relations. The question is, does perversion, with its important function of "metabolizing" aggression, have a role parallel to that of other "metabolizing" mechanisms in normal love relations (such as dissociated regressive interactions or submission to and rebellion against superego functions projected onto the partner)?

Aggression in a couple's relationship is expressed in the part-object relations activated in sexual play and intercourse, in sadistic and masochistic fantasies and activities, in the use of the partner as an object, and in the excitement of being used in this way. In terms of object relations, aggression is expressed in the normal ambivalence of total object relations and in the specific themes of oedipal competitiveness and rivalry and the activation of "reversed triangularization"—that is, the fantasy and wish for oedipal revenge by introducing a third party into a love relationship and thus threatening one's love object with a rival (Kernberg 1991a). Jealousy is a primary emotion expressing the love and hatred derived from the oedipal situation, perhaps condensed with preoedipal jealousy and envy.

In terms of superego functions, aggression is involved in the repression of pregenital components of infantile sexuality and of genital strivings themselves, insofar as these are too directly linked to the oedipal objects. Aggression is also involved in submission to conventional sexuality and to projected superego features directed against sexual wishes. At the same time, the integration of love and aggression in the superego permits firm, stable value systems and internal morality and a sense of concern and responsibility that reflects love as well. This function protects the couple's relationship against the excessive activation of aggression in the normal ambivalence of all intimate object relations, particularly the aggressive components of reversed oedipal triangularization.

I am suggesting that polymorphous perverse infantile sexuality serves an important function in the recruitment of aggression in the service of love that characterizes human sexuality. It is as if the transformations of the early experience of pain into sexual excitement, and of the experience of pleasure in aggressive behavior into pleasure in the expression of erotic hostility, provide a quality of elation to sexual arousal linked to the fantasy that sexual wishes as an expression of love and sexual wishes as an expression of aggression are no longer in contradiction (Kernberg 1991b). The resulting condensation provides a sense of power and freedom from conflict and, when contained by the security of a loving object relation, reassurance against the feared consequences of the aggressive side of unavailable ambivalence. Here, I believe, lies an important function of the polymorphous perverse aspects of normal sexuality: they cement the relation of the couple and limit the effects of infantile superego collusions and related social conventionalities. But where are the boundaries between normal polymorphous perverse sexuality and the regressive aspects of aggression in perversion?

MALIGNANT NARCISSISM, PERVERSION, AND PERVERSITY

This question introduces the third road leading to my encounter with perversion. I am referring to my recent proposals regarding the syndrome of malignant narcissism (see chap. 5 above). Because patients with malignant narcissism also may present the most severe types of perversions—those with life-threatening ego-syntonic aggression and/or self-directed aggression—psychoanalytic exploration of this spectrum of psychopathology may shed new light on the nature and functions of aggression in perversion.

The analytic exploration of patients with malignant narcissism led me to propose that they have superego pathology characterized by (1) the absence of idealized superego precursors (idealized self and object representations that would ordinarily constitute the early ego ideal) other than those integrated into the pathological grandiose self; (2) the predominance of the earliest level of sadistic superego precursors, which represent, because of their inordinate power, the only reliable internalized object representations available; and (3) the intrapsychic consolidation of a status quo, in fantasy, that permits survival when the only reliable object representations available would be of sadistic enemies.

The unopposed predominance of non-neutralized sadistic superego precursors, expressing a condensation of unmitigated preoedipal and oedipal aggression, constitutes a devastating pathological intrapsychic structure. The pathological grandiose self crystallizes around the sadistic self and object representations and also absorbs whatever idealized superego precursors are available.

The sexual fantasies of these patients are strikingly similar to those of patients with sadistic and masochistic sexual perversions. There is a consistent aggressivization of all sexual desires. Genital penetration becomes equivalent to destroying the genitals or to filling body cavities with excrement. The penis as a source of poison invading the body is the counterpart to teasingly unavailable breasts that can be incorporated only by cannibalistic destruction. The lack of differentiation of sexual aims, so that oral, anal, and genital fantasies are condensed and simultaneously express impulses and threats from all levels of sexual development, corresponds to a dedifferentiation of the sexual characteristics of male and female, so that homosexual and heterosexual impulses mingle chaotically. Patients with malignant narcissism present what Meltzer (1977) has called "zonal confusions" and "perverse transference" features. Sexual promiscuity may defend them from deep involvement with a sexual partner that would threaten them with the eruption of uncontrollable violence. These patients also typically present "analization," a type of object relations tending to deny sexual and generational differentiation, described by Chasseguet-Smirgel (1978, 1983).

Some of the patients with malignant narcissism I have seen have not manifested sexual perversion. In others, suicidal tendencies seemed to approximate masochistic perversions in their bizarre nature, and still others showed masochistic self-mutilation with clearly sexual implications. Some patients with malignant narcissism present sadistic perversions with dangerous aggressive behavior; others present bizarre perversions with direct expression of anal interests. Sadistic perversions in patients with antisocial personality proper (see chap. 5) are, by definition, extremely dangerous and even life-threatening.

For example, a patient in his early twenties, with an antisocial personality disorder, masturbated on rooftops while throwing bricks at women on the street below. He felt intense sexual excitement at the moment of throwing the brick without knowing whether or not it would hit the woman passing by, mixed with the excitement and fear of being caught in a criminal act. He reached orgasm in masturbation at the moment when the brick crashed on the street or on his victim and with the first evidence of shock from a passerby below; indeed, he waited for evidence of such shock before proceeding to escape.

Another patient with the syndrome of malignant narcissism together with homosexual and heterosexual promiscuity presented a pattern of sexual relations with women that represented the acting out of a perverse scenario. First he made it clear to the woman—one who was by this time obviously involved with him—that he intended to test her love for him by forcing her to submit to increasingly humiliating sexual experiences. After a number of preparatory encounters, he asked that she suck his penis and lick his ass in the presence of a male friend of his. It was during this culminating experience that he introduced his friend to the woman. He and his friend then engaged in bets on how long it would take him to get the woman to perform for the two of them. He then ended his relationship with the woman without any further explanation, although he had pretended, as part of his seductive efforts, to develop a deepening relationship with her. It was essential that the woman be truly involved with him; a prostitute would not do. The persistent paranoid fears that the woman would return to take revenge on him and what amounted to almost frankly paranoid psychotic episodes in this context, revealed both the depth of the pathology and the frailty of his personality organization.

Perversion and Perversity

The pretense of love in the service of aggression in this case leads us to the final characteristic of malignant narcissism, a quality of perversity in the transference and in object relations in general. By perversity I mean the conscious or unconscious transformation of something good into something bad: love into hatred, meaning into meaninglessness, cooperation into exploitation, food into feces. Perversity is clearly not the same as perversion, which can be defined as a deviation from a normal sexual function into an idiosyncratic and bizarrely rigidified one. In my experience, only the severest types of perversion, usually in patients with malignant narcissism, present characteristics of perversity in their transference and in other object relations. Perversity, as I see it, is a quality of object relations that reflects the conscious or unconscious recruitment of love, dependency, and/or sexuality in the ordinary sense in the service of aggression. It reflects the effort to exercise sadistic control and the omnipotence of the pathological grandiose self in malignant narcissism, a "mad" (Rosenfeld 1971, 1975), grandiose self-structure that causes the most severe negative therapeutic reactions. These patients relentlessly extract what is good in the analyst in order to empty him out and destroy him; they do the same in all other close object relations.

In his analysis of transference relationships, Bion (1970) described what he called "parasitic" transference as a relation between two people geared to destroying a third—namely, anything new, what might be called "the analytic baby," that might develop in the course of treatment. In essence, he suggested, in parasitic relations there is a malignant effort to destroy truth and truthfulness, and he pointed to the relationship between the liar and the analyst as the prototype of such a malignant distortion in the transference.

There exists a literature on perversity, from the plays of Harold Pinter (1965, 1973, 1978), at one extreme, to the plots of standard thrillers, at the other, built on similar lines: one person, sexually excited and falling in love with a second person, is exploited through this sexual bond by the second person, who, struggling internally with the contradiction between a wish to respond with sexual love and a secret predetermined commitment to betray the first person to a third one, finally yields to betrayal. The drama of this perverse triangle is significantly increased when the first person, knowing that he or she will be betrayed, willingly acquiesces in this destiny, thus internalizing the recruitment of love and sex in the service of aggression.

Chasseguet-Smirgel (1978, 1983), stressing the anal quality of the devaluation processes characteristic of narcissistic transferences, pointed to the transformation of all object relations into undifferentiated, devalued "segments" unconsciously representing feces. In her view, the omnipotent denial of the differences between the sexes and between generations and the omnipotent equalization of homosexuality and heterosexuality in multiple polymorphous perverse sexual activities reflect a perverse destruction of object relations by analizing them. I have observed some patients with malignant narcissism who took direct, conscious pleasure in their destructive engagement with the analyst as they first tried relentlessly to absorb everything from him and then relentlessly dismantled it. Moreover, the patient's wishful fantasy to destroy everything good in the analyst or to transform it into feces even before forcefully extracting it may lead to a frenzied and triumphant orgy of aggression. Typically, when this process cannot be resolved analytically, it culminates in the stage in which the patient feels that he has absorbed everything from the analyst, that what he learned he knew partially all along or discovered by himself, and that it was pretty much worthless anyhow. Interrupting the analysis under such conditions protects him against the fear of aggressive retaliation from the analyst and reinforces, in his fantasy, a sense of omnipotence, defenses against feelings of guilt over his own aggression, and the lack of mourning over object loss. These patients typically induce a sense of chaos and futility in the analyst at such crucial stages of their treatment, reflecting the chaos and futility that characterizes their own object world and even their physical environment.

The malignant sense of grandiosity expressed in perversity may find direct expression in actual sadistic perversions, as with the patient who lured women to participate in perverse rituals and then abandoned them. That abandonment had the function of "flushing the toilet," ridding the patient of anally destroyed and potentially poisonous objects. The combination of a fantasied sense of absolute power and control on the part of the pathological grandiose self with which the patient is totally identified under these conditions, of power over the world, with the induction of chaos as part of the anal destruction of the surrounding world leads us directly to the world of the novels of the Marquis de Sade, to the psychology of madness and chaos in the midst of absolute power in Orwell's *1984*, and to their counterparts in reality: the cases of sadistic tyrants exerting absolute control and the underlying chaos in the societies thus dominated.

The juxtaposition of order and chaos, Saul Friedlander suggests in *Reflections of Nazism: An Essay on Kitsch and Death* (1984), is a frightening yet strangely appealing aspect of certain regressive group processes. The fascination that Nazi Germany is exerting over a new generation of intellectuals trying to understand the appeal of totalitarian ideologies may relate to this fascination with total order and simultaneous destructive chaos.

If perversity is based on polymorphous perverse fantasies and activities that disregard the distinctions between the sexes and the generations and unconsciously equate not only all sexual activity but all object relations with fecal matter, and if the mad worlds of de Sade's *120 Days of Sodom* (1785), a fantasy, and of Auschwitz, a reality, represent the rock bottom condensation of aggression and perversion, then "ordinary perversions" that maintain a rigid, obligatory sexual scenario in the context of preserving ordinary genital relations and the capacity for maintaining differentiated object relations represent a truly "innocent" side of perversion.

PERVERSION AND NEUROTIC PERSONALITY ORGANIZATION

This brings me back to the traditional psychoanalytic view of perversion as the persistence or reemergence of a component part of sexuality, in which a permanent and obligatory change in the sexual aim and/or object is required in order to achieve orgasm. The traditional view is that a partial infantile sexual component serves as a defense against the unresolved Oedipus complex with its related castration anxiety and prohibitions against incest. In fact, in contrast to the recent tendency of the psychoanalytic literature (see chap. 16) to describe all perversions as if they represented a double layer of conflicts, with a strong predominance of preoedipal issues, I have found patients with typical neurotic personality organization who present an organized perversion as part of their symptomatology. In short, perversion is not limited to patients with borderline personality organization.

A college professor in his early thirties consulted because of a shoe fetish. The history of his childhood development revealed a benign but distant father and a large number of older female relatives, including sisters, aunts, and cousins, who created a constantly teasing atmosphere around him. He told of being harshly punished because he looked under women's skirts from a spot beneath the table and gradually becoming fascinated with women's feet and shoes. This led him to masturbate while holding and smelling the shoes of his older sisters, their friends, and eventually women co-workers at the college where he was now teaching. His adolescence had been marked by intense voyeuristic yearnings, and the shoe fetish acquired the function of satisfying his sexual excitement and providing him with a sense of independence from what he experienced as sadistically teasing and withholding women. This patient felt that masturbating with his secretary's shoes provided him with as much gratification as if he went to bed with her. The secrecy with which he went about obtaining her shoes also provided him with the symbolic gratification of invading mother's privacy without being caught. The professor was married and had a satisfactory relationship with his wife except that his sexual life with her lacked the intensity of the gratification he found in masturbating with shoes surreptitiously obtained.

Oedipal issues clearly predominated in his transference throughout five years of an analysis that ended with resolution of the shoe fetishism and a marked increase in his capacity for sexual pleasure with his wife. In fact, the treatment showed very little of the primitive ego defenses and object relations that have been highlighted in the recent contributions to perversion in general and to fetishism in particular, mentioned earlier in this chapter. Although primitive defensive mechanisms are prevalent in patients with perversions presenting borderline personality organization, their absence in patients presenting perversion with neurotic personality organization indicates that these mechanisms are related to the individual's ego organization and the level of organization of object relations rather than to the perversion itself.

POLYMORPHOUS PERVERSE SEXUALITY AND LEVELS
OF PERSONALITY ORGANIZATION

Polymorphous perverse fantasies, activities, and capabilities emerge as an essential part of human sexuality at all levels of pathology and normality. In fact, the absence of such fantasies and behaviors from sexual life may be considered a neurotic symptom. In patients with neurotic personality organization who have the capacity for heterosexual intercourse and orgasm with a stable heterosexual partner, the inhibition of polymorphous perverse infantile sexuality usually responds well to psychoanalytic treatment and in some cases to minor psychotherapeutic interventions, sex therapy, and even culturally facilitating pressures or opportunities.

In contrast, the absence of polymorphous perverse sexual tendencies in patients with borderline personality organization, particularly in those with narcissistic personality and malignant narcissism, may indicate a failure of earliest stimulation of erotogenic zones and extremely severe preoedipal conflicts in the mother-infant relation; such cases have a guarded prognosis. By the same token, polymorphous perverse sexual fantasies and behavior in patients with borderline personality organization are a prognostically favorable indicator and may lead, in the course of the resolution of borderline pathology, to a relatively easy integration of pregenital eroticism with full genital sexuality which includes and tolerates polymorphous perverse sexual components.

The consolidation of a specific perversion as an obligatory precondition for sexual gratification, to the detriment of ordinary freedom and flexibility of sexual gratification in a stable relation with a loved heterosexual object, may indicate a severe or moderate degree of pathology, depending on the patient's predominant level of ego organization and object relations. Specific sexual perversions in borderline personality organization have a more guarded prognosis and are more difficult to treat than sexual perversions in neurotic personality organization. For example, the treatment of male homosexuality reflecting unconscious submission to the oedipal father out of guilt for oedipal longings for mother and castration anxiety has a much more favorable prognosis than that of male homosexuality based upon the condensation of oedipal and preoedipal conflicts typical of borderline personality organization.

The prognosis for treatment is even more guarded for patients with narcissistic personality structure functioning on a borderline level, especially in malignant narcissism. Here, in contrast to the function of polymorphous perverse strivings under normal circumstances and even in many patients with borderline personality organization, sex and love are recruited in the service of aggression, sometimes leading to perversity in object relations and to actual violence.

So far, I have related perversion to the structural dimension of ego development, ranging from the most severe borderline cases to normality. Another crucial dimension that codetermines the severity of perversion is the developmental level and integration of superego functions. The overriding predominance of the earliest level of superego precursors—namely, the sadistic superego precursors (which are normally integrated with the later level of idealized superego precursors)—represents the most severely pathological precondition that facilitates the ego-syntonic expression of primitive aggression. Aggression in the form of criminal activity of the psychopath and aggression in the form of sadistic violence of the malignant narcissist may also be expressed in a violent sadistic perversion, illustrating the structural preconditions under which normal primitive polymorphous perverse activity may be replaced by the most dramatic and severe types of sexual perversion.

Superego pathology is both less severe and less important in the case of the ordinary borderline patient with polymorphous perverse sexuality and the corresponding chaos in object relations. The level of superego integration may be of general prognostic value in these cases in the sense that the treatment of all patients with borderline personality organization has a more favorable prognosis in the absence of antisocial features, but the direct link between superego pathology and perversion is less apparent here than in the psychopathic personality and malignant narcissism. In contrast, the relation between perversion and superego pathology in the case of neurotic personality organization is of great clinical importance. In these cases, the unconscious prohibitions against genital sexuality because of its unconscious oedipal meaning of incest and castration anxiety promote and maintain the perverse structure as a defense against these underlying oedipal conflicts.

Finally, at the level of normal sexual functioning, the mature superego should tolerate the expression of polymorphous perverse infantile sexual trends as part of sexual life. But, as we have seen, remnants of infantile prohibitions against adult sexuality are universal, so that the stable sexual couple must struggle against the tendency to submit unconsciously, through the mutual activation of superego functions, to the suppression of the perverse components of sexuality.

Having explored polymorphous perverse sexuality and perversion from the perspective of levels of ego organization with their corresponding object relations and defensive operations, and in terms of superego integration, I shall now explore this field in terms of the integration of aggression into sexual life. The direct expression of aggression as part of sexual behavior in psychotic patients is well documented in psychiatric literature: patients with schizophrenic illness and chronic paranoid psychosis may commit sexual murders because of their delusions. We might say that the direct expression of primitive aggression is facilitated by the absence of reality testing and by the confusion between self and nonself. Projective identification at a most primitive level reflects an attempt to establish distance from intolerable intrapsychic aggression by externalizing it onto an object; the object must then be destroyed because differentiation from it cannot be maintained.

The intensity of primitive aggression, whatever its origin, is a fundamental cause of the pathology of the earliest layer of sadistic superego precursors, which, having infiltrated the pathological grandiose self, determine the structure of malignant narcissism and psychopathy. One might speculate that in malignant narcissism, in contrast to the antisocial personality, there is at least the integration of some idealized superego precursors into the pathological grandiose self, so that a "self-righteous" ideology, as it were, replaces the ideologically nonrationalized aggression of the psychopath. In any case, perversion under these circumstances may reach the severest levels of direct expression of aggression and, in fact, may reflect the perverse recruitment of sexual excitement in the service of aggression.

In ordinary borderline personality organization, aggression is better defended against by generalized ego splitting and alternating object relations, which, in their multiplicity and chaos, protect the subject from total invasion and control by intolerable aggression. The polymorphous perverse activities at this level have a less directly sadistic quality than in malignant narcissism. In the ordinary borderline patient, the effort to integrate aggression into sexual excitement as part of the recruitment of aggression in the service of love has its beginning.

In the patient with neurotic personality organization, unconscious defenses against direct expression of aggression predominate, and aggression is significantly internalized as part of superego functioning. Aggression is also expressed in characterological reaction formations, so that the manifest characteristics of perversions are usually remarkably free from violent aggressive behavior. Paradoxically, it is at a normal level of sexual involvement that the more conscious awareness of aggressive fantasies implied in sadistic, masochistic, voyeuristic, and exhibitionistic behavior may become an important aspect of sexual play and activities and a source of intense sexual excitement.

Summarizing these vicissitudes of aggression in the perversions, one might say that aggression is an essential component of all sexuality and that, in expanding the repertoire of eroticized bodily functions and aspects of object relations recruited into genital sexuality, it actually enriches sexual experience and love in the form of polymorphous perverse components of human sexuality. Under normal circumstances, its recruitment in the service of sex and love enriches the love life; under extremely pathological circumstances, however, aggression may recruit sex and love for destructive purposes, reflected in the transformation of perversion into perversity. At intermediate levels of pathology, aggression is fundamental in linking unconscious conflicts from the preoedipal to the oedipal stage and in determining the condensation of all these conflicts. Throughout the entire spectrum of psychopathology, from neurosis to psychosis, perversion reflects the combined influence of object relations, the vicissitudes of superego development, the presence of pathological narcissism, and the intensity of aggression, as these jointly affect polymorphous perverse sexuality.

Chapter **16** A THEORETICAL FRAME FOR THE STUDY OF SEXUAL PERVERSIONS

If one were to draw up a schematic outline of the psychoanalytic theories of perversion, one could, I believe, roughly distinguish three groups of formulations. The first one, basically corresponding to Freud's (1927, 1940a, 1940b) original conclusions about the subject, defines perversion as a permanent and obligatory deviation from the normal in the sexual aim and/or object required to achieve orgasm. In this theory, an infantile sexual component (or partial) drive (anal, oral, and so on) serves as a defense against an underlying neurotic conflict—namely, the unresolved Oedipus complex. This concept stressing the centrality of castration anxiety and the Oedipus complex in the etiology of perversion views the perversion as a defense. In my view, this traditional concept of perversion continues to be valid for patients who present a neurotic rather than borderline personality organization and normal infantile rather than pathological narcissism.

A second concept of perversion is represented by the formulations of the British object relations theorists, particularly Fairbairn (1954), Klein (1945), and Winnicott (1953), who stress preoedipal contributions to its psychodynamics, psychopathology in the mother-infant relationship, and the central role of preoedipal aggression. In this view the child's pathologically intense pregenital and particularly oral aggression—whether inborn (Klein) or in reaction to frustration (Fairbairn, Winnicott)—is projected onto the parental figures, especially mother, thus causing a paranoid distortion of the early parental images. Because the child projects predominantly oral-sadistic but also anal-sadistic impulses, mother is experienced as potentially dangerous. The hatred of mother later expands to both parents, whom the child, in his unconscious fantasy, experiences as a unit. A contamination of the image of father by aggression, primarily projected onto mother and then displaced onto him, and a lack of differentiation between the images of the parents under the influence of primitive defensive operations dealing with this aggression produce in both boys and girls a dangerous combined father-mother image, with the result that all sexual relationships are conceived as dangerous and aggressively infiltrated. Under these circumstances, the primal scene acquires particularly dangerous and frightening characteristics and is perceived by the child with severely sadomasochistic distortions. These conditions lead to excessive aggressivization of oedipal conflicts, so that the image of the oedipal rival typically acquires terrifying, dangerous, and destructive characteristics; castration anxiety and penis envy become grossly exaggerated and overwhelming; and superego prohibitions against all sexual relations (because of their oedipal implications) acquire a savage, primitive quality, reflected in severe masochistic tendencies or paranoid projections of superego precursors.

In addition, idealization of the heterosexual love object in the positive oedipal relation and of the homosexual love object in the negative oedipal relation is also exaggerated and, as an expression of splitting operations, has marked defensive functions against the threatening condensation of primitive rage and oedipal aggressiveness. The exaggerated, unrealistic idealizations of the love object, matched by the unrealistic, paranoid distortions of the oedipal rival, intensify further oedipal inhibitions and castration anxiety. The genital strivings of these patients with predominant preoedipal conflicts serve important pregenital functions as well. In chapter 15, I described similar developments in borderline patients: how the penis may acquire symbolic functions of the feeding, withholding, or punishing mother, and the vagina the functions of the hungry, feeding, or aggressive mouth. Similar developments occur regarding anal and urinary functions. The existence of these features in combination with excessive aggressivization of the pregenital libidinal drive derivatives also contributes to intensifying castration anxiety and the fantasied dangers of sexual relations.

This second approach differs from Freud's thinking in that it stresses the crucial contribution of preoedipal conflicts, particularly preoedipal aggression, in the etiology of the perversions, but it continues to emphasize the importance of castration anxiety in blocking the full deployment of genital sexuality. The theory explains intense castration anxiety, the incapacity to identify normally with the oedipal parent of the same sex, and inhibition of the sexual approach to an object of the opposite sex as derived from aggressivization of the positive and negative oedipal relationship and the fantastic accentuation of castration fears as genital sexuality becomes the recipient of displaced preoedipal aggression.

A third approach to the psychodynamics of perversion is represented largely by the formulations of the French psychoanalytic school, particularly Chasseguet-Smirgel (1985b, 1986), Braunschweig and Fain (1971), Grunberger (1976), McDougall (1980), and Lussier (1983). Chasseguet-Smirgel (1985b), summarizing her view, points to the following central aspects. First, in agreement with Freud, she considers the perversions to be a regression to or fixation at a partial, pregenital component drive in replacement of a genital sexuality blocked by castration anxiety. Second, she stresses the universal potential for regression to the anal-sadistic phase, stating that "the anal universe can be considered as a preliminary sketch of the genital universe" (p. 157). This anal regression transforms the symbolic relation to the genital phallus into a relation to a pseudogenital fecal phallus that permits denial of the differences between the sexes (anal "equality" of the sexes in contrast to genital differentiation) and also implies the abolition of generational boundaries (the fecal phallus erases the differences between the little boy's penis and the father's and permits the boy to eliminate awareness of the vagina as the significant female genital organ). Third, in a secondary defense against and masking of the anal regression, an idealization of anality occurs, with a symbolic accentuation of the aesthetic and formal aspects of art, nature, physical objects, and interpersonal reality. There also develops an idealization of the specific perversion of the individual patient as vastly superior to "ordinary" genital relations (with their oedipal implications). Fourth, denial of the differences between sexes and generations and idealization of the pregenital, perverse component drive are accompanied by splitting, which permits, at the same time, a persistent recognition of reality. At a conscious level, the pervert still recognizes the reality of sexual and generational differences and the need to integrate his perverse strivings into his actual sexual behavior in some nonpsychotic fashion.

In short, in this formulation, perversions are characterized by regressive analization, denial of the differences of sexes and generations, defensive idealization of anality, persistent recognition of reality, and splitting (both denial and recognition of sexual differences) superimposed on repression.

Chasseguet-Smirgel (1986) stresses that, in both sexes, the early relation to mother is of fundamental etiological importance in perversions. In contrast to the British school, particularly to Klein's formulations, however, she considers aggression against mother to reflect archaic aspects of the oedipal situation deriving not from split, part-object relations to the breast but from fantastic distortions of the imagined interior of mother's body.

Chasseguet-Smirgel thinks perversion is ultimately derived from the need to deny the reality of mother's vagina and the "dark continent" of the interior of mother's belly, and from unconscious aggression against mother expressed in the archaic fantasy of destroying the contents of mother's body, including father's penis, other babies, and any other obstacle to a free-floating, endless expansion in mother's belly. She proposes that aggression against mother projected onto her as an engulfing primitive genital figure, the need to deny awareness of the vagina, and aggression against the content of mother's genitals underlie and reinforce castration anxiety of the later oedipal stage in both sexes.

The French concept of perversion reaffirms Freud's stress on the centrality of the oedipal complex and castration anxiety in determining the defensive regression to a component sexual drive, but it also stresses the archaic Oedipus complex linked to the primary relation to mother. This may be thought of as a modified version of the British view, with particular emphasis on the defensive denial of the differences between sexes and generations and the idealization of anality.

Chasseguet-Smirgel (1985b) has clarified this regressive analization in great detail. In my experience, this generalized destructiveness of all object relations—which seem to be regressively "digested" and then "fragmented" into symbolic feces—is a dramatic, quite concrete finding in the analytic exploration of most severe cases of perversions, such as those that threaten the physical integrity of the subject or his objects. I have explored the relation between these dynamics and the syndrome of malignant narcissism in earlier work (1984). Of relevance in this regard is Fairbairn's (1954, pp. 3–27) description of the defensive withdrawal from object relations in some patients with severe psychopathology and the replacement of object relations by a regressive accentuation of perverse sexual strivings.

Chasseguet-Smirgel's emphasis on the pathological consequences of severe early aggression for the process of separation-individuation from mother, particularly for the vicissitudes of the girl's identification with female functions and the boy's tolerance for the oedipal rivalry with father, dovetails with the ideas of American psychoanalysts who have stressed the importance of separation-individuation in the genesis of perversion. Stoller (1968) described the fear of femininity in men, an expression of men's anxiety about losing their sexual identity, as derived from the primary identification with mother, which must be undone in order for a masculine identity to be developed. Person and Ovesey (1974a,

1974b, 1974c, 1978, 1984) stress conflicts of separation-individuation and related disturbances in identity formation as common dynamic features of male transsexualism, transvestism, and homosexual cross-dressing. Blum (1988) points to the importance of shared unconscious fantasy in the mother-infant dyad as a key etiological factor in pre-oedipally determined gender identity disorders.

I concluded earlier that in clinical practice we do not find the same underlying dynamics for all cases of perversion. To the contrary, careful study of a broad spectrum of perverse psychopathology points to radical differences in the dynamic and structural preconditions of perverse behavior. More specifically, the study of perversion in men (chap. 17) and of the clinical syndromes of masochism (chap. 3) led me to conclude that polymorphous perverse fantasies, activities, and capabilities are an essential part of human sexuality at all levels of pathology and normality. The consolidation of a specific perversion as an obligatory precondition for sexual gratification, to the detriment of ordinary freedom and flexibility of sexual gratification in a stable relation with a loved heterosexual object, may indicate a severe or moderate or merely a mild degree of pathology, according to the patient's predominant level of ego organization and object relations.

Specific sexual perversions in the context of borderline personality organization have a more guarded prognosis and are more difficult to treat than sexual perversions in the context of neurotic personality organization. The prognosis is even more guarded for patients with borderline personality organization and the consolidation of a narcissistic personality structure, particularly for cases of malignant narcissism. Thus, the type and severity of the patient's character pathology are fundamental codeterminants of the structure, dynamics, and prognosis of perversion.

Another crucial dimension that, in my experience, codetermines the structure and prognosis of perversion is the developmental level and integration of superego functions. Aggression in the form of the criminal activity of the psychopath and sadistic violence in the malignant narcissist is characterized by the absence of an integrated superego. In contrast, the relation between perversion and superego pathology in neurotic personality organization has the paradoxical effect of consolidating the perversion (because of the unconscious prohibitions against genital sexuality, which represents incest and evokes castration anxiety) but also protecting the patient against uncontrolled expression of aggression and the related deterioration of object relations. An integrated although excessively severe superego guarantees the "boundaries of playfulness" of the perverse scenario, which has positive therapeutic and prognostic implications. The importance of the type and degree of superego pathology in determining the prognosis and treatment indications of perversions also reflects Rangell's (1974) emphasis on the general centrality of superego distortions in contemporary psychopathology.

Finally, in my view, the vicissitudes of aggression in the perversions emerge as an essential component of all sexuality, and the relationship between aggression and eroticism appears to be a basic psychodynamic factor throughout the entire spectrum of perverse psychopathology, from neurosis to psychosis.

In what follows, I shall stress the following ideas:

1. In contrast to the traditional view that polymorphous perverse features merely play a role in sexual foreplay, I consider them a crucial component of normal sexuality.
2. Organized perversions at a neurotic level of personality organization do present, in both sexes, the psychodynamics originally proposed by Freud. For all practical purposes, these cases follow the course of psychoanalytic treatment that is typical for other types of neurotic illness, including neurotic character pathology, and they should no longer be considered to be particularly severe.
3. Cases of stable perversion and borderline personality organization, in contrast, typically present the dynamics described by the British and French schools, with the centrality of different aspects of these dynamic constellations varying with each individual. In general, they present the same condensation of oedipal and preoedipal conflicts under the dominance of preoedipal aggression that is characteristic of borderline personality organization. I must stress that this condensation includes a regressive primitivization of the oedipal conflicts and an overriding predominance of aggressive over libidinal strivings; it is clinically very different from the more differentiated, defensive regression to preoedipal stages of development found in patients with neurotic personality organization. The fundamental question of why some patients with these dynamics develop a perversion and others do not is, in my view, still open.
4. Sexual perversions in the context of a narcissistic personality structure, particularly in cases of malignant narcissism, show the psychodynamics outlined by Chasseguet-Smirgel. In fact, the full deployment of a regressive "anal universe" pretty much overlaps with the syndrome of malignant narcissism plus an organized perversion. Even patients with multiple perverse tendencies and malignant narcissism display these psychodynamics.

5. Patients with total inhibition of all polymorphous perverse fantasies and impulses, derived not from repression but from lack of activation of early eroticism (that is, some extremely inhibited borderline but not hysterical patients), have the least favorable prognosis for treatment of their pathological sexuality. They tend to present almost insurmountable resistances to psychoanalysis and, in fact, to all psychotherapeutic treatments that attempt to resolve their sexual inhibitions.

6. The special position of homosexuality with regard to the perversions emerges as a major new development in psychoanalytic thinking. A consensus seems to be evolving that there exists not one homosexuality but a spectrum of homosexual psychopathology that parallels that of the other perversions (McDougall 1986). At the healthier end of the spectrum, homosexuality presents with the capacity for integration of genital and tender impulses in the same object relation and does not show the exclusive and rigid characteristics typical of other perversions. Also, in theory, homosexual impulses should be part of the available pattern of perverse fantasies and behaviors of normal sexuality as well. In fact, the continuity between such homosexual tendencies in neurotic personality organization and in patients who do not present significant character pathology seems to hold true for women but not for men. Many "normal" women are free to experience homosexual impulses and behaviors under socially facilitating circumstances that would trigger homosexual panic in nonhomosexual men. Openly bisexual men do usually have more severe character pathology than many openly bisexual women. The explanation for this difference may lie, as Stoller (1975) has suggested, in the more stable core gender identity of women, derived from their primary identification with mother, in contrast to the male, with his need to disidentify with mother in the course of separation-individuation. In addition, there is some evidence that the stronger social and cultural prohibitions against male as contrasted to female homosexuality may constitute a second reason for these differences (Liebert 1986).

POLYMORPHOUS PERVERSE INFANTILE SEXUALITY
AND NORMAL LOVE RELATIONS

I believe that we have not sufficiently explored the theoretical implications of the improvement in sexual functioning that we find in patients who obtain maximal benefit from psychoanalytic treatment. Regularly, in such cases, we observe that the patient's erotic excitement is inti-mately linked to derivatives of aggression, so that libidinal and aggressive impulses coalesce in sexual play and intercourse. We also observe the activation of implicit homosexual excitement and gratification in the mutual identification that takes place as part of intercourse and orgasm. In addition, it is striking how these normal polymorphous perverse fan-tasies and activities include a symbolic activation of the earliest object relation of the infant with mother and of the small child with both parents, condensing preoedipal and oedipal relations with them. Related to this finding is that such components of sexual intercourse as fellatio, cunnilingus, anal penetration, and exhibitionistic, voyeuristic, sadistic, and masochistic sexual play maintain erotic intensity because they rep-resent such unconscious fantasies regarding the oedipal and preoedipal objects.

If, as in narcissistic personalities, such internalized object relations have deteriorated, the sexual play also may deteriorate into mechanical activities that lose their erotic quality. An essential factor in maintaining the intensity of a passionate love relationship is the inclusion of poly-morphous perverse sexuality, which recruits in its function as the recep-tacle of unconscious fantasy the current conflicts that evolve between partners throughout time.

What is also of particular interest is that, insofar as sexual passion includes the freedom to unconsciously integrate love and hatred in poly-morphous sexual behavior, an implicit frame of a couple's safe object relation is developed, a frame that tolerates the playful use or "exploita-tion" of each other as part of sexual play. This frame represents a tempo-rary regressive splitting of the ego in the service of sexual excitement and love, which enters into a dialectic contradiction with the opposite ten-dency, also activated in sexual intimacy: the urge for temporary fusion experiences in the sexual act.

This sexual "use of the object" reflects a normal function of splitting of the sexual object or, rather, a duplication of it, in which the reality of the object relation is maintained while a fantastic, regressive one is playfully enacted as part of sexual desire and excitement. In fact, the inhibition of this sublimatory use of splitting is related to a decrease in sexual excite-ment in milder forms of sexual inhibition.

Another important mechanism operating in sexual excitement is ideal-ization of the sexual partner's genitals and body. I elsewhere (see chap. 17) refer to this as idealizing the sexual partner's anatomy (erotic idealiza-tion), a crucial aspect of the normal integration of tender and erotic strivings in both heterosexual and homosexual love relations. This erotic idealization parallels the normal idealization processes described by

Chasseguet-Smirgel (1985a)—namely, the projection of the ego ideal onto the loved object—which characterizes falling in love and which increases the narcissistic gratification provided by real encounters with this materialized version of the ego ideal. The idealization of the loved object also carries with it idealization of the genital encounter, of one's own and one's partner's body and genitals as they touch and merge with each other. Thus the defensive use of idealization and splitting that we encounter in perversion is also characteristic of mature sexuality.

"NORMAL" AND "TRANSITIONAL" HOMOSEXUALITY

The question of the boundaries between homosexuality in a neurotic personality organization and the normal homosexual components of male sexuality has no simple answer. One might assume theoretically that, in parallel to the existence of polymorphous perverse infantile sexual trends of other types, homosexual impulses would be freely available and would show in occasional homosexual excitement and experience. If homosexual tendencies simply behaved like other polymorphous perverse trends, we would expect a spectrum of homosexual responses— from perversion in the sense of the habitual and obligatory restriction at one extreme to occasional homosexual impulses, fantasies, and behaviors at the other. In clinical practice, however, we see very few cases of consistent homosexual behavior in male patients who otherwise present no major character pathology.

To the contrary, by far the large majority of male patients we encounter who present casual homosexual behavior or a casual bisexual orientation belong to the borderline spectrum of pathology. Thus, from a clinical viewpoint, there appears to be a discontinuity between neurotic male homosexuality and normality, and male orientation toward one or the other sex does not seem to follow the usual distribution of polymorphous perverse sexuality.

Regarding female homosexual behavior, however, the situation is different. In my experience, occasional homosexual involvements are quite common on the part of women who are essentially heterosexual and do not present severe characterological problems. But the defensive rejection of the normal preoedipal dependency on father on the part of adolescent boys may contribute to their rejection of longed-for closeness with other men (Blos 1987). The theoretically expected continuity between nonobligatory homosexual trends within a normal population, on the one hand, and an obligatory homosexual perversion at a neurotic level of personality organization, on the other, probably exists for women but not for men.

If this clinical observation is valid, one might speculate that two important factors may be operative here: first, as mentioned before, the hypothesis formulated by Stoller (1975) that female core gender identity is cemented in the primary identification with mother and that women may therefore be more secure in their gender role identity as well, accepting their homosexual impulses as derivatives of the unconscious psychological bisexuality without excessive anxiety. Men, in contrast, whose core gender identity implies disidentifying from mother and who therefore experience less certainty in their basic gender role identity, may be more prone to repudiate the feminine aspects of their sexual identity. A failure in mother's relating to her infant child as a little boy—which would further weaken the boy's identification with his own masculine gender as part of his identification with mother—may significantly contribute to this dynamic feature. A second factor may be the existence of strong cultural biases against male homosexuality in our society, even against any overt physical manifestation of closeness between men, which may discourage casual homosexual impulses and behavior in men. The fact that there is less cultural repudiation of female homosexuality and of physical closeness between women may facilitate the occasional manifestations of homosexual behavior in women.

PERVERSION AND HOMOSEXUALITY AND NEUROTIC PERSONALITY ORGANIZATION

In both men and women, obligatory homosexuality is commonly part of a neurotic personality organization. As mentioned before, the oedipal constellation and castration anxiety are dominant features in these types of perversion, and the most typical object relation is submission to the oedipal parent of the same sex—that is, the negative Oedipus complex—as a defense against the severe castration anxiety that interferes with the positive Oedipus complex.

Men's homosexual identification is with themselves as the child being loved by mother, while their longings for mother have been displaced onto motherly men who protect them both from a forbidden relation with mother and from rivalry with the dissociated, cruel, sadistic father. In other cases, and sometimes in the same case, the identification may be with the giving mother while the patient projects his sexually dependent self onto his homosexual object (Freud 1914).

Similar relations obtain in women, with the patient sexually submitting as a little girl to motherly women, thus avoiding the unconsciously forbidden relation with father; or the identification is with motherly and sexually available women while the submissive, dependent sexual self is projected onto the homosexual partner. Homosexual women who identify with the oedipal father while projecting their oedipally dependent self onto their homosexual object usually have a more complex and more pathological structure. Those who adopt a "male" role in the relationship and who in their gender role identity (physical appearance, clothing, and behavior) accentuate their identification with men usually also present significant repudiation of the feminine aspects of their personality and of their identification with mother in the preoedipal relation; by the same token, these indicate significant preoedipal conflictual roots condensed with oedipal conflicts. The "wish-fulfillment type" of the female castration complex described by Abraham (1920) thus presents more complex dynamics than those he suggested, and many cases of female homosexuality based on a narcissistic personality structure and borderline personality organization also present with a surface identification with a male role in relating to other women (thus revealing the preoedipal roots of their envy of men).

As has often been mentioned in the literature, all perversions except homosexuality and masochism are more prevalent in men than in women. This seems to be true at the level of both neurotic and borderline personality organizations. One also very frequently encounters masochistic and sadomasochistic fantasies and behavior in women that are not organized as a perversion but are quite freely expressed in masturbatory fantasy and in nonobligatory sexual behavior, whereas organized masochistic perversions in a strict sense seem to be more common in men. I have seen some typical cases of masochistic perversion in women with neurotic personality organization. One patient was able to achieve orgasm only if her arms were twisted severely during intercourse, producing intense pain. She related that behavior to the struggle with a boyfriend who forced her to have sexual intercourse by twisting her arms. She experienced intense pleasure on that occasion, which then organized her long-standing disposition to a masochistic perversion.

Similarly, women often have exhibitionistic fantasies and behavior that do not lead to an organized perversion. Fetishism, voyeurism, pedophilia, and sadistic perversion at any level of personality organization are relatively rare in women.

The generally held assumption that castration anxiety is a more powerful force in male than in female psychology may explain why this final common characteristic of all perversions is stronger in men. McDougall's (personal communication) observation, however, about the severity of primitive forms of castration anxiety in women with strong preoedipal conflicts suggests that this might remain an open question. Strong inhibition of all sexual enjoyment derived from preoedipal conflicts and predating the dominance of repressive mechanisms is more frequently seen in women, probably signaling the danger to the full expression of female sexuality when preoedipal conflicts around aggression toward the mother led to early repudiation of primary femininity.

PERVERSION AND HOMOSEXUALITY AND BORDERLINE PERSONALITY ORGANIZATION

At this level of psychopathology the dynamics of perversions described by the British and French schools appear to be central in the patients' unconscious life and coincide with the psychodynamics of borderline personality organization. Why some of these patients develop an organized perversion whereas most others instead present multiple polymorphous perverse infantile sexual traits has not yet been answered satisfactorily. The presence of the latter without an organized perversion is common in both male and female borderline patients. I have seen sadistic and masochistic, voyeuristic and exhibitionistic behavior in borderline women, and highly regressive, bizarre masochistic behaviors in both sexes. The most severe types of aggressive perversion, that I have seen however, and that are described in the literature have been almost exclusively in men. It is an open question to what extent biological aspects of the expression of aggression as well as cultural determinants contribute to both a higher intensity of aggression and its channeling into sadistic sexual behavior in men. There are, however, well-documented cases of sadistic perversions in women, and many such cases in the legal system may never reach a psychiatrist. The novel *Die Klavierspielerin* (The Pianist) by Elfriede Jelinek (1983) penetratingly describes the relation between a sadistic, voyeuristic, and masochistic perversion in a woman and her sadomasochistic and homosexual relation to an extremely envious, sadistic, and invasive mother.

When the borderline structure is not complicated by a narcissistic personality, the chaotic object relations overshadow the homosexual dynamics; but when the borderline personality organization exists in the context of a narcissistic personality, the homosexual orientation is much stronger. At the same time, object relations are not as chaotic—at least in ordinary social functioning. In these narcissistic patients one finds a dominant unconscious fantasy of incorporating, as part of the homosexual identity, the characteristics of both sexes so that envy of the other sex can be successfully denied. This development provides the background for extraordinarily severe resistances in psychoanalytic treatment.

I have found that in both men and women if the perverse tendencies are multiple and the organization of the personality is clearly borderline the overall prognosis for treatment depends on the intensity or severity of aggression, the degree to which superego functioning is maintained (so that at least ordinary conventional morality is available), and the presence or absence of a narcissistic organization—that is, the integration of a pathological grandiose self.

Borderline personality organization per se plus multiple perverse tendencies, in the absence of severe superego pathology, without primitivization of aggression, and without a narcissistic personality structure, has a relatively good prognosis for fundamental reorganization of the patient's sexual life and resolution of his psychopathology in general. Also, in these cases with better prognosis, the very availability of multiple perverse tendencies may improve sexual life at a time when the borderline personality organization has been resolved.

ELIMINATION OF ALL PERVERSE FEATURES

The study of borderline patients with severe inhibition of sexual desire, including significant limitations of the capacity for obtaining pleasure from masturbation or any sexual interaction with another person, has revealed the enormous difference between sexual inhibition resulting from repression (typical for neurotic personality organization) and inhibition derived from the unavailability or early repudiation of the erotic excitement of bodily stimulation in earlier stages of development. Serious conflicts in the mother-child relationship in the first few years of life, the absence of a sustained, gratifying mother-infant relationship that permits kindling of skin eroticism, seem leading etiological elements here.

Men with an incapacity for longing and tenderness and for erotic excitement have profound fears and experience deeply ingrained rejection of women, with paranoid tendencies that complicate their intense anxiety over their sexual functioning. One might say that their castration anxiety is so infiltrated by the fear of annihilation by a fantasied primitive sadistic mother image that all sensuality is suppressed or extinguished.

In women with borderline personality organization and severe conflicts around preoedipal aggression, these sexual inhibitions are particularly resistant to analytic treatment. They are usually linked to a profound repudiation of feminine identity and a conception of the female body as genitally destroyed and repugnant; by projection of their aggressive impulses, these women also experience male genitality as dangerous and repugnant. One female patient's exclusive masturbatory fantasy was that of a deeply humiliating scene in which she was prostrate on a hard bed, surrounded by groups of nuns who were watching her while the mother superior used a mechanical apparatus to penetrate her exposed genitals. This scenario contained no physical closeness, no contact of male and female genitals—only the awesome, frightening, humiliating atmosphere of a world dominated by sadistic and voyeuristic women. This patient had a history of problems of separation and individuation from a mother she experienced as extremely sadistic, overwhelming, and invasive. Mother forbade all expression of sexual curiosity in the family and dominated her passive and distant husband. The patient struggled with enormous difficulties in separating from an archaic, primitive maternal image that interfered with both her identification with a feminine role and her reaching out toward father and heterosexuality.

The task of treating perversion is to free infantile polymorphous perverse sexuality from its entanglement with the surrounding psychopathology. A point needs to be reached where the patient's polymorphous perverse infantile fantasies and experiences are expressed in the context of an object relation in depth, where tenderness and eroticism converge, and unavoidably also eroticism and aggression, and the deepest conflicts regarding the oedipal situation and castration anxiety emerge.

Chapter 17 A CONCEPTUAL MODEL FOR MALE PERVERSION (WITH PARTICULAR REFERENCE TO MALE HOMOSEXUALITY)

Discussing the history of the concept of perversion in Freud's thinking, Laplanche and Pontalis ask a central question about genitality: "It is . . . reasonable to ask whether it is merely its unifying character—its force as a 'totality' as opposed to the 'component' instincts—that confers a normative role upon genitality. Numerous perversions, such as fetishism, most forms of homosexuality, and even incest when it is actually practised, presuppose an organisation dominated by the genital zone. This surely suggests that the norm should be sought elsewhere than in genital functioning itself" (1973, p. 308).

In practice, most psychoanalysts restrict the concept of perversion to "deviations" from the normal in sexual aim or object choice that have a *habitual* and *obligatory* character (Moore and Fine 1990). This definition excludes a broad spectrum of behaviors and fantasies characteristic of normal sexuality, but it still presents the problem of what constitutes "normal" sexuality: Laplanche and Pontalis wonder whether Freud, after initially rejecting the descriptive classifications of perversions as not doing justice to the normal functions of polymorphous perverse sexual strivings throughout the individual's psychosexual development, did not end up by "categorising as perversions exactly what has always been so categorised" (p. 308).

I believe that "normal" sexual behavior may be more inclusive than the classical psychoanalytic definition has assumed. I think that the classification of sexual pathology, particularly of the perversions, must include the consideration of object relations; it cannot be based exclusively on the content of sexual behavior. I think too that the neglect or underestimation of the functions of polymorphous perverse fantasy and behavior in normal sexual interactions has led, in the classical psychoanalytic definition, to an underestimation of the function of perverse features in the idealization that is a normal constituent of the sexual aspects of love relations. Perverse features express early levels of object relations unconsciously activated in sexual intercourse, and these contribute to the intensity and the meaning of the sexual experience. In addition, Freud's (1905) assumption that neuroses are the negative of perversions falls short of our contemporary understanding of the complex relations among personality organization, perverse "structure," and pathology of object relations. Intimately linked with these questions is the relation between oedipal and preoedipal determinants of perversion and the extent to which oedipal and preoedipal components enter into certain perverse structures.

MALE POLYMORPHOUS PERVERSE SEXUALITY

What follows is an application of the general theoretical frame for analyzing perversions (spelled out in chap. 16) to male perversion.

One of the most striking and frequent fantasies of patients with clinical perversions is that their particular solution to their sexual needs provides them with such intense enjoyment or is of so "sublime" a nature that no other type of sexual behavior could possibly match it. Those who do not have this perversion, such patients believe, can experience only a pale reflection of the patients' sexual intensity and enjoyment (Lussier 1983). Chasseguet-Smirgel (1984) has pointed to the defensive nature of this idealization of the perversion, a defense that usually serves to justify the analization of all sexual relations, which is part of the perversion and also reinforces the denial of the importance of normal sexual intercourse, with its oedipal implications.

But idealization is also a central feature of normal love relations and sexual encounters. Men's idealization of female anatomy—the genitals, breasts, and skin—is part of the sexual excitement linked to falling in love. Idealization of the sexual partner's anatomy, which I call erotic idealization, depends on the ability to invest both tender and erotic feelings in the loved object. In addition, projection of one's ego ideal onto the loved object, which characterizes falling in love, increases the narcissistic gratification provided by the encounter; simultaneously, the love of the object expresses the gratification of object libidinal strivings. Idealization of the loved object, then, also carries with it idealization of the genital encounter, of one's own and one's partner's body and genitals as they touch and merge with each other. This comment may seem self-evident, but I make it because it is in contradiction to Freud's (1914, p. 88; 1921, p. 113) statement that narcissistic investment is depleted in the state of falling in love.

The voyeuristic, exhibitionistic, sadistic, and masochistic fantasies and wishes of the couple in love, the homosexual implications of their identification with the partner's excitement and orgasm, contribute to the symbolic expression of overcoming oedipal prohibitions. The couple in love and in a sexual union becomes the oedipal couple. Their fantasies, wishes, and interactions are also bridges for symbolic fusion or merger of two bodies that expresses preoedipal symbiotic longings, a fusion enacted in the sense of loss of control in mutual excitement and orgasm. The normal idealization of body parts of the loved object may also extend to the object's clothing and other possessions, which thus acquire fetishistic functions.

These erotic idealizations may inspire artistic or religious expression. In clinical perversions they may also serve the function of creating a "neosexuality" (McDougall 1985) or of evading the oedipal situation by idealizing preoedipal sexual precursors. I believe that these types of idealization normally blend with oedipal aspirations and give sexual love a transcendental quality, linking it to art and religion.

In contrast to the patient's fantasy that his clinical perversion is the ultimate in sexual enjoyment is the dramatic enrichment of sexual experience that can result when in the course of successful psychoanalytic treatment, polymorphous perverse sexuality is integrated with sexual fantasies and behavior that reflect the resolution of oedipal prohibitions against genital sexuality.

Erotic idealization thus may serve normal as well as pathological functions. All idealizations may be considered to stem from conflicts around ambivalence, and erotic idealization of polymorphous perverse sexuality is no exception. But the integration of hatred within a love relationship in general enriches that relationship and the accompanying erotic excitement, whereas idealization of a particular perversion is a secondary defense recruited in the service of denial of castration anxiety and regression to the anal phase.

The male heterosexual's idealization of a woman's body creates a sense of mystery and excitement that transcends ordinary aesthetic considerations and particularly the conventional limits of aesthetics. This idealization permits the man to tolerate the conflict between his wish to incorporate his beloved and his awareness of the ultimate impenetrability of both her body and her mind. In other words, this idealization facilitates tolerance for the impenetrable nature of the other while still keeping alive the endless desire for merger. Erotic idealization radiates sexual desire into social life and builds and maintains the interpersonal tensions that signal activation of oedipal fantasies and scenarios in the social structure.

Erotic idealization also strengthens the permanence of longing and preserves love under the condition of hatred that is a normal part of ambivalence, heightened in the intensity of the object relations of the couple in love. A man who is sexually excited by a woman who enrages him illustrates the function of erotic idealization in dealing with ambivalence.

The male homosexual's erotic idealization of his partner's body also reveals, upon analytic exploration, elements of heterosexuality in the fantasied relationship between the mother as oedipal object and the little boy, which Freud first described in his paper "On Narcissism" (1914). The little boy's wish to have mother admire his penis so that he can overcome his fears that his penis is inadequate and cannot compete with father's and fulfill the demands of mother's vagina (Chasseguet-Smirgel, 1984) and his need for assurance that he possesses a good, loving penis and not an aggressive, poisonous one are satisfied by the excited admiration of the homosexual partner's penis and by the partner's excitement and admiration of the homosexual patient's.

The exhibitionistic, voyeuristic, fetishistic, sadistic, and masochistic implications of the erotic idealization of the penis and of homosexual play with it are illustrated in the typical male fantasies of being sexually excited by manual stimulation without being permitted to achieve orgasm and the wish for passive stimulation of one's own penis, as well as the wish for aggressive penetration of the sexual partner's body cavities. Narcissistic identification with the partner's sexual excitement and orgasm and with the partner's admiration of the subject's own body is linked to oedipal and preoedipal fantasies that are remarkably alike for homosexual and heterosexual male patients; this similarity again points to the normal, universal function of polymorphous perverse fantasies and impulses. Similar observations could, of course, be made for the functions of homosexual components in a woman's exhibitionistic fantasies and excitement and in her excitement in erotic play with the erect penis that responds with excitement and orgasm to her control over it.

In my experience, psychoanalytic exploration regularly demonstrates that homosexual elements in both sexes enrich the erotic idealization of heterosexual sexual interactions. The problem, then, becomes one of tracing how normal perverse tendencies are transformed into restrictive, obligatory perversions, and how the concomitant erotic idealization is transformed into a defense that denies the importance of the dissociated or repressed sexual impulses that are linked to the forbidden oedipal realization. Although we may not yet have a definite answer to that question, the exploration of the dynamics of homosexuality in the context of significant personality disorders provides important information regarding some determinants of this transformation.

HOMOSEXUALITY IN A NEUROTIC PERSONALITY ORGANIZATION

Male homosexual patients with a neurotic personality organization and the corresponding structural characteristics of their world of object relations typically show the dominance of an unconscious submission to the oedipal father related to guilt over their oedipal longings for mother and to castration anxiety. In other words, they present a defensive structuralization of the negative oedipal complex within the context of a consolidated ego identity, the prevalence of total or integrated object relations, and a predominance of oedipal strivings and of defensive mechanisms centering upon repression.

In submitting to the oedipal father, they defensively identify with mother and often present the narcissistic homosexual object choice described by Freud (1914)—that is, they choose as their object a man who represents themselves as a child and whom they treat in a motherly way. In fact, there are patients whose homosexual identification is with themselves as the child being loved by mother, while their longings for mother have been displaced onto motherly men who protect them from both the forbidden relation with mother and the dissociated cruel and sadistic father. The same patient may identify alternately, in different homosexual love relationships, with the giving mother or with the dependent son.

These patients typically present an intensification of the erotic idealization of the male body, but often they are also capable of idealizing women's bodies provided the genitals are excluded. They may long for desexualized relationships with nonthreatening women while their relationships with soft, womanly men signals the rejection of aggressive, "brutally" heterosexual men representing the persecutory oedipal father.

In their love relationships, they are often able to have stable object relations that include both genital excitement and tenderness toward the same man, illustrating that here as well as in all neurotic perversions we find the capacity for integrating genital and tender feelings in the same object relation. These patients often tolerate polymorphous perverse fantasies and activities, and they may show a broad range of sexual behaviors so long as the obligatory homosexual condition is maintained. The idealization of art as a defense against significant regression and the dissociation of direct anal and oral enjoyment from such split-off idealizations are also typical of these cases.

What are the boundaries between homosexuality on the level of a neurotic personality organization and the normal homosexual components of male sexuality? From a traditional psychoanalytic view, we might say that neurotic homosexuality implies habitual, obligatory homosexual interests and relationships that signal the failure of the normal resolution of infantile oedipal conflicts and therefore of the capacity to identify with the oedipal father in a full relationship with an adult woman and to fully accept the function of paternity together with heterosexual sexuality. In recent years, this view has been challenged by psychoanalysts who propose a constitutionally determined homosexual orientation that, in some individuals, facilitates a normal homosexual organization, or a neurotic one if complicating developmental conflicts interfere with the establishment of normal homosexuality (Morgenthaler 1984; Isay 1989).

In addition, it may well be that the boundary between normal and pathological homosexual orientation is drawn very differently in different societies and historical periods; the exploration of this boundary by psychoanalysis may be hampered by the unavoidable cultural biases infiltrating all social sciences. I reexamine this question after exploring more severe levels of organization of homosexuality as well as of male perversions in general. Because of the great differences in prognosis mentioned in chapter 16, neurotic homosexuality must also be differentiated from homosexuality at the level of borderline personality organization and particularly from homosexuality rooted in a narcissistic personality structure.

Homosexuality at the Borderline Level

The clinical situations we encounter in homosexual patients with borderline personality organization differ in degrees of organization of perverse structure, qualities of narcissistic features, superego integration, and the intensity of aggressive drive.

We may descriptively differentiate, first of all, borderline patients who present multiple perverse features in chaotic coexistence, without any clear predominance over genital sexuality, from cases in which a dominant perversion (that is, a habitual and obligatory restriction of sexual fantasy and behavior) has crystallized. As I pointed out in chapter 16, borderline patients with chaotic, polymorphous perverse sexual fantasies and behaviors but without a consolidated perversion have a better prognosis for treatment than those with either an organized perversion or general unavailability of sexual eroticism.

It should be stressed that this unavailability is due not to repression but to lack of development or deterioration of the capacity for erotic excitement and idealization, a characteristic of some of the most severe cases of borderline patients, whose anhedonic quality of life experience continues to confront us with puzzling clinical and theoretical questions.

At this level of personality organization we find two dominant types of dynamics of male homosexuality. First is a consolidated homosexual perversion in a nonnarcissistic borderline patient in whom a dominantly preoedipal type of homosexuality usually involves the unconscious wish to submit sexually to father in order to obtain from him the oral gratifications that were denied by the dangerous, frustrating mother. Such a patient's relationship to the idealized partner may rapidly acquire demanding, greedy, eternally dissatisfied qualities that reflect oral needs and frustrations, efforts to control the sexual partner, and the tendency to extract by force the oral supplies the partner is suspected of withholding. These patients' sadistic impulses may be immediately projected and appear to have a strong potential for activating paranoid fantasies. Ongoing splitting operations facilitate the devaluation of sexual partners who frustrate the patient's oral needs and the idealization of new partners and lead to sexual promiscuity together with intense and chaotic clinging demandingness and sadomasochistic interactions.

These patients' idealization of desexualized women may also acquire a primitive, dependently clinging quality and may sometimes lead to revengeful identifications with women in the form of pseudofeminine behavior that expresses denial of the need for mother by identifying with a depreciated caricature of her. These patients' chaotic interactions, exploitativeness, ruthlessness, and yet desperate clinging illustrate their capacity for emotional involvement and their lack of capacity for object constancy.

The other alternative at this level of personality organization is, as mentioned before, the consolidation of a narcissistic personality structure with a dominant homosexual identification. This identification frequently reflects the unconscious fantasy of being both sexes at the same time and, therefore, denial of the narcissistic lesion of being condemned to belong to only one sex and to long eternally for the other one. The consolidation of a narcissistic personality structure and of homosexuality in this context leads to the search for other men who are idealized replicas of the pathological grandiose self. The relationship with such a man may be maintained as long as the patient's need for admiration is gratified by the partner without stirring up excessive envy, and the partner is not prematurely devalued in the course of defensive operations against envy. In practice, such carefully balanced homosexual relationships are difficult to maintain; male homosexuals with a narcissistic personality structure usually present either a stable but exploitative relationship with a nonnarcissistic, subservient, masochistic man with far greater capacity for object investment than they have, a long series of brief, exploitative relationships, or casual encounters with similarly inclined partners.

The surface functioning of these patients may be much better than that of the nonneurotic type mentioned earlier. Their relationships may be emotionally shallow and exploitative, but they are much less chaotic, and they have sublimatory capabilities in other areas. Their capacity for object investment in nonsexual areas is better maintained; they may, over the years, gradually devalue their conflict-ridden sexual encounters and end up in a relatively satisfactory asexual social equilibrium.

I have seen several patients with narcissistic personality and homosexuality who establish such an equilibrium by their early or late forties. They may have occasional sexual encounters or fleeting affairs, but they also have other friendships with men (often previous lovers) that may develop into socially gratifying and sometimes even close relationships without sexual involvement. Similarly, they may establish somewhat distant but stable relationships with women friends; their sexual gratifications eventually become dissociated and somewhat mechanical, while their mostly asexual life provides them with stability. This is in dramatic contrast to the later life experiences of homosexual men at a neurotic level of personality organization, who are able to maintain a stable and gratifying relationship with another man throughout many years or even a lifetime.

Male homosexuals with malignant narcissism show paranoid, sadistic, and antisocial tendencies, as is often the case with male prostitutes and the aggressive type of male transvestite (the drag queen). The infiltration of the pathological grandiose self in malignant narcissism leads to a failure of the defensive function of homosexuality against the direct expression of primitive aggression. In contrast to the function of perverse tendencies under normal circumstances to recruit aggression in the service of sex and love, sex and love are here recruited in the service of aggression. This leads in extreme circumstances to perversity of object relations characterized by ruthless exploitation, symbolic destruction of objects, and actual violence.

A DIAGNOSTIC FRAME FOR MALE PERVERSION

I trust it has become clear that I think one cannot speak of a perverse structure or integrate all the pathology included under male perversion within a single frame or category. There may be greater differences, for example, between male homosexuality on a neurotic level of personality organization and male homosexuality on a borderline or narcissistic level than between neurotic homosexuality and other types of neurotic character pathology in men. And there may be greater differences between nonhomosexual perversions in the context of a neurotic personality organization and similar perversions at the level of a borderline personality organization than between such perversions and other nonperverse neurotic character pathology. It seems to me that in terms of indications and contraindications for psychoanalysis, in terms of analyzability and prognosis, these observations have long been recognized, and that in this area differences between clinical practice and theoretical outlooks may have been influenced, at least in part, by cultural biases.

I am suggesting a classification of male perversion based on the pathology of internalized object relations, superego pathology, dominance of aggression, and level of ego organization.

Normal Polymorphous Perverse Sexuality. The point here is that the clinician often overlooks the inhibition of polymorphous perverse sexuality, which is of great importance in normal enjoyment of love and sex. It is of interest, for example, that in patients presenting sexual inhibitions, it is only when polymorphous perverse tendencies are freed in a sexual relationship that a full resolution of oedipally determined sexual conflicts can take place. Another advantage in adopting the criteria I am suggesting is that they help in detecting areas requiring further analytic exploration. Patients in transition, for example, from a borderline personality organization with multiple polymorphous sexual tendencies to a neurotic personality organization, a change that otherwise indicates definite improvement, may develop a sexual inhibition replacing the previously "free" polymorphous perverse sexual trends and may require renewed analytic work in this area within the context of dominant oedipal conflicts and neurotic symptomatology.

Organized Perversion in Neurotic Personality Organization. This category includes the typical perversions of which neurosis may be considered the negative. These patients present dominant oedipal conflicts with anal and oral regression but without a dominance of preoedipal conflicts or preoedipal aggression or the loss of ego identity. They evince object constancy or the corresponding capacity for object relations in depth.

Polymorphous Perverse Sexuality as Part of Borderline Personality Organization. Here we have polymorphous perverse sexual fantasies and behavior without an organized perversion—that is, the typical sexual chaos of borderline patients, with homosexual, heterosexual, exhibitionistic, voyeuristic, sadistic, masochistic, and fetishistic features. These cases are definitely not perversions in a clinical sense. To focus on their polymorphous perverse tendencies is warranted only in that they indicate a prognostically favorable development, contrasting with that of borderline cases who present a severe inhibition of all eroticism and erotic idealizations.

Structured Perversion in Borderline Personality. These patients present a lack of identity integration and object constancy and predominantly primitive defensive operations. They do not show the idealization, denial, reaction formation, and projection based on repression typical of the neurotic level of personality organization. These cases are more difficult to treat than ordinary borderline pathology and have a more guarded prognosis. Here we find hysteroid male patients who present cross-dressing and predominantly passive and effeminate character traits.

Perversion and Narcissistic Pathology. These cases are even more difficult to treat, and, as mentioned before, the homosexual identity may be intimately integrated into the pathological grandiose self. In this connection, many male homosexual patients with narcissistic personality structure display powerful defenses that rationalize and protect their homosexuality as an ego-syntonic part of the pathological grandiose self. Therefore, they do not wish to be treated and may even offer an ad hoc "ideology" regarding the superiority of male homosexuality.

This phenomenon illustrates that the extent to which homosexuality is ego-syntonic or ego-alien has no relation to whether the patient's personality structure is neurotic, borderline, or narcissistic. The homosexuality of a neurotic personality structure may also be ego-syntonic. Many patients with neurotic personality structure and a severe symptomatic neurosis or character pathology request psychoanalytic treatment but insist that they want to maintain their homosexuality. In my experience, it is difficult or impossible to predict what the patient's sexual orientation will be at the completion of the treatment. In many cases of both neurotic or narcissistic character pathology, an initially ego-syntonic homosexuality will change into heterosexuality, but there are cases in which a resolution of character pathology coincides with the consolidation of a more adaptive and satisfactory homosexuality. Whether this indicates the existence of normal homosexuality or a limitation in the psychoanalytic treatment is discussed below.

Perversion and Malignant Narcissism. This group includes many drag queens—male homosexuals with antisocial tendencies and life-threatening, sadistic homosexual perversions. The prognosis for psychotherapeutic treatment of this category is unusually poor and practically zero for patients with antisocial personality proper.

Perversion in Psychosis. Organized perversions in patients with psychotic functioning have many features in common with malignant narcissism and life-threatening sadism. When sadistic features are prominent, these patients are usually extremely dangerous.

Does it make sense to use the term *perverse structure* to refer to any of these groups? I would reserve this term for patients with an organized perversion and borderline personality organization, with the understanding that the term perversity in the transference should be restricted to patients who unconsciously attempt to transform all help received, all love and concern, into a destructive or self-destructive force. This process may develop both in patients with perversions and in patients without sexual deviations. The severity of borderline pathology, the guardedness of the prognosis, and the enormous difficulties in treating these cases, it seems to me, warrant applying the term *perverse structure* to these subgroups. In contrast, my classification tends to reduce the diagnostic and prognostic differences between perversion at the neurotic level of personality organization, on the one hand, and ordinary neuroses and neurotic character pathology, on the other. If I am right in assuming that this is a clinically reasonable conceptual shift, it would raise new questions regarding the spectrum of psychoanalytically treatable patients with perversions.

MALE HOMOSEXUALITY AND NORMALITY

We can now return to the question of how to distinguish between homosexuality imbedded in a neurotic personality organization and homosexual tendencies that might be considered equivalent to other polymorphous perverse aspects of normal sexuality. Here we encounter theoretical, clinical, and cultural problems.

Theoretically, within a psychoanalytic frame of reference, one may ask whether homosexuality can ever be considered a "normal" variant of sexual life. If overcoming the oedipal constellation means that a man must be able to identify with the sexual and paternal functions of the father, then any homosexual orientation would imply a limitation in this regard. If, in clinical practice, we encountered cases that indeed corresponded to a homosexual object choice without significant evidence of conflicts involving castration anxiety, fear of a full genital and tender involvement with a woman, fear of competing with the oedipal father in the sexual realm, or fear of an overwhelming, persecutory mother image, the psychoanalytic theory of the crucial importance of infantile sexuality in determining unconscious sexual conflicts and orientation would have to be revised.

One might, of course, cynically assume that, given psychoanalysts' theoretical bias, we will never find what we do not want to see. Against this argument, however, stands the reality of sharply differing opinions regarding these matters among psychoanalysts and determined tendencies in some quarters to radically reexamine basic psychoanalytic assumptions in this area. Morgenthaler (1984), for example, proposes that polymorphous perverse sexuality reflects basic, objectless sexual drives, and that both homosexuality and heterosexuality constitute organized, object-related structures that may be either normal or pathological. Isay (1989), on the basis of a psychoanalytic exploration of more than forty homosexual men, concludes that homosexuality is a nonpathological variant of human sexuality. Friedman (1988), while stressing the psychological determinants of homosexual orientation, also points to the possible relationships between male childhood aversion to aggressive play and prenatal endocrine influence on sexual orientation. Although the influence of psychosocial factors on homosexual orientation seems dominant (Green 1987; Money 1988; Arndt 1991), the influence of prenatal hormonal factors on brain structures influencing sexual behavior may account for recent findings suggesting a biological substrate for sexual orientation in homosexual men (LeVay 1991).

From a clinical viewpoint, the situation is equally complex. If homosexual tendencies simply expressed themselves like other polymorphous perverse trends, we would expect a spectrum of homosexual responses, from a perversion in the sense of a habitual and obligatory restriction, at one extreme, to occasional homosexual impulses, fantasies, and behavior—what I have described as the normal homosexual components of polymorphous perverse aspects of heterosexual interaction—at the other. These ideas, however, are not supported by my own clinical experience over the years or that of colleagues. I have seen very few cases of occasional homosexual behavior in male patients who otherwise would present no major character pathology.

By far the large majority of patients we encounter who present casual homosexual behavior or a bisexual orientation belong to the borderline spectrum of pathology. In other words, the casual or occasional selection of homosexual partners and "bisexuality" in a loose sense are usually found in patients who are more severely disturbed than those having a neurotic personality organization.

When, on the other hand, a homosexual orientation is dominant and the sexual behavior and/or fantasy is exclusively or dominantly directed toward men, we also find varying degrees of character pathology; only rarely do we find cases of male homosexuality without such pathology. It could be argued, of course, that normal homosexual males do not consult a psychoanalyst and that the cultural bias against male homosexuality present even in early child rearing traumatizes the homosexual boy and contributes to his character pathology.

In addition, although not all male patients with neurotic personality organization and homosexuality resolve their homosexual orientation in the course of psychoanalytic treatment, those who do usually resolve major neurotic character pathology as well. These treatments, however, are long and difficult. In contrast, some patients with borderline personality organization and narcissistic personalities find it easier to abandon their homosexual behavior without a major resolution of their character pathology. That is, some patients with severe pathology of object relations find it easier to switch their overt sexual orientation than do healthier, neurotic patients with homosexual structure who have a deeper investment in object relations.

Clinically, then, there appears to be a discontinuity between neurotic male homosexuality and normality, and orientation toward one or the other sex does not follow the usual distribution of polymorphous perverse sexuality.

We might ask to what extent strong cultural biases against male homosexuality may have something to do with this observed discontinuity. Are there conventional social pressures that discourage male homosexual behavior even though the disposition to it is more prevalent than actual behavior would indicate? One argument in support of this hypothesis is that in women we may indeed observe a range of casual homosexual behavior that follows the theoretically expectable range for all polymorphous perverse sexual trends.

The higher frequency of occasional, nonobligatory homosexual interaction in women is illustrated in Bartell's (1971) sociological study of group sex, which suggests that it is relatively easy for ordinarily heterosexual women to engage in homosexual encounters in the context of group sex, in contrast to the enormous reluctance, fear, or revulsion found in men without previous homosexual behavior to engage in such encounters. It may be that men are more concerned or uncertain about their sexual identity than women are about theirs. This may be explained in terms of a cultural bias more strongly directed against male than female homosexuality; or it might be explained in terms of gender differences in early psychosexual development—that is, the fact that the first object of both sexes is a woman and that girls but not boys normally have to undergo a change in libidinal object as part of their oedipal development.

Still another explanation of the relation between homosexual behavior and psychosexual development—or, rather, the hypothesis that homosexuality may develop for reasons other than psychosocial and/or psychodynamic determinants—refers to genetic predispositions. Although some recent research would seem to support a genetic or prenatal hormonal disposition to homosexual behavior in animals, the current evidence as applied to humans is inconclusive (Ehrhardt and Meyer-Bahlburg 1981; Friedman 1988; Money 1988; Arndt 1991). Also, from a theoretical viewpoint it is questionable to what extent one can assume a genetic predisposition to homosexuality that would not be importantly influenced by psychosexual development in early childhood.

It seems to me that we are left with the impression that male homosexuality, at least as we can explore it psychoanalytically, tends to present itself clinically as linked to significant character pathology. From a clinical viewpoint, then, the boundary between male homosexuality and normal polymorphous perverse sexual trends is more defined than we would expect theoretically.

SOME TECHNICAL PROBLEMS IN THE PSYCHOANALYSIS OF PERVERSION

It seems to me essential that the analyst who treats patients with well-structured perversions, whether at a neurotic or at a borderline and narcissistic level, maintain an attitude of technical neutrality in terms of the final outcome regarding the patient's sexual orientation. This does not mean that the analyst should maintain impassive indifference with patients who present, for example, a sadistic perversion that might endanger others or themselves. Technical neutrality always includes concern for the safety of the patient and those with whom he interacts and protection of the treatment situation itself.

It is essential that the analyst permit the patient to determine his own sexual orientation and object choice. Whether the analyst genuinely respects the patient's freedom to define himself as homosexual or heterosexual or simply pays lip service to that freedom can crucially influence the nature and helpfulness of the analytic treatment. The analyst may have to free himself from a conventional bias that might apply to situations other than the psychoanalytic one. The analyst's freedom to experience his or her own polymorphous perverse sexual tendencies in the emotional reactions to the patient's material, to identify with the patient's sexual excitement as well as with that of the patient's objects as part of the ebb and flow of countertransference, may help bring to the surface the patient's primitive fantasies linked to the preoedipal determinants of polymorphous perverse sexuality that will otherwise remain dissociated, repressed, or even consciously suppressed.

Patients with organized perversions often present a false or pseudo-incorporation of the analyst's interpretation as part of an extremely subtle devaluation of the oedipal father projected onto the analyst (Chasseguet-Smirgel 1984), thereby creating particular difficulties in the treatment. The patient acts "as if " he were incorporating the interpretation, in an unconscious mockery of the analytic process; this represents unconscious mockery of the power of the oedipal father and pseudo-identification with him based on anal regression and destructive spoiling of what is received.

This development may take the form of the patient's asking clarifying questions indicating that he has heard the analyst's interpretations "but not quite" and is trying subtly to adjust them for better understanding. It is as if the patient were "just about" to obtain some understanding; the analyst is frequently left with a vague uneasiness about whether authentic work is being carried out. The fact that deep transference regressions can take place under these circumstances and that a significant change of transference paradigms can be ascertained may reassure the analyst about the authenticity of the interaction, yet a doubt remains about what is real and what is "as if."

This defensive constellation should be differentiated from the unconscious spoiling of interpretations and the greedy incorporation and destruction of them that are typical of narcissistic personalities. In fact, the analyst's awareness that this process also obtains with organized perversions in nonnarcissistic patients may alert him that this particular defense is active and permit him to interpret it. The defense may take the form of the patient's childlike boasting about what he is learning in his analysis or discussing his analysis with other people in a subtle ridiculing of the oedipal father—symbolically, we might say, sharing his penis and degrading it in the process.

It is important to carefully explore a patient's indifference to or revulsion against the female genitals. Repression of sexual excitement underlying such devaluation should be differentiated from an incapacity for erotization of body surfaces in general, which is characteristic of some severely ill borderline and narcissistic patients. In the latter instances, no change can be expected before a regression in the transference develops that permits the reactivation of what may amount to a very early mother-child relationship, the development of a new capacity for tenderness that reinvests skin eroticism, the idealization of body parts, and the early roots of polymorphous perverse sexuality in general. In contrast, in better-functioning patients in whom loathing and disgust of the female body is a regressive defense against extreme castration anxiety, the working through of that anxiety, of the fear of and revulsion against a powerful and cruel father, and of the inhibition of the capacity for identification with him usually precedes the capacity for tolerating the reemergence of sexual excitement with female genitals.

In perversions as well as in all other cases with severe sexual inhibition, the patient's sexual fantasies as well as activities in masturbation and actual sexual interactions should be carefully explored. Frequently, subtle defensive avoidance of such exploration occurs in the form of the patient's willingness to openly discuss some aspects of his sexual experiences while carefully leaving out other aspects; it sometimes takes many months for the analyst to become aware of the areas that have been avoided.

In other cases, the patient may profusely display chaotic sexual fantasies and activities—in apparently total "freedom" of sexual expression—defensively to avoid central aspects of the transference, particularly primitive types of negative transference dispositions. The patient's chaotic sexual life that characterizes all his other interactions is utilized as a defense against an object relation in depth involving the analyst, and the task is very different: the analysis of the object relation in the transference has to be highlighted and linked to the defensive "smearing" of the analytic situation with primitive sexual material.

REFERENCES

Abraham, K. (1920). Manifestations of the female castration complex. In *Selected Papers on Psychoanalysis*. New York: Brunner/Mazel, 1979, pp. 338–369.

Alexander, F. (1930). The neurotic character. *International J. Psychoanalysis*, 11:292.

Alexander, F., and Healy, W. (1935). *The Roots of Crime*. New York: Knopf.

American Psychiatric Association. (1952). *Diagnostic and Statistical Manual of Mental Disorders (DSM-I)*. Washington, D.C.: Mental Hospital Service.

————. (1968). *Diagnostic and Statistical Manual of Mental Disorders (DSM-II)*. Washington, D.C.: American Psychiatric Association.

————. (1980). *Diagnostic and Statistical Manual of Mental Disorders (DSM-III)*. Washington, D.C.: American Psychiatric Association.

————. (1987). *Diagnostic and Statistical Manual of Mental Disorders (Third Edition-Revised): (DSM-III-R)*. Washington, D.C.: American Psychiatric Association.

Anzieu, D. (1984). *The Group and the Unconscious*. London: Routledge and Kegan Paul.

Arndt, W. B., Jr. (1991). *Gender Disorders and the Paraphilias*. Madison, Conn.: International Universities Press.

Arnold, M. B. (1970a). Brain function in emotion: A phenomenological analysis. In *Physiological Correlates of Emotion*, ed. P. Black. New York: Academic Press, pp. 261–285.

————. (1970b). Perennial problems in the field of emotion. In *Feelings and Emotions*, ed. M. B. Arnold. New York: Academic Press, pp. 169–185.

————. (1984). *Memory and the Brain*. Hillsdale, N.J.: Erlbaum Associates, chapters 11, 12.

Asch, S. (1985). The masochistic personality. In *Psychiatry 1*, ed. R. Michels and J. Cavenar. Philadelphia: Lippincott, 27:1–9.

Bartell, G. D. (1971). *Group Sex*. New York: Signet Books.

Berliner, B. (1958). The role of object relations in moral masochism. *Psychoanalytic Quarterly*, 27:38–56.

Bion, W. R. (1957a). On arrogance. In *Second Thoughts: Selected Papers on Psychoanalysis*. New York: Basic Books, 1968, pp. 86–92.

————. (1957b). Differentiation of the psychotic from the nonpsychotic personalities. In *Second Thoughts: Selected Papers on Psychoanalysis*. New York: Basic Books, 1968, pp. 43–64.

———. (1959). Attacks on linking. In *Second Thoughts: Selected Papers on Psychoanalysis*. New York: Basic Books, 1968, pp. 93–109.

———. (1967). Notes on memory and desire. In *Psychoanalytic Forum*, 2:271–280.

———. (1968). *Second Thoughts: Selected Papers on Psychoanalysis*. New York: Basic Books.

———. (1970). *Attention and Interpretation*. London: Heinemann.

———. (1974). *Brazilian Lectures 1, São Paulo, 1973*, ed. J. Salomao. Rio de Janeiro: Imago Editora.

———. (1975). *Brazilian Lectures 2, Rio/São Paulo, 1974*, ed. J. Salomao. Rio de Janeiro: Imago Editora.

Blacker, K. H., and Tupin, J. P. (1977). Hysteria and hysterical structures: Developmental and social theories. In *Hysterical Personality*, ed. M. J. Horowitz. New York: Jason Aronson, 2:97–140.

Blos, P. (1987). The role of the dyadic father in male personality formation. In *Sigmund Freud Haus Bulletin*. Vienna: Sigmund Freud Society, 10:7–14.

Blum, H. P. (1988). Shared fantasy and reciprocal identification, and their role in gender disorders. In *Fantasy, Myth, and Reality*, ed. H. Blum, Y. Kramer, A. Richards, and A. Richards. New York: International Universities Press.

Braunschweig, D., and Fain, M. (1971). *Eros et Antéros*. Paris: Payot.

———. (1975). *Le nuit, le jour: Essai psychanalytique sur le fonctionnement mental*. Paris: Payot.

Brenner, C. (1959). The masochistic character: Genesis and treatment. *J. American Psychoanalytic Association*, 7:197–266.

Brierley, M. (1937). Affects in theory and practice. In *Trends in Psychoanalysis*. London: Hogarth, 1951, pp. 43–56.

Call, J. D. (1980). Attachment disorders of infancy. In *Comprehensive Textbook of Psychiatry*, ed. H. I. Kaplan et al. Baltimore: Williams and Wilkins, 3:2586–2592.

Cavenar, J. O., and Walker, J. I. (1983). Hysteria and hysterical personality. In *Signs and Symptoms in Psychiatry*, ed. J. O. Cavenar, Jr., and H. F. Brodie. Philadelphia: J. B. Lippincott, 4:59–74.

Chasseguet-Smirgel, J. (1970). Feminine guilt and the Oedipus complex. In *Female Sexuality*, ed. J. Chasseguet-Smirgel. Ann Arbor: University of Michigan Press, pp. 94–134.

———. (1978). Reflexions on the connexions between perversion and sadism. *International J. Psychoanalysis*, 59:27–35.

———. (1983). Perversion and the universal law. In *Creativity and Perversion*. New York: Norton, 1984, pp. 1–12.

———. (1984). *Creativity and Perversion*. New York: Norton.

———. (1985). *The Ego Ideal: A Psychoanalytic Essay on the Malady of the Ideal*. New York: Norton.

_____. (1986). *Sexuality and Mind: The Role of the Father and the Mother in the Psyche.* New York: New York University Press.

Chodoff, P. (1974). The diagnosis of hysteria: An overview. *American J. Psychoanalysis,* 131:1073–1078.

Chodoff, P., and Lyons, H. (1958). Hysteria, the hysterical personality and "hysterical" conversion. *American J. Psychotherapy,* 14:734–740.

Cleckley, H. (1941). *The Mask of Sanity.* St. Louis: Mosby.

Cooper, A. (1985). The masochistic-narcissistic character. In *Masochism: Current Psychoanalytic and Psychotherapeutic Perspectives,* ed. R. A. Glick and D. I. Meyers. New York: Analytic Press.

Diatkine, G. (1983). *Les transformations de la psychopathie.* Paris: Presses Universitaires de France.

Dicks, H. V. (1972). *Licensed Mass Murder: A Socio-Psychological Study of Some SS Killers.* New York: Basic Books.

Easser, B. R., and Lesser, S. R. (1965). Hysterical personality: A re-evaluation. *Psychoanalytic Quarterly,* 34:390–415.

_____. (1966). Transference resistance in hysterical character neurosis: Technical considerations. In *Developments in Psychoanalysis,* ed. G. Goldman and D. Shapiro. New York: Hafner, pp. 69–80.

Eissler, K. R. (1950). Ego-psychological implications of the psychoanalytic treatment of delinquents. *Psychoanalytic Study of the Child,* 5:97–121.

Emde, R. (1987). Development terminable and interminable. Plenary Presentation at the thirty-fifth International Psychoanalytical Congress, Montreal, Canada, July 27, 1987.

Emde, R., Kligman, D. H., Reich, J. H., and Wade, T. D. (1978). Emotional expression in infancy: I: Initial studies of social signaling and an emergent model. In *The Development of Affect,* ed. M. Lewis and L. Rosenblum. New York: Plenum Press.

Erhardt, A., and Meyer-Bahlburg, H. (1981). Effects of prenatal sex hormones on gender-related behavior. *Science,* 211:1312.

Erikson, E. H. (1954). The dream specimen of psychoanalysis. *J. American Psychoanalytic Association,* 2:5–56.

Fairbairn, W. (1943). *An Object-Relations Theory of the Personality.* New York: Basic Books.

Fenichel, O. (1941). *Problems of Psychoanalytic Technique.* Albany, N.Y.: Psychoanalytic Quarterly.

_____. (1945). *The Psychoanalytic Theory of Neurosis.* New York: Norton, 20:501–502.

Fraiberg, A. (1983). Pathological defenses in infancy. *Psychoanalytic Quarterly,* 60: 612–635.

Frank, J. D., et al. (1952). Two behavior patterns in therapeutic groups and their apparent motivation. *Human Relations,* 5:289–317.

Freud, S. (1894). The neuro-psychoses of defence. *Standard Edition,* 3:43–61. London: Hogarth Press, 1962.

———. (1905). Three essays on the theory of sexuality. *S.E.*, 7:125–245. London: Hogarth Press, 1953.

———. (1914). On narcissism. *S.E.*, 14:69–102. London: Hogarth Press, 1957.

———. (1915a). Instincts and their vicissitudes. *S.E.*, 14:109–140. London: Hogarth Press, 1957.

———. (1915b). Repression. *S.E.*, 14:141–158. London: Hogarth Press, 1957.

———. (1915c). The unconscious. *S.E.*, 14:159–215. London: Hogarth Press, 1957.

———. (1916). Some character-types met with in psycho-analytic work. *S.E.*, 14:309–333. London: Hogarth Press, 1957.

———. (1919). "A child is being beaten": A contribution to the study of the origin of sexual perversions. *S.E.*, 17:175–204. London: Hogarth Press, 1955.

———. (1920). Beyond the pleasure principle. *S.E.*, 18:1–64. London: Hogarth Press, 1955.

———. (1921). Group psychology and the analysis of the ego. *S.E.*, 18:69–143. London: Hogarth Press, 1955.

———. (1924). The economic problem of masochism. *S.E.*, 19:157–170. London: Hogarth Press, 1961.

———. (1926). Inhibitions, symptoms and anxiety. *S.E.*, 20:87–156. London: Hogarth Press, 1961.

———. (1927). Fetishism. *S.E.*, 21:147–158. London: Hogarth Press, 1961.

———. (1933). New introductory lectures on psycho-analysis. *S.E.*, 22. London: Hogarth Press, 1964.

———. (1937). Analysis terminable and interminable. *S.E.*, 23:209–253. London: Hogarth Press, 1964.

———. (1940a). An outline of psycho-analysis. *S.E.*, 23:143, 202–204. London: Hogarth Press, 1964.

———. (1940b). Splitting of the ego in the process of defence. *S.E.*, 23:273–274. London: Hogarth Press, 1964.

Friedlander, S. (1984). *Reflections of Nazism*. New York: Harper and Row.

Friedman, R. (1988). *Male Homosexuality: A Contemporary Psychoanalytic Perspective*. New Haven: Yale University Press.

Gaensbauer, T., and Sands, K. (1979). Distorted affective communications in abused and neglected infants and their potential impact on caretakers. *J. American Academy Child Psychiatry*, 18:236–250.

Galenson, E. (1986). Some thoughts about infant psychopathology and aggressive development. *International Rev. Psychoanalysis*, 13:349–354.

Gill, M. (1982). *Analysis of Transference. Vol. 1, Theory and Technique*. New York: International Universities Press.

Glover, E. (1955). *The Technique of Psychoanalysis*. New York: International Universities Press.

Glueck, S., and Glueck, E. (1943). *Criminal Careers in Retrospect*. New York: Commonwealth Fund.

Green, A. (1977). Conceptions of affect. In *On Private Madness*. London: Hogarth Press, 1986, pp. 174–213.

Green, R. (1987). *The "Sissy Boy Syndrome" and the Development of Homosexuality*. New Haven: Yale University Press.

Grinberg, L. (1979). Projective counteridentification and countertransference. In *Countertransference*, ed. L. Epstein and A. H. Feiner. New York: Jason Aronson, pp. 169–191.

Gross, H. (1981). Depressive and sadomasochistic personalities. In *Personality Disorders: Diagnosis and Management*, ed. J. R. Lion. Baltimore: Williams and Wilkins, 13:204–220.

Grossman, W. (1986). Notes on masochism: A discussion of the history and development of a psychoanalytic concept 1. *Psychoanalytic Quarterly*, 55:379–413.

———. (1991). Pain, aggression, fantasy, and concepts of sadomasochism. *Psychoanalytic Quarterly*, 60:22–52.

Grunberger, B. (1976). Essai sur le fetichisme. *Revue Française de Psychanalyse*, 40(2):235–264.

Guntrip, H. (1961). *Personality Structure and Human Interaction*. New York: International Universities Press.

———. (1968). *Schizoid Phenomena, Object Relations, and the Self*. New York: International Universities Press.

———. (1971). *Psychoanalytic Theory, Therapy, and the Self*. New York: Basic Books.

Guze, S. B. (1964a). Conversion symptoms in criminals. *American J. Psychiatry*, 121:580–583.

———. (1964b). A study of recidivism based upon a follow-up of 217 consecutive criminals. *J. Nervous and Mental Diseases*, 138:575–580.

Henderson, D. K. (1939). *Psychopathic States*. London: Chapman and Hall.

Henderson, D. K., and Gillespie, R. D. (1969). *Textbook of Psychiatry: For Students and Practitioners*, 10th ed., rev. I. R. C. Batchelor. London: Oxford University Press.

Hoffman, M. (1978). Toward a theory of empathic arousal and development. In *The Development of Affect*, ed. M. Lewis and L. Rosenblum. New York: Plenum Press, pp. 227–256.

Holder, A. (1970). Instinct and drive. In *Basic Psychoanalytic Concepts of the Theory of Instincts*, ed. H. Nagera. New York: Basic Books, 3:19–22.

Horowitz, M. J. (1977). *Hysterical Personality*. New York: Jason Aronson.

———. (1979). *States of Mind*. New York: Plenum.

Isay, R. A. (1989). *Being Homosexual*. New York: Farrar, Straus, and Giroux.

Izard, C. (1978). On the ontogenesis of emotions and emotion-cognition relationships in infancy. In *The Development of Affect*, ed. M. Lewis and L. Rosenblum. New York: Plenum Press, pp. 389–413.

Izard, C., and Buechler, S. (1979). Emotion expressions and personality integration in infancy. In *Emotions in Personality and Psychopathology*, ed. C. Izard. New York: Plenum Press.

Jacobson, E. (1953). On the psychoanalytic theory of affects. In *Depression*. New York: International Universities Press, 1971, pp. 3–47.

———. (1957a). Denial and repression. In *Depression*. New York: International Universities Press, 1971, pp. 107–136.

———. (1957b). Normal and pathological moods: Their nature and functions. In *Depression*. New York: International Universities Press, 1971, pp. 66–106.

———. (1964). *The Self and Object World*. New York: International Universities Press.

———. (1967). *Psychotic Conflict and Reality*. New York: International Universities Press.

———. (1971a). Acting out and the urge to betray in paranoid patients. In *Depression*. New York: International Universities Press, pp. 302–318.

———. (1971b). *Depression*. New York: International Universities Press.

James, W. (1884). What is an emotion? *Mind*, 9:188–205.

Jaques, E. (1982). *The Form of Time*. New York: Crane, Russak.

Jelinek, E. (1983). *Die Klavierspielerin*. Reinbek bei Hamburg: Rowohlt.

Johnson, A. M. (1949). Sanctions for superego lacunae of adolescents. In *Searchlights on Delinquency*, ed. K. R. Eissler. New York: International Universities Press, pp. 225–245.

Johnson, A. M., and Szurek, S. A. (1952). The genesis of antisocial acting out in children and adults. *Psychoanalytic Quarterly*, 21:323.

Kernberg, O. F. (1974a). Barriers to falling and remaining in love. *J. American Psychoanalytic Association*, 22:486–511.

———. (1974b). Mature love: Prerequisites and characteristics. *J. American Psychoanalytic Association*, 22:743–768.

———. (1975). *Borderline Conditions and Pathological Narcissism*. New York: Jason Aronson.

———. (1976). *Object Relations Theory and Clinical Psychoanalysis*. New York: Jason Aronson.

———. (1980a). Adolescent sexuality in the light of group processes. *Psychoanalytic Quarterly*, 49(1):27–47.

———. (1980b). *Internal World and External Reality: Object Relations Theory Applied*. New York: Jason Aronson.

———. (1983). Psychoanalytic studies of group processes: Theory and applications. In *Psychiatry 1983: APA Annual Review*. Washington, D.C.: American Psychiatric Press, 2:21–36.

———. (1984). *Severe Personality Disorders: Psychotherapeutic Strategies*. New Haven: Yale University Press.

———. (1991a). Aggression and love in the relationship of the couple. *J. American Psychoanalytic Association*, 39:45–70.

———. (1991b). Sadomasochism, sexual excitement, and perversion. *J. American Psychoanalytic Association*, 39:333–362.

———. (1992). "Mythological encounters" in the psychoanalytic situation. In *The Personal Myth in Psychoanalytic Theory*, ed. P. Hartocollis and I. Graham. Madison, Conn.: International Universities Press, pp. 37–48.

Kernberg, O. F.; Burstein, E.; Coyne, L.; Appelbaum, A.; Horwitz, L.; and Voth, H. (1972). *Psychotherapy and Psychoanalysis: Final Report of the Menninger Foundation's Psychotherapy Research Project*. Bulletin Menninger Clinic, 36:1–275.

Klein, M. (1940). Mourning and its relation to manic-depressive states. In *Contributions to Psychoanalysis, 1921–1945*. London: Hogarth Press, 1948, pp. 311–338.

———. (1945). The oedipus complex in the light of early anxieties. In *Contributions to Psychoanalysis, 1921–1945*. London: Hogarth Press, 1948, pp. 311–338.

———. (1946). Notes on some schizoid mechanisms. In *Developments in Psychoanalysis*, ed. J. Riviere. London: Hogarth Press, 1952, pp. 292–320.

———. (1952a). Some theoretical conclusions regarding the emotional life of the infant. In *Developments in Psychoanalysis*, ed. J. Riviere. London: Hogarth Press, pp. 198–236.

———. (1952b). The origins of transference. In *Envy and Gratitude*. New York: Basic Books, 1957, pp. 48–56.

———. (1955). On identification. In *Envy and Gratitude*. New York: Basic Books, 1957, pp. 141–175.

———. (1957). *Envy and Gratitude*. New York: Basic Books.

Knapp, P. H. (1978). Core processes in the organization of emotions. In *Affect: Psychoanalytic Theory and Practice*, ed. M. B. Cantor and M. L. Glucksman. New York: Wiley, pp. 51–70.

Kohut, H. (1971). *The Analysis of the Self*. New York: International Universities Press.

———. (1977). *The Restoration of the Self*. New York: International Universities Press.

Krause, R. (1988). Eine Taxonomie der Affekte und ihre Anwendung auf das Verständnis der frühen Störungen. *Psychotherapie und Medizienische Psychologie*, 38:77–86.

Krause, R., and Lutolf, P. (1988). Facial indicators of transference processes in psychoanalytical treatment. In *Psychoanalytic Process Research Strategies*, ed. H. Dahl and H. Kachele. Heidelberg: Springer, pp. 257–272.

Krohn, A. (1978). *Hysteria: The Elusive Neurosis*. New York: International Universities Press.

Lange, C. (1885). *The Emotions*. Baltimore: Williams and Wilkins, 1922.

Laplanche, J., and Pontalis, J. B. (1973). *The Language of Psychoanalysis*. New York: Norton.

Laughlin, H. (1967). *The Neuroses*. New York: Appleton-Century-Crofts.

Lazare, A. (1971). The hysterical character in psychoanalytic theory. *Archives of General Psychiatry*, 25:131–137.

Lazare, A., Klerman, G. L., and Armor, D. J. (1966). Oral, obsessive, and hysterical personality patterns: An investigation of psychoanalytic concepts by means of factor analysis. *Archives of General Psychiatry*, 14:624–630.

———. (1970). Oral, obsessive and hysterical personality patterns. *J. Psychiatric Research*, 7:275–290.

LeVay, S. (1991). A difference in hypothalamic structure between heterosexual and homosexual men. *Science*, 253:1034–1037.

Lewis, D., et al. (1985). Biopsychosocial characteristics of children who later murder: A prospective study. *American J. Psychiatry*, 142:1161–1167.

Liebert, R. S. (1986). The history of male homosexuality from ancient Greece through the Renaissance: Implications for psychoanalytic theory. In *The Psychology of Men: New Psychoanalytic Perspectives*, ed. G. I. Fogel, F. M. Lane, and R. S. Liebert. New York: Basic Books, pp. 181–210.

Liebowitz, M. R., and Klein, D. F. (1981). Interrelationship of hysteroid dysphoria and borderline personality disorder. *Psychiatric Clinics of North America*. Philadelphia: Saunders. 4:67–88.

Lorenz, K. (1963). *On Aggression*. New York: Bantam Books.

Luborsky, L. (1977). Measuring a pervasive psychic structure in psychotherapy: The core conflictual relationship theme. In *Communicative Structures and Psychic Structures*, ed. N. Freedman and S. Grand. New York: Plenum.

Luisada, P. V., Peele, R., and Pittard, E. A. (1974). The hysterical personality in men. *American J. Psychiatry*, 131:518–521.

Lussier, A. (1983). Les dèviations du dèsir. Etude sur le fetichisme. *Revue Française Psychanalyse*, 47:19–142.

McDougall, J. (1970). Homosexuality in women. In *Female Sexuality*, ed. J. Chasseguet-Smirgel. Ann Arbor: University of Michigan Press, pp. 171–212.

———. (1980). *Plea for a Measure of Abnormality*. New York: International Universities Press.

———. (1985). *Theatres of the Mind*. New York: Basic Books.

———. (1986). Identifications, neoneeds and neosexualities. *International J. Psychoanalysis*, 67:19–31.

Mahler, M. S. (1971). A study of the separation-individuation process and its possible application to borderline phenomena in the psychoanalytic situation. *Psychoanalytic Study of the Child*, 26: 403–424.

———. (1972). On the first three subphases of the separation-individuation process. *International J. Psychoanalysis*, 53:333–338.

Mahler, M. S., and Furer, M. (1968). *On Human Symbiosis and the Vicissitudes of Individuation*. New York: International Universities Press.

Mahler, M. S., Pine, F., and Bergman, A. (1975). *The Psychological Birth of the Human Infant*. New York: Basic Books.

Main, T. (1957). The ailment. *British J. Medical Psychology*, 30:129–145.

Mann, H. (1932). *Professor Unrat oder Das Ende eines Tyrannen*. Suhrkamp: Bibl. Suhrkamp 1981.

Marmor, J. (1953). Orality in the hysterical personality. *J. American Psychoanalytic Association*, 1:656–671.

Massie, H. (1977). Patterns of mother-infant behavior and subsequent childhood psychoses. *Child Psychiatry and Human Development*, 7:211–230.

Meltzer, D. (1977). *Sexual States of Mind*. Perthshire, Scotland: Clunie Press, pp. 132–139.

———. (1984). *Dream Life*. London: Clunie Press.

Merksy, H. (1979). *The Analysis of Hysteria*. London: Baillière Tindall.

Milgram, S. (1963). Behavioral study of obedience. *J. Abnormal and Social Psychology*, 67:371–378.

Millon, T. (1981). *Disorders of Personality*. New York: Wiley.

Money, J. (1988). *Gay, Straight, and In-Between: The Sexology of Erotic Orientation*. New York: Oxford University Press.

Moore, B. E., and Fine, B. D. (1990). *Psychoanalytic Terms and Concepts*. New Haven: American Psychoanalytic Association and Yale University Press.

Morgenthaler, F. (1984). *Homosexualität, Heterosexualität, Perversion*. Paris: Qumran.

Moser, U. (1978). Affektsignale und aggressives Verhalten: Zwei verbal formulierte Modelle der Aggression. *Psyche*, 32:229–258.

Ogden, T. H. (1979). On projective identification. *International J. Psychoanalysis*, 60:357–373.

O'Neal, P., et al. (1962). Parental deviance and the genesis of sociopathic personality. *American J. Psychiatry*, 118:1114.

Orwell, G. (1949). *1984*. New York: Harcourt Brace.

Osofsky, J. D. (1988). Affective exchanges between high risk mothers and infants. *International J. Psychoanalysis*. 69:221–232.

Ovesey, L. (1983). The cross-dressing phenomenon in men. Paper presented at the twenty-sixth annual Sandor Rado Lecture delivered at the New York Academy of Medicine, New York (unpublished).

Ovesey, L., and E. Person (1973). Gender identity and sexual psychopathology in men: A psychodynamic analysis of homosexuality, transsexualism, and transvestism. *J. American Academy of Psychoanalysis*, 1(1):53–72.

———. (1976). Transvestism: A disorder of the sense of self. *International J. Psychoanalytic Psychotherapy*, 5:219–236.

Parin, P., Morgenthaler, F., and Parin-Matthéy, G. (1971). *Fürchte Deinen Nächsten Wie Dich Selbst*. Frankfurt: Suhrkamp.

Person, E. S. (1978). Transvestism: New perspectives. *J. American Academy of Psychoanalysis*, 6(3):301–323.

———. (1984). Homosexual cross-dressers. *J. American Academy of Psychoanalysis*, 12(2):167–186.

Person, E. S., and Ovesey, L. (1974a). The psychodynamics of male transsexualism. In *Sex Differences in Behavior*, ed. R. C. Friedman, R. M. Richart, and R. L. VandeWiele. New York: Wiley, pp. 315–331.

————. (1974b). The transsexual syndrome in males. I. Primary transsexualism. *American J. Psychotherapy*, 28:4–20.

————. (1974c). The transsexual syndrome in males. II. Secondary transsexualism. *American J. Psychotherapy*, 28:174–193.

————. (1978). Transvestism: New perspectives. *J. American Academy of Psychoanalysis*, 6(3):301–323.

————. (1984). Homosexual cross-dressers. *J. American Academy of Psychoanalysis*, 12(2):167–186.

Piaget, J. (1954). *Intelligence and Affectivity*. Palo Alto: Annual Review Press, 1981.

Pinter, H. (1965). *The Homecoming*. New York: Grove Press.

————. (1973). The Quiller memorandum. In *Five Screenplays*. New York: Grove Press.

————. (1978). *Betrayed*. New York: Grove Press.

Plutchik, R. (1980). *Emotions: A Psychoevolutionary Synthesis*. New York: Harper and Row.

Plutchik, R., and Kellerman, H. (1983). *Emotions: Theory, Research, and Experience*. Vol. 2, *Emotions in Early Development*. New York: Academic Press.

Racker, H. (1957). The meaning and uses of countertransference. *Psychoanalytic Quarterly*, 26:303–357.

————. (1968). *Transference and Countertransference*. New York: International Universities Press.

Rangell, L. (1974). A psychoanalytic perspective leading currently to the syndrome of the compromise of integrity. *International J. Psychoanalysis*, 55:3–12.

Rapaport, D. (1953). On the psychoanalytic theory of affects. In *The Collected Papers of David Rapaport*, ed. M. M. Gill. New York: Basic Books, 1967, pp. 476–512.

————. (1960). *The Structure of Psychoanalytic Theory: A Systematizing Attempt*. Psychological Issues, Monograph 6. New York: International Universities Press.

Reed, G. S. (1987). Rules of clinical understanding: Classical psychoanalysis and self psychology. *J. American Psychoanalytic Association*, 35:421–446.

Reich, W. (1933). *Character Analysis*. New York: Farrar, Straus, and Giroux, 1972.

Reid, W. H. (1981). *The Treatment of Antisocial Syndromes*. New York: Van Nostrand Reinhold.

Rice, A. K. (1965). *Learning for Leadership*. London: Tavistock.

Robins, L. N. (1966). *Deviant Children Grown Up: A Sociological and Psychiatric Study of Sociopathic Personality*. Baltimore: Williams and Wilkins.

Roiphe, H., and Galenson, E. (1981). *Infantile Origins of Sexual Identity*. New York: International Universities Press.

Rosenfeld, H. (1964). On the psychopathology of narcissism: A clinical approach. *International J. Psychoanalysis*, 45:332–337.

_____. (1965). *Psychotic States: A Psychoanalytical Approach*. New York: International Universities Press.

_____. (1971). A clinical approach to the psychoanalytic theory of the life and death instincts: An investigation into the aggressive aspects of narcissism. *International J. Psychoanalysis*, 52:169–178.

_____. (1975). Negative therapeutic reaction. In *Tactics and Techniques in Psychoanalytic Therapy*. Vol. 2, *Countertransference*, ed. P. L. Giovacchini. New York: Jason Aronson, pp. 217–228.

_____. (1978). Notes on the psychopathology and psychoanalytic treatment of some borderline patients. *International J. Psychoanalysis*, 59:215–221.

_____. (1987). *Impasse and Interpretation*. New York: Tavistock.

Roy, A., ed. (1982). *Hysteria*. New York: Wiley.

Rutter, M., and Giller, H. (1983). *Juvenile Delinquency: Trends and Perspectives*. New York: Penguin.

Sacher-Masoch, L. (1881). *La Venus de las Pieles*. Madrid: Alianza Editorial, 1973.

Sade, D.-A.-F. (1785). *The Marquis de Sade: The 120 Days of Sodom and Other Writings*. Comp. and trans. A. Wainhouse and R. Seaver. New York: Grove Press, 1966.

Sandler, J., and Rosenblatt, R. (1962). The concept of the representational world. *Psychoanalytic Study of the Child*, 17:128–145.

Sandler, J., and Sandler, A. (1978). On the development of object relationships and affects. *International J. Psychoanalysis*, 59:285–296.

Sandler, J., and Sandler, A. (1987). The past unconscious, the present unconscious and the vicissitudes of guilt. *International J. Psychoanalysis*, 68:331–341.

Schwartz, F. (1981). Psychic structure. *International J. Psychoanalysis*, 62:61–72.

Searles, H. (1961). Phases of patient-therapist interaction in the psychotherapy of chronic schizophrenia. *British J. Medical Psychology*, 34:169–193.

Segal, H. (1967). Melanie Klein's technique. In *Psychoanalytic Techniques: A Handbook for the Practicing Psychoanalyst*, ed. B. Wolman. New York: Basic Books, pp. 168–190.

Shapiro, D. (1965). *Hysterical Styles, Neurotic Styles*. New York: Basic Books.

Sroufe, L. A. (1979). Socioemotional development. In *Handbook of Infant Development*, ed. J. Osofsky. New York: Wiley, pp. 462–518.

Sroufe, L. A., Waters, E., and Matas, L. (1974). Contextual determinants of infant affective response. In *The Origins of Fear*, ed. M. Lewis and L. A. Rosenblum. New York: Wiley, pp. 49–72.

Stanton, A., and Schwartz, M. (1954). *The Mental Hospital*. New York: Basic Books.

Sterba, R. (1934). The fate of the ego in analytic therapy. *International J. Psychoanalysis*, 15:117–126.

Stern, D. (1977). *The First Relationship*. Cambridge: Harvard University Press.

_____. (1985). *The Interpersonal World of the Infant*. New York: Basic Books.

Stoller, R. (1968). *Sex and Gender*. Vol. 1, *Splitting*. New York: Science House.

_____. (1975). *Sex and Gender*. Vol. 2, *The Transsexual Experiment*. London: Hogarth Press.

_____. (1976). *Perversion: The Erotic Form of Hatred*. New York: Pantheon.

_____. (1985). *Observing the Erotic Imagination*. New Haven: Yale University Press.

Stone, M. H. (1980). *The Borderline Syndromes*. New York: McGraw-Hill.

_____. (1983). The criteria of suitability for intensive psychotherapy. In *Treating Schizophrenia Patients: A Clinical-Analytical Approach*, ed. M. H. Stone, M. D. Albert, D. V. Forrest, and S. Arieti. New York: McGraw-Hill, pp. 119–138.

Sullivan, H. S. (1953). *The Interpersonal Theory of Psychiatry*. New York: Norton.

_____. (1962). *Schizophrenia as a Human Process*. New York: Norton.

Ticho, E. (1966). Selection of patients for psychoanalysis or psychotherapy. Paper presented at the twentieth anniversary meeting of the Menninger School of Psychiatry Alumni Association. Topeka, Kansas.

Tinbergen, N. (1951). An attempt at synthesis. In *The Study of Instinct*. New York: Oxford University Press, pp. 101–127.

Tomkins, S. S. (1970). Affect as the primary motivational system. In *Feelings and Emotions*, ed. M. B. Arnold. New York: Academic Press, pp. 101–110.

Tupin, J. P. (1981). Histrionic personality. In *Disorders: Diagnosis and Management*, ed. J. R. Lion. Baltimore: Williams and Wilkins, pp. 85–96.

Turquet, P. (1975). Threats to identity in the large group. In *The Large Group: Dynamics and Therapy*, ed. L. Kreeger. London: Constable, pp. 87–144.

Wallerstein, R. (1986). *Forty-two Lives in Treatment: A Study of Psychoanalysis and Psychotherapy*. New York: Guilford Press.

Wilson, E. O. (1975). *Sociobiology: The New Synthesis*. Cambridge: Harvard University Press.

Winnicott, D. W. (1949). Hate in the countertransference. In *Collected Papers*. New York: Basic Books, 1958, pp. 194–203.

_____. (1953). Transitional objects and transitional phenomena. In *Collected Papers*. New York: Basic Books, 1958, pp. 229–242.

_____. (1960). The theory of the parent-infant relationship. In *The Maturational Processes and the Facilitating Environment*. New York: International Universities Press, 1965, pp. 37–55.

_____. (1965). *The Maturational Processes and the Facilitating Environment*. New York: International Universities Press.

_____. (1971). *Playing and Reality*. New York: Basic Books.

Wittels, F. (1931). Der hysterische Charakter. *Psychoanal. Bewegung*, 3:138–165.

Zetzel, E. R. (1968). The so-called good hysteric. In *The Capacity for Emotional Growth*. New York: International Universities Press, pp. 229–245.

Zinoviev, A. (1984). *The Reality of Communism*. New York: Schocken.

PERMISSIONS

Permission to reprint material in the following chapters is hereby acknowledged.

Chapter 1: Adapted from "New Perspectives in Psychoanalytic Affect Theory," in *Emotion: Theory, Research, and Experience*, ed. R. Plutchik and H. Kellerman, 1990, pp. 115–130. Published with permission of the Academic Press. "The Dynamic Unconscious and the Self," in *Theories of the Unconscious and Theories of the Self*, ed. R. Stern, 1987, pp. 3–25. Published with permission of the Analytic Press.

Chapter 2: Adapted from "The Psychopathology of Hatred," Journal of the American Psychoanalytic Association 39 (1991), Supplement. Published with permission of the *Journal of the American Psychoanalytic Association*.

Chapter 3: Adapted from "Clinical Dimensions of Masochism," *Journal of the American Psychoanalytic Association* 36 (1988): 1005–1029. Published with permission of the *Journal of the American Psychoanalytic Association*.

Chapter 4: Adapted from "Hysterical and Histrionic Personality Disorders," in *Psychiatry*, vol. 1, ed. R. Michels and J. O. Cavenar, 1985, pp. 1–11. Published with permission of J. B. Lippincott.

Chapter 5. Adapted from "The Narcissistic Personality Disorder and the Differential Diagnosis of Antisocial Behavior," in *Psychiatric Clinics of North America: Narcissistic Personality Disorder*, vol. 12, no. 3, ed. Otto F. Kernberg, 1989, pp. 553–570. Published with permission of W. B. Saunders.

Chapter 6: Adapted from "Object Relations Theory in Clinical Practice," *Psychoanalytic Quarterly* 57 (1988): 183–207. Published with permission of the *Psychoanalytic Quarterly*.

Chapter 7: Adapted from "An Ego-Psychology–Object Relations Theory Approach to the Transference," *Psychoanalytic Quarterly* 56 (1987): 197–221. Published with permission of the *Psychoanalytic Quarterly*.

Chapter 8: Adapted from "Psychic Structure and Structural Change: An Ego Psychology–Object Relations Theory Viewpoint," *Journal of the*

American Psychoanalytic Association 36 (1988): 315–337. Published with permission of the *Journal of the American Psychoanalytic Association.*

Chapter 9: Adapted from "Transference Regression and Psychoanalytic Technique with Infantile Personalities," *International Journal of Psychoanalysis* 72 (1991): 189–200. Published with permission of the *International Journal of Psychoanalysis.*

Chapter 10: Adapted from "Projection and Projective Identification: Developmental and Clinical Aspects," *Journal of the American Psychoanalytic Association* 35 (1987): 795–819. Published with permission of the *Journal of the American Psychoanalytic Association.*

Chapter 11: Adapted from "Projective Identification, Countertransference and Hospital Treatment," in *Psychiatric Clinics of North America: Intensive Hospital Treatment of Psychotic and Borderline Patients,* vol. 10, no. 2, ed. Eric Marcus, 1987, pp. 257–272. Published with permission of W. B. Saunders.

Chapter 12: Adapted from "Identification and Its Vicissitudes as Observed in Psychosis," *International Journal of Psychoanalysis* 67 (1986): 147–159. Published with permission of the *International Journal of Psychoanalysis.*

Chapter 13: Adapted from "Hatred as Pleasure," in *Pleasure beyond the Pleasure Principle: Developmental and Psychoanalytic Concepts of Affect,* ed. R. A. Glick and S. Bone, 1990, pp. 177–188. Published with permission of Yale University Press.

Chapter 14: Adapted from "Psychopathic, Paranoid, and Depressive Transferences," *International Journal of Psychoanalysis,* In press. Published with permission of the *International Journal of Psychoanalysis.*

Chapter 15: Adapted from 'The Relation of Borderline Personality Organization to the Perversions," in *Psychiatrie et psychanalyse: Jalons pour une fecondation reciproque,* ed. W. Reid, 1985, pp. 99–116. Published with permission of Gaetan Morin Editeur.

Chapter 16: Adapted from "A Theoretical Frame for the Study of Sexual Perversions," in *The Psychoanalytic Core: Essays in Honor of Leo Rangell,* ed. H. P. Blum, E. M. Weinshel, and F. R. Rodman, 1989, pp. 243–263. Published with permission of International Universities Press.

Chapter 17: Adapted from "A Conceptual Model for Male Perversion," in *The Psychology of Men: New Psychoanalytic Perspectives,* ed. G. I. Fogel, F. M. Lane, and R. S. Liebert, 1986, pp. 152–180. Published with permission of Association for Psychoanalytic Medicine.

INDEX